JACQUI JONES & JOAN WILMOT

THE BOXING CLEVER COOKBOOK

Twelve Recipe Books in One

FRONT COVER PHOTOGRAPH BY PETER JONES
OTHER PHOTOGRAPHS BY KATE BEWICK AND PETER JONES
EDITING AND PROOF READING BY SUSAN KEMP

PUBLISHERS J&J PUBLISHING

Published by J&J PUBLISHING, 2002
First Re-print 2004
Second Re-print 2005

TO

ROBIN, BEN, JOE, SAM, ZAC, PETE, AND SEB

J & J Publishing Tel: 01309 672001
Design & Print: Posthouse Printing and Publishing, Findhorn, Scotland Tel: 01309 691641

Some people are put off by CSA because they feel they get too much food. They are neither accustomed to this bounty of fresh, raw food, nor educated about it. A common complaint heard by CSA farmers: "This is too much. I don't know what to do with it, and I don't want to waste it – because then I will feel guilty."

FROM

'Farms of Tomorrow Revisited'

BY

Trauger Groh & Steven McFadden

ACKNOWLEDGEMENTS

A book like this is rarely the product of one or two people. Throughout the three-year gestation period of the Boxing Clever Cookbook there have been many enthusiastic supporters who have given freely of their time and experience.

Special thanks must go to Mathis Rosenbusch and Christopher Raymont for the time they gave answering our many questions about growing, and also about CSA schemes, and to the rest of the EarthShare team for providing us with such a fabulous scheme on which to base our book.

We would also like to thank: Mark Williamson for the authors' portrait photographs; Pam Bochel, who writes the EarthShare newsletters and box notes, and has been available to answer any queries along the way; Fay Blackburn, for help with the storage methods; Harvey Pettit, whose knowledge of publishing and computer expertise has been invaluable; Susan Kemp, for editing and proof reading; Helen Trussell, for donating the EarthShare Year diagram and her input into the nature of the EarthShare celebrations and their part in the agricultural calendar; Kate Bewick and Peter Jones, for their beautiful photographs; and Pam Rodway, who was there at the beginning when we started the project, for her continuing support. We'll be right behind you Pam when you finally have time to write that book of yours.

Many friends and EarthShare subscribers have donated recipes and they are named and woven into the text. Many thanks for your contributions. We would like to thank Peter Jones and Robin Shohet, our respective partners, for their tremendous support and help with re-writes. Thanks to our children Sam, Zac and Seb for their interest in the book and sampling the many meals. We include in this the successes as well as the failures, such as the bulgar cabbage parcels, which looked too much like boiled gonads to be palatable!

FOREWORD

"If fresh food is necessary to health in man and beast then that food must be provided not only from our own soil but as near as possible to the sources of consumption".
Lady Eve Balfour, founder of the Soil Association

Community Supported Agriculture (CSA) connects the consumer, as directly as possible, to 'the sources of consumption'. This book grew out of the CSA, EarthShare, and its authors know only too well the importance of this link. Millions of people live in an urban existence with little sense of a connection with farming. The Soil Association believes that this link is imperative if we are to halt the juggernaut of industrialised agriculture and its relentless drive towards ever cheaper food. The impact of this disconnection is that many farmers, both organic and non-organic, are selling at or below the cost of production. This downward pressure on prices threatens to bring about their extinction.

People like you are preventing small farmers becoming an endangered species. By buying their produce at a farm shop or farmers' market, by having a vegetable box or being part of a CSA, you are keeping that connection alive. This is not altruism but an act of mutual reward, because the benefits are immense. Economically, buying direct (with no 'middleman' to take a profit) means more for your money and more for the farmer. Environmentally, the nearer we are to the place where organic food is grown or reared, the more food miles are reduced, and so is environmental pollution. Healthwise, food that is produced locally, that has not been stored or chilled or has travelled for days, is fresher and more nutritious. And culturally, local organic food has its own 'story', bringing a shared meaning at mealtimes and a deeper connection to the land.

The Soil Association pioneeered the first vegetable box scheme in 1992 – now there are over 300 organic box schemes across the country. In 1999 the Soil Association helped found the National Association of Farmers' Markets; now there are over 400 markets. Direct sales – when farmers sell directly to the public – have topped £90 million, in 2003, for the first time. This is an unstoppable movement because it is so human to want that connection between food and field. Everytime you cook a meal with local organic ingredients, you are revitalising that link. The local organic revolution has begun.

PATRICK HOLDEN
Director of the Soil Association

INTRODUCTION TO THE BOXING CLEVER COOKBOOK

It is difficult to pinpoint the exact eureka moment when we decided to put this book together.

For Joan it grew from several years of struggling with ever-increasing piles of boxes, all half full with vegetables in varying degrees of decay.

Jacqui had subscribed to a vegetable box scheme in her native Wales, but time constraints led to her giving it up, making her feel guilty that she had not managed the box very well. Like Joan, she had piled up boxes and often resorted to throwing unused, rotten vegetables in the bin.

We met when Joan's partner, Robin, formed an improvisational theatre group, called the Findhorn Playback Theatre. Joan wanted to write a cookbook as a way of managing her weekly box of vegetables and over conversations with Jacqui, who always has excesses of home grown vegetables, it evolved into a joint venture and the book was born.

As the book took shape, it became clear that it had a life of its own, and four strands emerged:
1. Recipes, as befits any cookbook
2. A manual for managing the box
3. The attitudes of the producers and consumers
4. The bigger picture from earth to table

It became clear to us that the people who were subscribing to a box, ourselves included, fell into particular character types when it came to attitudes to 'the box'. From that **THE SPROUT RATING** evolved. This light-hearted system is one we created to relate to the producers and consumers, and we called them '**The Sprouters**'.

We rated our families, and ourselves, and subsequently found that it's fun to apply to anyone and anything.

Throughout the book, constant reference is made to EarthShare, the CSA scheme operating on the Moray Firth coast in the north-east of Scotland, and the one to which Joan, Jacqui and their families subscribe. A key premise of all CSA schemes is that through them people become better informed about the journey of the food from earth to table. There are CSAs all over the world, but it's easier to write about what you know, and we know EarthShare and the people in it.

We started in January and followed the farming year through. We were particularly interested in the growing side of food. We thought if we could appreciate not using pesticides, understanding the effect of the weather on the produce, and using vegetables in season we would have a better relationship with the vegetables in the box.

In writing this book we thought that, for many, this would be one way of making the transition from using vegetables bought in the supermarkets to those that are locally grown, seasonal and organic.

Felipe Fernandez-Armesto, author of 'Food: A History', observes, "...mealtimes are our oldest rituals, companionable effects of eating together help to make us human. The little links which bind households together are forged at the table."

The links may well be forged at the dinner table, but there's a whole chain already built by the time it gets there.

SO WHAT IS CSA?

Pete, along with many people, used to think that CSA stood for the Child Support Agency, although Robin is adamant that it should stand for Chuck Swedes Away. What it actually stands for is **Community Supported Agriculture**. Its aims are to connect local farmers with local consumers. It is a partnership between a farm and a community of subscribers, which provides a direct link between the production and consumption of food. This means that the produce won't have come from all the way round the world. CSA farmers typically use organic or biodynamic farming methods, and strive to provide fresh, high-quality foods.

This type of farming originated in the 1970's in Europe and Japan starting as simple, isolated 'test plots'. One story relating to the origins was that of a group of women in Japan about 30 years ago. The women were concerned about the increase in food imports and the decrease in the farming population, so they initiated a direct growing and buying relationship between their group and local farms. It was called 'teikei' which means 'putting the farmers face on food'. By the 1980's the concept travelled to the USA, and was labelled 'Community Supported Agriculture' by those at Indian Line Farm, Massachusetts, USA, in 1985. CSAs developed in the UK during the 1990's.

Typically, subscribers would purchase a share of the season's harvest, either in one lump sum before the seeds are sown in early spring, or in several instalments throughout the growing season. As members they make a commitment to support the farm throughout the season, and take on the costs, as well as the highs and lows of growing food along with the farmer. The subscribers help to pay for the seeds, fertilizer, equipment, maintenance and labour. They share the risks, including poor harvests, unfavourable weather, and pests.

In some CSA schemes, subscribers have the option of committing to an agreed amount of time to help the farm in exchange for a discount on membership cost. This is known as having 'a working share'. The net result is that production expenses are met and the farmer starts receiving income as soon as work begins.

In return for their investment, CSA subscribers receive a box of fresh, locally-grown, organic, produce once a week throughout the year, which they pick up from a local drop-off point. Once they have committed to the scheme, they have to receive a box every week. However, in the words of one subscriber, "this can have a positive outcome because if you go on holiday, it allows you to pass on your box to other friends or family, or to someone who may want to sample the boxes before committing to the scheme". She adds, "once you have paid your subscription, it almost feels as though you are receiving free vegetables throughout the year. Every week you feel as though you get interest on your share investment. There is also an element of surprise every week because you do not know exactly what is going to be in the box".

As crops rotate throughout the season, weekly boxes vary by size and types of produce, reflecting local growing seasons and conditions. There is a period at the end of the winter season and the beginning of the spring months where it is difficult to grow sufficient quantity and variety. This is known as the 'hungry gap'. The box will contain fewer vegetables during this period than at other times in the season.

Some CSA schemes provide flowers, meat, honey, eggs and dairy produce as well as vegetables and fruit.

As a result of receiving weekly vegetables in one go, rather than buying them from the supermarket on a need basis, subscribing to a scheme does mean that more planning is needed.

In their excellent book on the subject, 'Farms of Tomorrow Revisited', Trauger Groh & Steven McFadden sum up the real value of CSAs:

"*So one gift that CSA gives to individuals, to families, and to culture in general, is a vehicle for re-establishing a conscious connection with the rhythm of life, the rhythm of the seasons, and the rhythm of the farm that gives rise to the food which eventually becomes the molecules and cells of our bodies. Thus, joining a CSA is an act not just of economy or ecology, but also of health at its most fundamental leve*l."

Tatties, glorious tatties!

planted out. EarthShare relies on Cullerne for this element of the box and allows Mathis to concentrate on the staple crops like brassicas, potatoes and root vegetables suited to EarthShare's more extensive field and tractor-based systems. The partnership works well. Cullerne Garden provides tunnel crops mainly from May to September; but in a typical year there is at least something in the box every month from Cullerne. The field crops provide subscribers with the bulk of their vegetables between October and May.

The fruit growing is based on land owned by **John Salt**, a carpenter and part-time beekeeper at nearby **RAFFORD**. Blackcurrants, raspberries, rhubarb and strawberries are grown on this site, as well as garlic.

Crops are harvested each week and boxes packed each Friday. Since the beginning of EarthShare, **Manfred Hafner**, a former businessman from Germany, has run the all-important box-packing operation with the required quiet efficiency. The labelled boxes are then taken to three local pick-up points where subscribers collect their own, and are encouraged to share in a rota scheme to collect for their nearest neighbours. Recycling and environmental awareness are also promoted – the return of empty boxes, punnets and bags are welcomed.

Although not part of EarthShare, **WESTER LAWRENCETON** an organic farm overlooking the Moray Firth, three miles south of Forres, plays a vital role in the CSA scheme's fight against pests and diseases. Soil fertility is boosted through a complex crop rotation and EarthShare takes part in this.

The farm is a partnership between **Nick and Pam Rodway** and **Julia Hilton** that began in 1997. Their land adjoins the EarthShare fields, sharing boundaries as well as a common purpose. The farm's 65 acres has organic laying hens, dairy cows and sheep, and a herd of milking goats.

Wester Lawrenceton farm demonstrates the importance of adding value to its produce, especially through on-farm cheese making. Pam says, "I feel passionately committed to preserving traditional, high-quality cheese-making here in the north of Scotland where once the women of the crofts produced cheese and butter for their families and neighbours".

Its award-winning cheese is available widely in Scotland and England. Oatcakes, haggis, sausages and wool are produced on the farm and are processed by small businesses in the area.

The farm has also established a 'cowshare' scheme, where local people invest £500 in the dairy herd. In return they get £40 worth of dairy produce each year as interest on their loan. Joan has had a cowshare since 1997.

Wester Lawrenceton cheeses

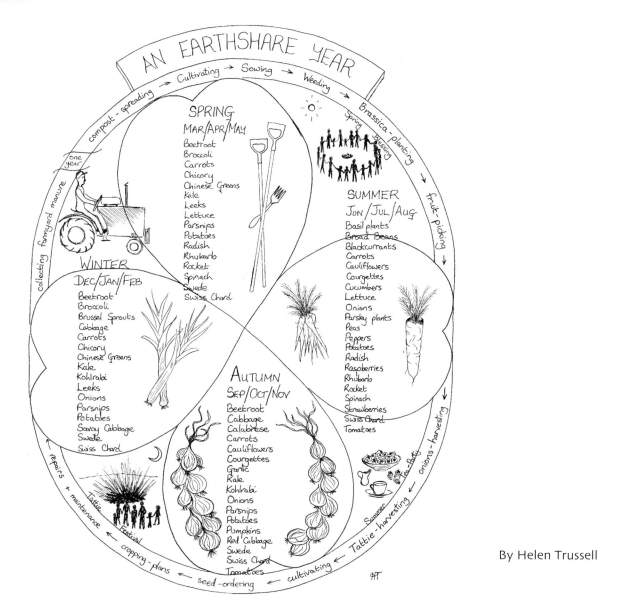

AN EARTHSHARE YEAR

compost - spreading → Cultivating → Sowing → Weeding → Brassica - planting → Fruit - picking

one year

collecting farmyard manure

SPRING
MAR/APR/MAY
Beetroot
Broccoli
Carrots
Chicory
Chinese Greens
Kale
Leeks
Lettuce
Parsnips
Potatoes
Radish
Rhubarb
Rocket
Spinach
Swede
Swiss Chard

Spring blessing

SUMMER
JUN/JUL/AUG
Basil plants
Broad Beans
Blackcurrants
Carrots
Cauliflowers
Courgettes
Cucumbers
Lettuce
Onions
Parsley plants
Peas
Peppers
Potatoes
Radish
Raspberries
Rhubarb
Rocket
Spinach
Strawberries
Swiss Chard
Tomatoes

WINTER
DEC/JAN/FEB
Beetroot
Broccoli
Brussel Sprouts
Cabbage
Carrots
Chicory
Chinese Greens
Kale
Kohlrabi
Leeks
Onions
Parsnips
Potatoes
Savoy Cabbage
Swede
Swiss Chard

AUTUMN
SEP/OCT/NOV
Beetroot
Cabbage
Calabrese
Carrots
Cauliflowers
Courgettes
Garlic
Kale
Kohlrabi
Onions
Parsnips
Potatoes
Pumpkins
Red Cabbage
Swede
Swiss Chard
Tomatoes

onions - harvesting

Summer festival

Tattie - harvesting

← cultivating ← seed - ordering ← cropping - plans ← Festival

Tattie

repairs + maintenance

By Helen Trussell

SPROUT RATING
A DO-IT-YOURSELF GUIDE

In the introduction we talked about our unique 'sprout ratings' and here is your chance to rate yourselves and others. Using this exclusive, scientifically-tested formula you will be able to categorise those around you, even develop your own personal code for judging performance in all areas – even the bedroom. Experts have predicted that 'sprout ratings' will soon replace star signs as the opening chat-up gambit, so get in there first with this free guide.

ONE SPROUT RATING
CHARACTERISTICS
- Starts the box scheme because they think it is a good idea

- By nature would prefer to buy organic vegetables from the supermarket on a need basis

- Has a broad-based approach to food and is willing to include a box scheme as part of their food shopping

- Often will give up the box after a period of time and will revert back to supermarket shopping

FORGIVABLE FAULTS
- Quickly loses interest in the box if vegetables are dirty or mis-shapen

- Good at ideas but poor to follow through. Needs instant gratification – wonders why the lettuce doesn't come with a salad dressing

- Bit of a green slut when it comes to food – easily persuaded to eat out or get a takeaway when faced with cooking a meal from the box

TWO SPROUT RATING
CHARACTERISTICS
- Often chooses to lead a busy life but keen to take on the extra challenge of managing a vegetable box

- Can be a sinner or a saint in relation to the box, depending on their mood

- Often has boxes stacked up like London buses, over-whelmed by the very abundance of vegetables in the box

- Wants to be more creative with the box but finds it easier to compost than to cook

FORGIVABLE FAULTS
- Won't give up the box and risk feeling a failure

- With audience present, will punish themselves by eating 4-week old vegetables

- Gives vegetables generously to friends and family to lessen guilt trip to compost heap

- Over-committed to everything but the box

THREE SPROUT RATING
CHARACTERISTICS
- Starts off with good intentions, and believes in the box scheme

- Occasionally gets behind with the boxes and fights to use them up weekly

- Will bail themselves out with creative use of freezer, becoming local expert on vegetable cryogenics

- Takes on too much

FORGIVABLE FAULTS
- Wracked with guilt when vegetable cryogenics fail and forced to empty year old frozen vegetables into wheelie bin

- Can exude self-confidence which, as we all know, often belies self-doubt

- An ideal candidate for a self-help group
- One sprouter or five sprouter wannabees, depending on mood

FOUR SPROUT RATING
CHARACTERISTICS

- Thoroughly researches all the issues involved between growing the food to serving it up on the table
- Even then, mulls everything over before making a choice
- Committed to eating locally grown organic food
- Keeps in touch with farming issues in the 'outside world'
- Often has an extensive network of personal contacts and a lively interest in anything that is happening with food
- Can be creative with food, researches recipes, and will manage the box well

FORGIVABLE FAULTS

- Works hard to promote the scheme – the Billy Graham of box schemes
- Earnest and Queen-like, their duty lies within the box
- **Never** leaves anything to chance
- Makes simplicity complicated

FIVE SPROUT RATING
CHARACTERISTICS

- The box is one of the highlights of their week
- Could probably use twice as many vegetables as they receive
- Uses up all vegetables by midweek and hungry for more
- Shows genuine shock when told that some struggle with the contents of their box
- Managing the box is second nature, can turn any vegetable in the box into a meal.

FORGIVABLE FAULTS

- Crusader
- Lowers morale in lesser box subscribers
- Sometimes inflexible on that special dinner date. Requires mouth-to-mouth resuscitation if shown prices on a restaurant menu, preferring to buy a new garden fork instead

THE SPROUTERS

Using the do-it-yourself guide we tested the sprout ratings on our family and the farmers, or 'Sprouters' as they affectionately became known. After much laughter and leg-pulling we eventually rated them as below, along with some of their characteristics.

JOAN AND JACQUI   3 SPROUTERS

Co-authors of this book, co-members of Findhorn Playback Theatre, and co-conspirators in the kitchen to convert vegetable haters in the family. They are drinkers of real coffee, G and T's and good red wine. How to tell them apart? Jacqui has the better boobs.

ROBIN   1 SPROUTER

Long-time partner of Joan. Closet vegetable hater, particularly paranoid about swede and beetroot. Has to be dragged every year to the weeding shifts but always enjoys the work and sense of community once he gets there.

PETE   2 SPROUTER

Husband of Jacqui. Can find or recycle anything and has a built-in log radar. Can spot free firewood through brick walls. Loves vegetables but prefers meat, best of all if it's free off the side of the road (deer, pheasant, hare). When Pete suggests to Jacqui that they go for a moonlight drive, she knows he's not being romantic but looking for food.

SAM   1 SPROUTER

Trainee cheese maker at Wester Lawrenceton Farm and resident teenager of Joan and Robin. Makes a mean lemon meringue pie.

ZAC   1 SPROUTER

Can spot a speck of onion in a dish at a distance of 60 paces. The onion-free recipes are dedicated to him. Younger brother of Sam.

SEB   1 SPROUTER

Resident teenager of Jacqui and Pete. Ate vegetables until he lived in a vegetarian community. Loves pasta and is a chocoholic.

MATHIS   5 SPROUTER

Teutonic, indefatigable farmer, inventor, loving owner of a grey Ferguson tractor and part-time pig farmer. Director of EarthShare, our local CSA scheme.

CHRISTOPHER   5 SPROUTER

Loves growing crops in polytunnels. Dreams about building a glasshouse, which would double the crop. Director of EarthShare, our local CSA scheme.

WHERE IS EARTHSHARE?

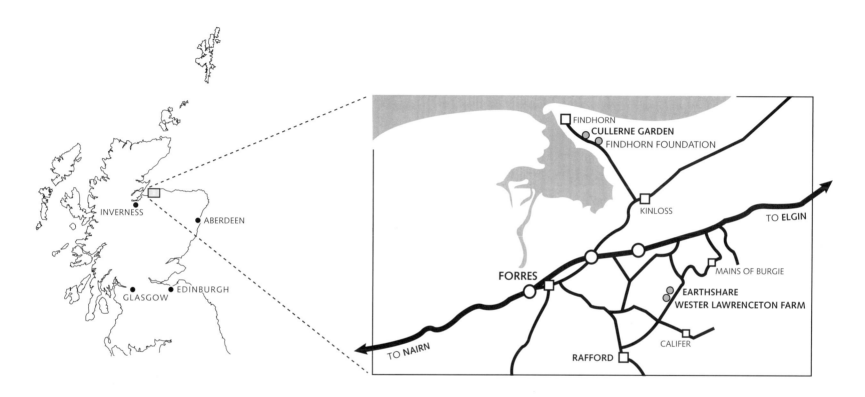

EARTHSHARE MONTHLY VEGETABLE
BOX CONTENTS (Variety names are examples and vary from year to year)

JANUARY

FIELD CROPS - BRASSICAS	FIELD CROPS - ROOT VEGETABLES	FIELD CROPS - ONION FAMILY	FRUIT
Brussels sprouts (Igor)	Beetroot (Crimson King)	Leeks (Musselburgh)	
Cabbage, green (Primo)	Carrots (Bolero & Tip Top)	Onions (Centurion & Sturon)	
Cabbage, white (Castello)	Parsnips (Tender & True)		
Curly kale (Dwarf Green Curled)	Potatoes (Remarka)		
Red cabbage (Marner Lager Rot)			
Swede (Lizzy)			
Winter kohlrabi (Superschmelz)			

FEBRUARY

FIELD CROPS - BRASSICAS	FIELD CROPS - ROOT VEGETABLES	FIELD CROPS - ONION FAMILY	FRUIT
Brussels sprouts (Igor)	Beetroot (Crimson King)	Leeks (Musselburgh)	
Brussels sprouts tops (Igor)	Carrots (Bolero & Tip Top)	Onions (Centurion & Sturon)	
Cabbage, green (Primo)	Parsnips (Tender & True)		
Curly kale (Dwarf Green Curled)	Potatoes (Remarka)		
Green cauliflower (Romanesco Minaret)			
Greens			
Purple sprouting broccoli (Late)			
Red cabbage (Marner Lager Rot)			
Swede (Lizzy)			
CULLERNE TUNNEL CROPS			
Oriental greens (Ta Tsai, Mizuna)			
Green salad (Lambs lettuce)			

MARCH

FIELD CROPS - BRASSICAS	FIELD CROPS - ROOT VEGETABLES	FIELD CROPS - ONION FAMILY	FRUIT
Brussels sprouts (Igor)	Carrots (Bolero & Tip Top)	Leeks (Musselburgh)	**RAFFORD**
Cabbage, green (Primo)	Parsnips (Tender & True)		Rhubarb
Curly kale (Dwarf Green Curled)	Potatoes (Remarka)		
Purple sprouting broccoli (Late)			
Red cabbage (Marner Lager Rot)			
Swede (Lizzy)			
CULLERNE TUNNEL CROPS			
Chicory (Brussels Witloof)			
Oriental greens (Ta Tsai, Mizuna)			
Pak Choi (Joy Choi)			
Spinach (Primo)			

EARTHSHARE MONTHLY VEGETABLE BOX CONTENTS

APRIL

FIELD CROPS - BRASSICAS	FIELD CROPS - ROOT VEGETABLES	FIELD CROPS - ONION FAMILY	FRUIT
Beetroot leaf (Crimson King)	Beetroot (Crimson King)		RAFFORD
Brussels sprouts (Igor)	Carrots (Bolero & Tip Top)		Rhubarb
Cabbage, green (Primo)	Parsnips (Tender & True)		
Purple sprouting broccoli (Late)	Potatoes (Remarka)		
Swede (Lizzy)			
CULLERNE TUNNEL CROPS			
Chicory (Brussels Witloof)			
Coriander			
Lettuce (Wendel)			
Parsley (Curly and Italian Flat)			
Radish (French, Breakfast, Cherry Belle)			
Rocket			

MAY

FIELD CROPS - BRASSICAS	FIELD CROPS - ROOT VEGETABLES	FIELD CROPS - ONION FAMILY	FRUIT
Purple sprouting broccoli (Late)	Carrots (Bolero & Tip Top)		RAFFORD
CULLERNE TUNNEL CROPS	Potatoes (Remarka)		Rhubarb
Parsley (Curly and Italian flat)	CULLERNE TUNNEL CROPS		
Radish (French, Breakfast, Cherry Belle)	New carrots (Amsterdam Forcing, Earls Nantes, indoor)		
Spinach (Medania)			

JUNE

FIELD CROPS - BRASSICAS	FIELD CROPS - ROOT VEGETABLES	FIELD CROPS - ONION FAMILY	FRUIT
	Potatoes (Remarka)		RAFFORD
CULLERNE TUNNEL CROPS	CULLERNE TUNNEL CROPS		Rhubarb
Basil plants	New carrots (Amsterdam Forcing, Earls Nantes, indoor)		
Lettuce			
Oak leaf lettuce			
Parsley (Curly and Italian Flat)			
Parsley plants			
Spinach (Medania)			
Swiss Chard			

EARTHSHARE MONTHLY VEGETABLE BOX CONTENTS

JULY

FIELD CROPS - BRASSICAS	FIELD CROPS - ROOT VEGETABLES	FIELD CROPS - ONION FAMILY	FRUIT
CULLERNE TUNNEL CROPS	Potatoes (Remarka) – first half of month		**RAFFORD**
Broad beans (Aquadulce)	New potatoes (Aminka) – second half of month		Blackcurrants
Coriander	**CULLERNE**		Raspberries
Cucumber (Hana, Flamingo)	New carrots – outdoor (Nantes & Tip Top)		Strawberries
Lettuce (6 or 7 varieties)			
Peas/Mange tout (Podding and Sugar Snap)			
Parsley (Curly and Italian Flat)			

AUGUST

FIELD CROPS - BRASSICAS	FIELD CROPS - ROOT VEGETABLES	FIELD CROPS - ONION FAMILY	FRUIT
Calabrese (Samson)	Beetroot (Crimson King)	Onions (Centurion & Sturon)	**RAFFORD**
Cauliflower (All year round)	New potatoes (Aminka)	**RAFFORD**	Blackcurrants
CULLERNE TUNNEL CROPS	**CULLERNE**	Garlic (Christo)	Raspberries
Broad beans (Aquadulce)	Carrots (Bolero & Tip Top)		
Courgettes (All Green Bush)			
Cucumber			
French beans (Climbing and Dwarf)			
Lettuce (Cos, Crisphead, Little Gem, Oakleaf)			
Parsley (Curly and Italian Flat)			
Peas (Podding and Sugar Snap)			
Tomatoes (Matina, Sungold, Clementine)			

SEPTEMBER

FIELD CROPS - BRASSICAS	FIELD CROPS - ROOT VEGETABLES	FIELD CROPS - ONION FAMILY	FRUIT
Cabbage (Primo)	Beetroot (Crimson King)	Onions (Centurion & Sturon)	
Calabrese (Samson)	New potatoes (Aminka)		
Cauliflower (All year round)	Carrots (Bolero & Tip Top)	**RAFFORD**	
CULLERNE TUNNEL CROPS	**CULLERNE**	Garlic (Christo)	
Cucumber	Courgette (All Green Bush)		
French beans (Climbing and Dwarf)	Daikon		
Lettuce (6 or 7 varieties)			
Small leaf greens			
Tomatoes (Matina, Sungold , Clementine)			

EARTHSHARE MONTHLY VEGETABLE BOX CONTENTS

OCTOBER

FIELD CROPS - BRASSICAS	FIELD CROPS - ROOT VEGETABLES	FIELD CROPS - ONION FAMILY	FRUIT
Cabbage (Primo)	Beetroot (Crimson King)	Leeks (Musselburgh)	
Cauliflower (All year round)	Carrots (Bolero & Tip Top)	Onions (Centurion & Sturon)	
Red cabbage (Marner Lager Rot)	Parsnips (Tender & True)		
RAFFORD	Potatoes (Remarka)		
Pumpkin	**CULLERNE**		
CULLERNE TUNNEL CROPS	Courgette (All Green Bush)		
Cucumber			
Spinach (Perpetual)			
Tomatoes (Matina, Sungold, Clementine)			

NOVEMBER

FIELD CROPS - BRASSICAS	FIELD CROPS - ROOT VEGETABLES	FIELD CROPS - ONION FAMILY	FRUIT
Cabbage, green (Primo)	Beetroot (Crimson King)	Leeks (Musselburgh)	
Curly kale (Dwarf Green Curled)	Carrots (Bolero & Tip Top)	Onions (Centurion & Sturon)	
Red cabbage (Marner Lager Rot)	Parsnips (Tender & True)		
Swede (Lizzy)	Potatoes (Remarka)		
Winter kohlrabi (Superschmelz)			
RAFFORD			
Pumpkin			
CULLERNE TUNNEL CROPS			
Green tomatoes			
Lettuce			
Oriental Greens (Ta Tsai, Mizuna)			
Spinach (Giant Winter Prickly)			

DECEMBER

FIELD CROPS - BRASSICAS	FIELD CROPS - ROOT VEGETABLES	FIELD CROPS - ONION FAMILY	FRUIT
Brussels sprouts (Igor)	Beetroot (Crimson King)	Onions (Centurion & Sturon)	
Cabbage, green (Primo)	Carrots (Bolero & Tip Top)		
Curly kale (Dwarf Green Curled)	Parsnips (Tender & True)		
Red Cabbage (Marner Lager Rot)	Potatoes (Remarka)		
Swede (Lizzy)			
Winter kohlrabi (Superschmelz)			

STORAGE OF VEGETABLES

Once you have collected your box from the pick-up point, the following table may help you to store the vegetables so that they will keep fresher for longer. The leafy greens are the most vulnerable, needing either to be eaten or put in the fridge on the same day. Root vegetables will store well for a long time, the ideal place is the old-fashioned back kitchen, damp and cold. If root vegetables are stored in a dry place, cover them with a damp newspaper. If you like to keep vegetables in the fridge, investing in a larger fridge gives more space for storage.

VEGETABLE	HOW TO STORE
BEETROOT	Upon storage the greens will quickly draw the moisture from the root, greatly reducing flavour and shrivelling the beetroot. Leave a 2.5cm (1") stem and the taproot intact to retain moisture and nutrients. After separating, beetroot will store well for about a week in perforated plastic bags in the fridge. Try to use the beetroots while they are still firm and fresh.
BROAD BEANS	Put into a perforated plastic bag in their skins and they will keep for up to 7 days in the fridge.
BRUSSELS SPROUTS	Remove any damaged outer leaves and store fresh unwashed sprouts in plastic bags in the fridge. The fresher the sprouts the better the flavour. Use within 2 days.
CABBAGE	Put unwashed into plastic bags and refrigerate. If you plan to eat the cabbage raw, eat within a few days. Cabbage that you plan to cook can be stored for about 2 weeks.
CAULIFLOWER/CALABRESE	Place in a perforated plastic bag in the fridge for up to 5 days. Pre-cut florets do not keep well, so store whole.
CARROTS	Store carrots with the green tops trimmed. The tops rob the carrots of moisture and nutritional value. Carrots will keep for several weeks in the salad drawer of the fridge in perforated plastic bags. If you plan to use the green tops in soups or stews, store them separately, as they will only keep for a few days. Of all the root vegetables, carrots have a longer shelf life if kept in the fridge.
CHARD, SWISS CHARD, LEAF BEET, SPINACH OR ANY LEAFY GREENS	These greens are extremely perishable. Put them straight into the fridge in newspaper and they will keep for up to three days. The leaves go limp, but as long as they are green they can be thoroughly refreshed by placing them in a bowl of cold water half an hour before use. Alternatively, put the unwashed leaves in plastic bags in the salad drawer for 2-3 days. The stalks can be kept for longer if separated from the leaves.
CHICORY	Chicory is delicate and ideally should be eaten right away. It can be stored for a few days covered in a cool place or in the salad drawer of the fridge.
CHINESE GREENS, PAK CHOI	Same as chard above.
COURGETTES	Refrigerate unwashed in plastic bags for up to 7 days.
CUCUMBER	Put in loose or perforated plastic bags for up to 3 days in the fridge.
CURLY KALE	Put in a perforated plastic bag, unwashed in the fridge. It will keep fresh for up to a week.

STORAGE OF VEGETABLES

VEGETABLE	HOW TO STORE
GARLIC	If garlic is stored around 12°C (55°F), fungi and other pathogens and pests are much less active than they are with the temperature in the 24–26°C (75-80°F) range. Keeping it cool, but not cool enough to sprout is the key to storing garlic well. Basically, any dark, cool place is fine as long as the humidity is not excessive. Garlic stored in oil at room temperature poses a danger of botulism. Garlic in oil can be kept in the refrigerator for a maximum of three weeks.
KOHLRABI	Kohlrabi stores well in the fridge for weeks in a sealed plastic bag. They can also be stored in a cool, dark place.
LEEKS	Loosely wrap in plastic, unwashed, and refrigerate for up to 5 days.
LETTUCE	Lettuce leaves should be free of wilt, rot and rust. Put fresh, unwashed leaves in plastic bags and refrigerate for up to 3 days.
MUSHROOMS	Mushrooms need to breathe because they deteriorate quickly when stored in plastic bags. Store in a brown paper bag in the fridge, or loose on a plate lined with kitchen paper.
ONIONS	Lay onions in a single layer of newspaper in a warm, well-ventilated place to cure for a few days. Leave undisturbed until the outer skin becomes papery and crispy dry. Rub off stringy roots. Hang in strings or in mesh bags away from moisture. If stored in a cool place they will last for months.
PARSLEY	Thoroughly wash fresh parsley and shake off excess moisture, wrap in paper towels, place in a plastic bag and refrigerate for up to one week; OR put stems in a glass of water, cover with a secured plastic bag and refrigerate and change the water every few days; OR put parsley in plastic bags and freeze.
PEAS	Store unwashed peas in perforated plastic bags in the fridge for a few days. The sugar in them quickly begins to turn to starch even when under refrigeration; so the sooner they are eaten the better.
POTATOES	Potatoes must be stored properly – thick brown paper bags are best – and kept in the dark at all times. A cool place with good ventilation is important. Do not refrigerate potatoes. If potatoes start to sprout they can be eaten if the potato is still firm. Remove the sprouts and discard.
PUMPKIN	Pumpkins should not be stored in the fridge or in a damp place. Moisture causes rapid deterioration. Whole unblemished pumpkin can be stored for up the 3–6 months in a cool, dry place.
PURPLE SPROUTING BROCCOLI	Put into plastic bags, unwashed in the fridge for up to 3 days.
RADISHES	Cut off tops because the leaves cause moisture and nutrient loss during storage. Topped radishes, placed in plastic bags and refrigerated, will keep for 5-7 days. Radish tops, stored separately in plastic bags in the fridge, will last for 2-3 days.
RHUBARB	Freshly harvested, unwashed stalks can be kept refrigerated in plastic bags, for up to three weeks.
SWEDE	Swede stores well in the fridge for weeks in a sealed plastic bag. They can also be stored in a cool, dark place.
TOMATOES	Keep in the salad drawer of the fridge.

HOW TO STRING GARLIC AND ONIONS

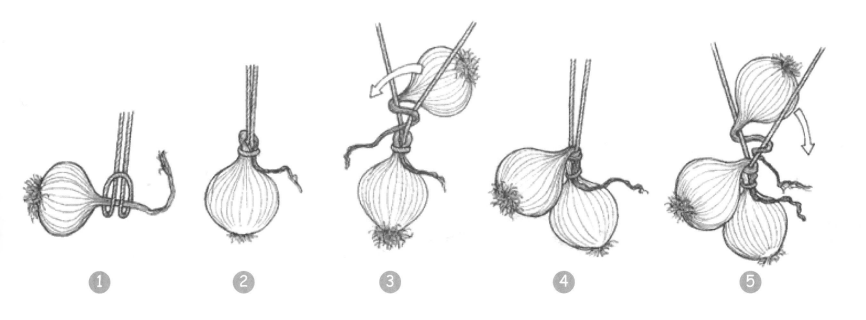

Once garlic and onion are dried until the skins rustle, make into strings as above. For onions, cut a piece of string about 1.6 m (5 ft) long. Fold the string in half and tie a knot at the loose ends to fasten. For garlic, half the length of string is needed. Hang in a cool, dry place where air can circulate.

THE STORE CUPBOARD

Apart from the vegetables in your box, the following ingredients have been used in the recipes. It could be helpful to build up a store cupboard to include these items so that you will be able to attempt any recipe without extra shopping. We have also included in the list the different types of cheese, dairy produce and fresh food used.

ALCOHOL
Beer
Cider
Gin
Orange liqueur
Red Wine
Sherry
Vermouth
Whisky
White wine

BAKING
Apple juice
Baking powder
Bicarbonate of soda
Bread flour
Brown sugar
Caster sugar
Cocoa powder
Cornflour
Creamed coconut
Crystallized ginger
Dark chocolate
Demerara sugar
Desiccated coconut
Dried active yeast
Evaporated milk
Fresh yeast
Granulated sugar
Honey
Icing sugar

Lemon juice
Lime juice
Maple syrup
Marmalade
Molasses
Muscovado sugar
Orange juice
Pineapple juice
Plain flour
Self-raising flour
Semolina
Vanilla essence
Wholewheat flour

CHEESE
Brie
Camembert
Cheddar
Cottage
Cream
Edam
Feta
Gorgonzola
Gruyère
Mozzarella
Parmesan
Red Leicester
Ricotta
Roquefort
Stilton

COOKING OILS
Margarine
Olive oil
Sesame oil
Sunflower oil
Vegetable oil
Walnut oil

DAIRY
Butter
Crème fraîche
Double cream
Eggs
Milk
Single cream
Sour cream
Whipping cream
Yoghurt, plain

DRIED FRUIT
Apricots
Currants
Dates
Prunes
Raisins

ESSENTIALS
Balsamic vinegar
Bouillon
Cider vinegar
Citric acid

Dijon mustard
English mustard
English mustard powder
Horseradish, creamed
Malt vinegar
Mango chutney
Mayonnaise
Miso
Red wine vinegar
Soy sauce or Tamari
Sundried tomatoes
Tofu
Tomato paste/purée
Vegetable suet
White wine vinegar
Wholegrain mustard
Worcestershire sauce

FRESH FOODS
Apples
Celery
Elderberries
Elderflowers
Ground elder
Lemons
Limes
Mushrooms
Olives, green and black
Oranges
Red/green chillies

FROZEN
Filo pastry
Puff pastry
Shortcrust pastry

GRAINS & CEREALS
Bran
Bulgar
Oat bran
Oatmeal
Pearl barley

HERBS & SPICES
Allspice
Basil
Bay leaves
Black peppercorns
Caraway seeds
Cardamom
Cayenne pepper
Celery salt
Celery seed
Chilli powder
Cinnamon
Cloves
Coriander seed
Coriander, ground
Cumin
Curry powder
Dill weed
Fennel seeds

Garam masala
Garlic, fresh
Ginger powder
Ginger, fresh root
Juniper berries
Lavender flowers
Lemongrass
Marjoram
Mint
Mixed herbs
Mustard seeds
Nutmeg
Oregano
Paprika
Parsley
Poppy seeds
Rosemary
Sage
Salt
Sesame seeds
Sunflower seeds
Tamarind paste
Tarragon
Thyme
Turmeric

NUTS
Almonds
Cashew
Dry roasted peanuts
Ground almonds
Hazelnuts

Peanut butter
Peanuts
Pecan
Pine
Walnuts

PASTA
Cannelloni
Macaroni
Pasta shapes
Spaghetti
Tagliatelle

PULSES
Brown lentils
Chickpeas
Red lentils

RICE
Arborio
Basmati
Brown
Jasmine
Long-grain

TINS & CARTONS
Butter beans
Cannellini beans
Chestnuts
Chickpeas
Coconut milk
Tomatoes
Passata
Water chestnuts

INTRODUCTION TO RECIPES

"Some of the vegetables that CSA members receive as part of their weekly share may be new and unfamiliar. Not everyone has experience with collards or greens, beet greens, and so forth – and they may be a hard sell for finicky children. Getting people to broaden their diet from the four or five basic vegetables they are now accustomed to, thanks to mass production, is a real tricky thing. Dietary habits are set deep and, naturally, of great emotional importance to each individual. Consequently, there can be lots of personal resistance to different ways of eating."

From 'Farms of Tomorrow Revisited'
by Trauger Groh & Steven McFadden

The recipes in this book may help you cope with your abundance of vegetables. Most of them are quickly and easily prepared and add flavours that are interesting. We have also included many recipes for familiar and unfamiliar vegetables. Many of the recipes have been tested on our own children, and we have commented where we have had a positive response. They have also been tested on our friends and other family members. Many hours of cooking, talking, drinking and laughing have taken place since our decision to write the book. We are hoping that the recipes will encourage subscribers to persevere with the boxes.

There are two fundamental and practical tips on how to use up left-overs and coping with vegetables that appeal least to your family. An easy way is to turn leftover cooked vegetables into quiches. Put them into a pastry case, with a mixture of 2 eggs and 150 ml ('/4 pint/5 fl oz) milk or soya milk and/or yoghurt, cream, crème fraîche. You can also top the quiches with cheese, from blue to Cheddar.

Joan's most successful quiche made from leftovers was one she made from the previous night's spaghetti bolognaise, bound with an egg.

When making pastry it is useful to make more than one pie case and freeze for another day. Blind bake the ones you are not using for 5 minutes and freeze.

You can curry anything. Although we have included curry recipes, you can make up your own spice mix. For Jacqui, the art is not to use ready-made curry powder, but to make up your own blend. To get the full flavour from the spices, fry onions until soft, then add the spices and cook for 2-3 minutes before you add anything else. Suggested blends are coriander, cumin, turmeric and ginger. Add coconut milk, or creamed coconut, when making a curry for children or adults who do not like a hot curry. To adjust the blend and spice it up, just add chilli powder, fresh chilli, or serve with hot pickles. You can also add poppy seeds, mustard seeds, cinnamon and cardamom. Experiment until you get a flavour that suits you or your family.

To make things easier for you, we've listed the ingredients in each recipe in the order that you'll need them whilst cooking. On top of that, we've given you a brand new recipe book each month to keep you inspired all year round as one of our aims was to look at the box of vegetables with a fresh eye.

In this book, every month's recipes has a farming news preamble that will introduce you to who does what, the jobs that must be done, and to the planning needed at all levels to ensure continuity. Most of us have lost touch with the hard work that produces our most basic food, so part of our aim is to inform any future subscribers on the year-round activity that takes place in a typical CSA scheme. The farming news also shows how CSA schemes have a habit of developing relationships, contacts and friends. There's a special bond between those who have completed work shifts in sunny weather, crisp frosty days, or waded through muddy fields, braved the freezing wind and rain to weed a row of cabbages.

FARMING NEWS FOR JANUARY

The main activity is harvesting. Potato grading or dressing is done weekly. This is where the potatoes are put across a grader and the small, green and rotten ones are taken out.

HARVESTING

As EarthShare fields are close to the sea, they do not suffer from hard frosts. As a result, Mathis is able to leave the following vegetables in the ground and harvest them weekly or as needed: Brussels sprouts, red and green cabbage, carrots, chicory, curly kale, kohlrabi, leeks, parsnips and swede.

Mathis has a rhythm of harvesting twice a week. On Tuesdays he crops for the Findhorn Foundation kitchens and on Thursdays for EarthShare subscribers. The freshly-picked vegetables are driven from the fields to the box-packing sheds at Cullerne on Thursday evenings.

Two to three people are normally needed to compile an average of 120 boxes – currently Manfred and Barbara Hafner, and Julie Adams – who start packing the boxes at 8.30 on Friday mornings.

Robust field crops are packed first. During the morning the more fragile produce – just picked from the tunnels at Cullerne – arrives at the packing shed, and this is placed on top.

To complete the boxes are weekly 'box notes' which include news, views and recipes, and the quarterly newsletter, 'The Onion String', to which subscribers are encouraged to contribute. These are produced by EarthShare Director and Administrator, Pam Bochel, who took over from Carol Shaw, another Director of EarthShare who is now in charge of finance. The completed boxes are then driven to three separate pick-up points at Elgin, Forres and the Findhorn Foundation for subscribers to collect.

MAINTENANCE AND MACHINERY

In addition to the general maintenance tasks, Mathis often undertakes a project or two to occupy himself during this time of year. One year he converted the grey 'Fergie' tractor from its paraffin/petrol mixture to run on LPG – probably the first such eco-friendly tractor in the UK.

At Cullerne, Christopher looks after the tools. He sharpens them and oils the wooden handles. The rotovator and power tools receive their winter maintenance.

PESTS AND DISEASES

At this time of year the crops still in the ground are relatively disease free. The only disease evident is parsnip canker – or rust, as gardeners call it – where they can crack a little and go brown but that has not been too much of a problem to date. Cabbages and other brassicas can suffer from the cabbage root fly, which eats the roots away and kills the plant.

Scotland is the perfect place for growing swede (sorry Robin!) because it is windy and cool so there is less chance of it being affected by root fly.

PLANTING

The early potatoes are put into boxes for chitting – this is to allow the tubers to sprout. However, they are put in the light so as not to become leggy.

WEATHER

The weather can be very cold and windy in Scotland at this time of year, but thankfully the working days are short. The sun doesn't peek over the horizon until nearly 8am, and it starts to get dark at about 3pm.

Mathis and Milan on the Ferguson tractor

Manfred and Barbara Hafner box packing

BEETROOT AND CARROT CURRY

1 tsp whole coriander seed
½ tsp ground cinnamon
¼ tsp freshly ground black pepper
Pinch of chilli powder
2 tbsp olive oil
450 g (1 lb/2 cups) beetroot, peeled and diced
450 g (1 lb/2 cups) carrots, peeled and diced
300ml (10 fl oz/½ pint) water
Salt to taste   (Serves 4)

1   Roughly grind all the spices together in a spice grinder or
    with a pestle and mortar.
2   Heat olive oil in pan. Add the spices, and stir for 30
    seconds.
3   Add beetroot and carrot and stir for 2 minutes.
4   Add water and salt to taste, cover and cook on low heat
    for about 15 minutes, stirring occasionally, or until
    vegetables are cooked.
5   Serve with rice.

BEETROOT, ORANGE KISSED

450 g (1 lb/2 cups) beetroot, scrubbed but not topped
and tailed
1 tbsp butter or margarine
½ tsp cornflour
150 ml (¼ pint/5 fl oz) orange juice
2 tbsp brown sugar
¼ tsp ground ginger
Salt and freshly ground pepper to taste
2 tbsp raisins

Strips of orange peel   (Serves 4)

1   Place beetroot in a saucepan with cold, salted water.
    Bring to the boil, cover the pan and quickly return to the
    boil. Reduce heat and simmer until cooked, about one
    hour depending on size.
2   Drain, allow to cool, peel and slice.
3   In a saucepan, over medium heat, melt butter or mar-
    garine and add cornflour with orange juice, brown sugar,
    ginger, salt and pepper. Stir continuously until thick.
4   Add the beetroot and raisins to the sauce and heat
    through.
5   Garnish with strips of orange peel.

SPROUT SNIPPET: You can make any root vegetable into
chips and deep-fry them. You can also make crisps. Slice the vegetable with a potato peeler or a cheese slice and deep fry or lay
vegetable slices on a baking tray, brush with oil and sprinkle with
herb of your choice. Serve with salt.

BEETROOT PESTO

Apart from the fabulous colour of this dish, this was the first time
Robin had ever eaten beetroot and was even spotted having a
second helping. The children also liked it.

200 g (7 oz) beetroot, scrubbed but not topped and tailed
2 tbsp olive oil
150 g (5 oz) toasted pine nuts
5 crushed cloves of garlic
2 tbsp fresh chopped basil
Zest and juice of one lemon
225 ml (8 fl oz/1 cup) olive oil
150 g (5 oz) grated Parmesan cheese
Season to taste

1 Place beetroot on a baking tray, brush with olive oil and roast in the oven 180°C (350°F/Gas 4) for about one hour or until cooked, depending on size. Skin and quarter cooked beetroot.
2 Toast the pine nuts in a dry frying pan over medium heat, stirring frequently, until golden and nutty, about 5 minutes.
3 Place all ingredients in a blender and zap until smooth. You may need to add a little more olive oil. We found it kept well for up to 3 days if stored in a jar in the fridge.
4 Serve as a dressing, in sandwiches, dip, with crackers, vegetable sticks or with pasta.

SPROUT SNIPPET: Because beetroot contains more natural sugar than starch, it is particularly delicious roasted. Roasting concentrates the sugar rather than leaching it out into cooking liquid.

BRUSSELS SPROUTS WITH CARAWAY SEEDS

450 g (1 lb/2 cups) Brussels sprouts, trimmed with outer leaves removed
50 g (2 oz) butter or margarine
150 ml (¼ pint/5 fl oz) water
2 garlic cloves, peeled and crushed
½ tsp caraway seeds
Salt and freshly ground black pepper to taste   (Serves 4)

1 Thinly slice the sprouts lengthwise.
2 Place the butter or margarine and water into a saucepan over a medium heat.
3 Add sprouts when water boils. Return to boil quickly. Cover, reduce heat and simmer for about 5 minutes, or until the sprouts are just cooked.
4 Add garlic and caraway seeds. Continue to cook until water has almost evaporated. Season and transfer to serving dish.

BRUSSELS SPROUTS AND CHESTNUTS WITH MAPLE GLAZE

175 g (6 oz/¾ cup) tinned chestnuts
450 g (1 lb/2 cups) Brussels sprouts, trimmed with outer leaves removed
5 tbsp maple syrup
25 g (1 oz) butter or margarine
Salt and freshly ground black pepper to taste   (Serves 4)

1 Drain and dry chestnuts.
2 Cut an X in the base of each sprout and put into boiling salted water. Return to boil quickly, reduce heat and simmer until tender, about 10 minutes. Drain and rinse with cold water. Leave to cool.
3 Quarter each Brussels sprout.
4 Put maple syrup into a pan and warm. Add the sprouts, chestnuts, and butter. The syrup and butter will thicken and glaze the sprouts. Season and, when warmed through, serve.

BRUSSELS SPROUTS WITH LEMON

450 g (1 lb/2 cups) Brussels sprouts, trimmed with outer leaves removed
4 tbsp fresh chives or spring onions, chopped
25 g (1 oz) butter or margarine
1½ tsp grated lemon peel
Salt and freshly ground black pepper to taste   (Serves 4)

1 Place Brussels sprouts into a saucepan of boiling salted water and cook until sprouts are just tender and still slightly crisp, about 5 minutes.
2 Drain and put back into saucepan.
3 Combine rest of the ingredients together in a bowl, and add this to the sprouts. Stir well and transfer to serving dish.

BRUSSELS SPROUTS WITH WINE AND HONEY-GLAZED

We tried this recipe using sprouting broccoli instead of Brussels sprouts and it worked well. We also felt it our duty not to waste the wine.

450 g (1 lb/2 cups) Brussels sprouts, trimmed with outer leaves removed
150 ml (¼ pint/5 fl oz) water
4 tbsp dry red wine
3 tbsp honey
1 tbsp soy sauce
1 tsp cornflour   (Serves 4)

1   Cut an X into the base of each Brussels sprout about ¼" deep and put into a pan of boiling salted water and cook for about 5 minutes.
2   In a small bowl combine the wine, honey, and soy sauce and add to Brussels sprouts. Stir well. Bring back to the boil, reduce heat, and simmer for a further 5 minutes.
3   Mix cornflour with a little water and stir into the saucepan quickly, then cook for another 5 minutes until thickened.
4   Transfer to serving dish.

CABBAGE AND CELERY BAKE

At this point, you can drink the rest of the beer or let it go flat and make the carrot fritters with beer batter on page 134.

450 g (1 lb/2 cups) cabbage, coarsely chopped
175 g (6 oz) celery, sliced
Salt to taste
1 tsp caraway seeds or fennel seeds (optional)

Sauce
25 g (1 oz) butter or margarine
50 g (2 oz/½ cup) plain flour
425 ml (¾ pint/2 cups) milk
150 ml (¼ pint/5 fl oz) beer
225 g (8 oz/1 cup) Cheddar cheese, grated
Salt and freshly ground black pepper to taste   (Serves 4)

1   Bring one litre, (1¾ pints) water to the boil in a saucepan. Add cabbage, celery, salt, and caraway or fennel seeds. Bring back to the boil, reduce heat and simmer for about 5 minutes and drain well. Transfer to buttered oven dish.
2   Melt the butter or margarine in a pan, add flour and cook, stirring continuously for 1 minute. Slowly add milk, again stirring continuously until sauce is smooth and thick. Add beer and continue stirring until foam disappears. Cook until heated through.
3   Add cheese and stir until melted. Season to taste.
4   Pour sauce over vegetables and bake in oven 180°C (350°F/Gas 4) for 30 minutes.

VARIATION: Can decorate with slices of tomato or sprinkle with a mixture of 4 tablespoons wholemeal breadcrumbs and a tablespoon of cheese before baking. You can also use leeks instead of celery.

SPROUT SNIPPET: The notorious odour problem of cabbage is a result of overcooking. Cabbage contains isothiocynates that break down into smelly sulphur compounds during cooking. The reaction is even stronger in aluminium pans. The longer the cabbage is cooked, the more smelly the compounds become. The solution: brief cooking time in stainless steel pans.

CABBAGE WITH SPICES, GINGER AND COCONUT MILK

2 tbsp olive oil
½ tsp black mustard seeds
1 onion, chopped
2 garlic cloves, crushed
1 green chilli, seeded and finely chopped (optional)
1 tsp turmeric
2.5 cm (1") piece fresh root ginger, peeled and finely chopped
2 tsp ground coriander
1 tsp ground cumin
1 bay leaf
1 pinch ground cinnamon
Salt and freshly ground black pepper to taste
450 g (1 lb) cabbage, cut into medium sized strips
2 tbsp cider vinegar
1 x 400 ml (14 fl oz) tin coconut milk   (Serves 4)

1   Heat oil in a pan and fry the mustard seeds until they crackle.
2   Add the onion, garlic, chilli (if used), turmeric, ginger, coriander, cumin, bay leaf, cinnamon, salt and pepper to taste. Fry for about another 2 minutes.
3   Add the cabbage and vinegar.
4   Stir in the coconut milk and simmer gently, stirring occasionally for about 15 minutes or until the cabbage is cooked.
5   Serve with rice.

SPROUT SNIPPET: To relieve an upset stomach and stimulate digestion, drink 1 tbsp of olive oil before eating.

CARROT, LEEK AND OLIVE ~~STEW~~ RAGOUT

In deference to Robin we had to rename this recipe. Why does stew sound better in another language?

1 tbsp olive or vegetable oil
3 medium leeks, sliced
2 cloves garlic, crushed
3 medium carrots peeled and diced
1 medium potato, finely diced
2 tbsp tomato paste or purée
Large pinch dried thyme
Large pinch dried oregano
Salt and freshly ground black pepper to taste
500 ml (16 fl oz/2 cups) water or vegetable stock
90 g (3 oz/½ cup) ripe olives, pitted & chopped   (Serves 4)

1   Heat oil in pan, sauté leek and garlic until soft.
2   Add all other vegetables and seasonings.
3   Add water or vegetable stock, cover and bring to boil.
4   Reduce heat and simmer for about 45 minutes.
5   During last 5 minutes of cooking, stir in olives.
6   Serve with rice, wholewheat crackers, roast potatoes or breads.

CURLY KALE PESTO

225 g (8 oz/1 cup) curly kale, chopped
1½ tsp dried basil
2-4 garlic cloves
2 tbsp Parmesan
50 g (2 oz/¼ cup) sunflower seeds
175 ml (6 fl oz/¾ cup) olive oil
Salt and freshly ground black pepper to taste

1 Blend curly kale, basil, garlic, Parmesan and seeds in a blender or food processor.
2 With blender running slowly, gradually add olive oil. Season to taste. You may need to add a little more olive oil.
3 Keeps well in jars in the refrigerator for up to 3 days.

SPROUT SNIPPET: We found that keeping food in jars in the fridge rather than in a dish with cling-film encouraged the family to eat it.

CURLY KALE AND POTATO RISOTTO

2 tbsp olive oil
25 g (1 oz) butter or margarine
1 medium onion, chopped
2 medium potatoes, peeled or with skin, cut into 1.25 cm (½") chunks
350 g (12 oz/1½ cups) curly kale, chopped finely
350 g (12 oz/1½ cups) Arborio rice
150 ml (¼ pint/5 fl oz) white wine
950 ml (32 fl oz/1½ pints/4 cups) vegetable stock, heat to boiling
2 tbsp Parmesan cheese
Salt and freshly ground black pepper to taste   (Serves 6-8)

1 In a large pan, heat the oil and butter or margarine. Add onion, potatoes and curly kale.
2 Sauté over medium-high heat until kale wilts, about 5-10 minutes.
3 Add rice and stir briefly, until rice turns opaque, about one minute.
4 Add wine and stir until evaporated.
5 Add boiling stock. Simmer until rice is cooked, about 18 minutes.
6 Add the Parmesan and season to taste.

SPROUT SNIPPET: Arborio rice is a pearly-looking, round, fat, Italian, white rice and forms the foundation of risotto. Riso means rice in Italian. Like other rices, Arborio is a member of the grass family. What distinguishes it is a higher than normal amount of soluble starch that is released during cooking. The starch makes the risotto creamy. It takes about 18 minutes to cook. It is done when it is *al dente*: tender on the outside and firm in the centre.

CURLY KALE WITH TOASTED SESAME SEEDS

1¼ tsp sesame oil
2 garlic cloves, crushed
450 g (1 lb/2 cups) curly kale, cut into fine strips
2 tbsp vegetable stock
2 tsp soy sauce
Salt and freshly ground black pepper to taste
1¼ tsp sesame seeds, toasted   (Serves 4)

1 In a pan, heat the oil. Add the garlic and sauté for 10 seconds.
2 Add the curly kale and stock. Cover and steam for 5-10 minutes until the kale has wilted. Check the liquid, you may need to add more.
3 Add the soy sauce. Season if necessary.
4 Put into a serving dish and keep warm.
5 Toast the sesame seeds by putting them on a baking tray and grill for about 2 minutes, or toast in a dry frying pan. Watch that they do not burn.
6 Top the kale with sesame seeds and extra freshly ground black pepper.

SPROUT SNIPPET: When you get curly kale in your box, one way to store it short-term is to put it in a glass of water for a few days to keep it fresh, rather like a bunch of flowers. You will find that it will start to sprout from the top and more curly kale will grow – a one sprouter nightmare and a five sprouter dream!

A Burns' Night dinner is traditionally held on 25th January, the date when Scotland's most famous poet, Robert Burns, was born. He wrote his 'Address to the Haggis' during his first visit to Edinburgh in 1786. The poem, which is highly patriotic and atmospheric, is very suitable for reciting in a loud voice.

Burns' Night is a key event in the Scottish year, and is celebrated not only in Scotland, but wherever people of Scottish descent live. It has an established ritual, which Burns would no doubt have revelled in. The centrepiece is the haggis, borne on a silver platter by the cook, preceded by a kilted bagpiper. Others follow, bearing the dishes of swede (neeps) and potato (tatties). The 'Address' is declaimed and the haggis is then ceremonially stabbed with the black knife (sgean dhu), kept in the Scot's stocking. Traditionally, large amounts of whisky are consumed at the same time.

We thought we could not write this book without including a haggis recipe. This is a completely different and unusual way to cook haggis.

HAGGIS BURGERS WITH WHISKY AND WHITE WINE SAUCE

Burgers
450 g (1 lb) haggis
1 egg, beaten
Coating
50 g (2 oz) flour
1 egg, beaten

125 g (4 oz) breadcrumbs
2 tbsp olive oil for frying
Sauce
1 medium onion, finely chopped
2 tbsp white wine
150 ml (¼ pint/5 fl oz) vegetable stock
4 tbsp double cream
4 tbsp whisky
Salt and freshly ground black pepper to taste   (Serves 4)

1   Take the haggis out of its skin and put into a bowl.
2   Add the beaten egg and mix together.
3   Form into burgers, coating each one with flour.
4   Now dip each burger into egg and then breadcrumbs.
5   Heat olive oil in a pan and fry burgers until golden brown, turning once.
6   For the sauce, place chopped onion in a pan with the white wine and vegetable stock. Bring to the boil, and reduce by half.
7   Remove from heat, add double cream, return to heat and cook until the sauce thickens. Remove from heat.
8   Add whisky and season to taste. Pour sauce over burgers.
9   Serve with neeps and tatties.

KOHLRABI WITH BROWN SUGAR AND GINGER

700 g (1½ lb/3 cups) kohlrabi, peeled and sliced 0.6 cm (¼") thick
25 g (1 oz) butter or margarine
2 tbsp brown sugar
½ tsp ground ginger
Salt and freshly ground black pepper to taste   (Serves 6)

1   Put kohlrabi into a pan with salted water. Bring to the boil, reduce heat and simmer until tender, about 10-15

minutes. Drain.

2. Melt butter or margarine in a pan. Add brown sugar, ginger, salt and pepperand stir. Pour over the kohlrabi, mix well and serve.

KOHLRABI, SWEDE AND POTATO SOUP

1 tbsp olive oil
1 medium onion, chopped
2 garlic cloves
450 g (1 lb/2 cups) kohlrabi, peeled and diced
450 g (1 lb/2 cups) swede, peeled and diced
450 g (1 lb/2 cups) potato, peeled and diced
950 ml (32 fl oz/1¾ pints/4 cups) vegetable stock
Salt and freshly ground black pepper to taste
¼ tsp ground nutmeg
To serve: 150 ml (5 fl oz/¼ pint) sour cream   (Serves 6-8)

1. Heat oil in pan, add onion and garlic and sauté for about 4 minutes or until onion is transparent.
2. Add kohlrabi, swede, potato and stock and stir well.
3. Bring to the boil, cover, reduce heat and simmer for about 40 minutes or until the vegetables are tender.
4. In a food processor, blend until smooth.
5. Return to pan and add salt, pepper and nutmeg.
6. Ladle into bowls and top with sour cream.

LEEK, CARAMELISED PEAR, AND BRIE TART

Sam loved this so much that he learnt how to cook it himself.

Pastry
175g (6 ozs/1½ cups) plain flour
¼ tsp sea salt

Filling
3 medium sized pears
4 tbsp oil
3 large leeks, sliced

Pinch of sugar
90g (3 oz) butter/margarine
4-5 tbsp cold water

90 g (3oz/½ cup) pine nuts
Salt and freshly ground black pepper to taste
Pinch of nutmeg
225 g (8 oz/1 cup) Brie cheese
(Serves 4)

1. To make pastry, combine flour, salt and sugar in a bowl.
2. Cut butter or margarine into cubes and rub into flour until it looks like fine breadcrumbs.
3. Add water to form a dough. Knead on a floured board.
4. Wrap up in plastic and allow to rest in fridge for at least 30 minutes.*
5. On lightly floured board, roll out dough, roughly circular, and place in a 24 cm (9 ½") pie dish.
6. Prick pastry with fork and blind bake in the oven for 5-10 minutes 200°C (400°F/Gas 6) until it has just a hint of colour.
7. Peel, core and dice pears 1.25 cm (½").
8. Heat 2 tbsp oil in frying pan, sauté pears at a high heat until golden brown. (Be mindful that the pears will burn very easily, so stir frequently). Remove from the pan and set aside.
9. Heat the remaining oil in the frying pan and sauté leeks over a medium heat until translucent.
10. Lightly toast the pine nuts in a dry frying pan.
11. Combine pears, leeks, pine nuts, salt, pepper and nutmeg in a bowl.
12. Spoon mixture into tart case and dot top of tart with all of the Brie cheese.
13. Bake at 180°C (350°F/Gas 4) for about 10 minutes, or until cheese has melted.

14 Serve warm. Makes a lovely starter, or lunch with salad.

*If you are busy, pastry doesn't seem to suffer if used straight away.

LEEK, POTATO, PRUNE AND APPLE PIE WITH STOUT

50 g (2 oz) dried prunes
150 ml (¼ pint/5 fl oz) stout such as Black Bishop or Guinness
275 g (10 oz) frozen puff pastry
50 g (2 oz) butter or margarine
1 medium onion, thinly sliced
225 g (8 oz/1 cup) potatoes, thinly sliced
1 leek, sliced and washed
1 medium cooking apple, cored, peeled and sliced
6 sage leaves, finely chopped
3 cloves
Pinch of cinnamon, salt and freshly ground pepper to taste
2 tbsp double cream or yoghurt
Beaten egg to glaze   (Serves 4)

1 Marinate the prunes in stout for 2 hours or overnight.
2 De-frost pastry and roll out to line medium pie dish with large flaps overlapping.
3 Melt butter or margarine in frying pan, sauté onions and potatoes gently until softened.
4 Add leek and sauté for 2 minutes.
5 Remove from heat and stir in apple, sage, cloves, cinnamon, salt and pepper.
6 Stir in 2 tablespoons of double cream or yoghurt.
7 Drain prunes (retaining marinade), chop and add to mixture.
8 Pour into pie dish.
9 Pull over pastry flaps, leaving hole in the centre.

10 Brush with beaten egg and bake in a preheated oven 200°C (400°F/Gas 6) for 30 minutes or until golden.
11 Use prune marinade to make extra gravy. Melt 25 g (1 oz/2 tbsp) butter or margarine in a pan, blend in 25 g (1 oz) plain flour, and cook over a low heat for 2-3 minutes, stirring constantly with a wooden spoon. Gradually add the prune marinade and up to ½ pint of vegetable stock until desired thickness is achieved. Season to taste.
12 Serve with green vegetables.

PARSNIP AND CARROT PURÉE

450 g (1 lb/2 cups) parsnips, peeled and sliced
450 g (1 lb/2 cups) carrots, peeled and sliced
225 ml (8 fl oz/1 cup) milk or single cream
50 g (2 oz) butter or margarine
½ tsp vanilla essence
Salt and freshly ground black pepper to taste   (Serves 4)

1 Put parsnips into salted water. Bring to the boil, reduce heat and simmer until tender. Drain.
2 Put carrots into salted water. Bring to the boil, reduce heat and simmer until tender. Drain.
3 Place cooked parsnips in a blender or food processor. Add half the milk or cream, half the butter or margarine, and blend until smooth. Season to taste. Set aside and keep warm.
4 Rinse and dry food processor. Place carrots in the blender with the remaining milk and butter or margarine, all of the vanilla essence and blend until smooth. Season to taste.
5 Spoon parsnip mixture into half of a small serving bowl.

Spoon carrot in the other half. Pull a small rubber spatula through the mixture to create a marbled pattern.

PARSNIP AND POTATO CASSEROLE

225 g (8 oz/1 cup) parsnips, peeled and chopped
225 g (8 oz/1 cup) potatoes, peeled and chopped
90 g (3 oz) cream cheese
1 tbsp grated Parmesan cheese
2 tbsp evaporated milk
25 g (1 oz) margarine or butter
2 tbsp parsley, chopped
Salt and freshly ground black pepper to taste   (Serves 4)

1   Preheat oven to 190°C (375°F/Gas 5).
2   Place parsnips and potatoes in saucepan with salted water. Bring to the boil, reduce heat and simmer until tender, about 10 minutes.
3   Drain and return vegetables to saucepan.
4   Mash well and stir in rest of ingredients.
5   Season with salt and pepper to taste.
6   Pour mixture into a greased baking dish and bake for about 20 minutes until mixture is bubbly.

PARSNIP CAKE WITH WALNUT AND CINNAMON FROSTING

Do you remember the Fawlty Towers episode about not mentioning the war? We found this also applies to parsnips if you know someone who does not like them – if you make this cake don't tell them that there are parsnips in it, even after they have tried it. Joan's neighbour, Karl, loved the cake, but sounded a little sick when she mentioned the parsnips, even though it was a week later.

125 g (4 oz/½ cup) butter or margarine
150 ml (¼ pint/5 fl oz) vegetable oil
225 g (8 oz/1 cup) granulated sugar
225 g (8 oz/1 cup) brown sugar
4 eggs
225 g (8 oz/2 cups) plain flour
1 tsp baking powder
1 tsp bicarbonate of soda
1 tsp ground cinnamon
1 pinch salt
700 g (1½ lb/3 cups) parsnips, peeled and grated
150 g (5 oz/1 cup) walnuts, chopped
1 tsp vanilla essence
For the frosting
175 g (6 oz) cream cheese
125 g (4 oz/½ cup) butter or margarine
150 g (5 oz/1 cup) walnuts, chopped
1 tsp ground cinnamon
350 g (12 oz) icing sugar

1   Preheat oven to 180°C (350°F/Gas 4).
2   Grease 2 x 24 cm (9½") cake tins.
3   Combine butter or margarine, oil, granulated sugar and brown sugar and cream the mixture until smooth.
4   Add the eggs, one at a time.
5   Sieve the flour, baking powder, bicarbonate of soda, cinnamon and salt into a bowl and mix well.
6   Fold in the flour mixture to the butter/sugar mixture.
7   Add the parsnips, walnuts and vanilla. Mix well.
8   Pour the mixture into the prepared cake tins and spread evenly.
9   Bake in the oven for 30-40 minutes, or until a knife inserted into the centre of the cake comes out clean.

10 Remove from the oven and cool.
11 For the frosting, combine the cream cheese, butter or margarine, and mix well.
12 Add the walnut pieces and cinnamon and mix well.
13 Add the icing sugar a little at a time and mix until the frosting is spreadable.
14 Spread half the frosting between the cake pieces and the other half on top of the cake.

POTATO CAKES WITH GOAT'S CHEESE

450 g (1 lb) potatoes, coarsely grated
1 tsp dried thyme
2 garlic cloves, crushed
1 onion, finely chopped
Salt and freshly ground black pepper to taste
2 tbsp olive oil
50 g (2 oz) butter or margarine
125 g (4 oz) goat's cheese   (Makes 4 cakes)

1 After grating the potatoes, using your hands, squeeze out as much of the thick starchy liquid as possible.
2 Add the thyme, garlic, onion and seasoning.
3 Heat olive oil and butter or margarine in a pan, divide mixture into 4 four large spoonfuls and place in a frying pan, spacing them well apart. Press firmly down with a spatula.
4 Cook for 3-4 minutes on each side or until golden. Drain on kitchen paper.
5 Preheat the grill.
6 Put a slice of cheese on top of each potato cake and grill for 2-3 minutes until lightly golden.
7 Serve with a light salad.

RED CABBAGE WITH APRICOTS AND BALSAMIC VINEGAR

50 g (2 oz) butter or margarine
1 onion, thinly sliced
½ tsp allspice
¼ tsp ground nutmeg
700 g (1½ lb/3 cups) red cabbage, thinly sliced
125 g (4 oz/½ cup) dried apricots, sliced
4 tbsp balsamic vinegar
Salt and freshly ground black pepper to taste   (Serves 6–8)

1 Melt butter or margarine in large pan over medium heat. Add onion, allspice and nutmeg and stir for one minute.
2 Add cabbage and apricots. Sauté until well coated, about 2 minutes.
3 Add vinegar and cook until cabbage is crisp-tender, about 5 minutes.
4 Season with salt and pepper.

SPROUT SNIPPET: Traditional balsamic vinegar is made in the hills near Modena, Italy. The vinegar is made through the natural fermentation of Trebbiano grapes. Through each iteration, the vinegar is poured into a series of wooden casks, typically made of oak, chestnut, cherry ash and mulberry, each imparting a different flavour to the concoction. Like a good malt whisky, it takes 12 years to make a 'tradizionale' balsamic vinegar and 25 years to make a 'tradizionale extra vecchio'. Non traditional or commercial balsamic vinegar is usually what you would buy in your local supermarket. It constitutes a more economic alternative to the very expensive traditional product. Look for commercial products of high quality that are suitable for use in marinades, salad dressings and sauces.

RED CABBAGE WITH CHESTNUT SAUCE

1 tbsp olive oil
2 onions, chopped
2 cloves garlic, crushed
½ tsp ground coriander
1 large red cabbage, sliced
450 g (1 lb/2 cups) chestnuts, peeled
225 ml (8 fl oz/1 cup) vegetable stock
2 tbsp red wine vinegar
Salt and freshly ground black pepper
2 ripe pears, peeled and sliced   (Serves 6)

1   In a large pan, heat oil and cook onions, garlic and
    coriander until onions are tender.
2   Add cabbage and cook for 3–5 minutes.
3   Add chestnuts, stock, vinegar, salt and pepper.
    Cover and cook on a low heat for about 20 minutes.
4   Add pears and cook for another 10 minutes.
5   Serve with crispy roast potatoes.

RED CABBAGE, SWEET AND SOUR

1 tbsp olive oil
700 g (1½ lb/3 cups) red cabbage, chopped finely
225 g (8 oz/1 cup) carrots, grated
1 onion, finely chopped
2 cloves garlic, crushed
½ tsp ground ginger
¼ tsp cayenne pepper

For the blender

125 g (4 oz/½ cup) prunes, pitted
150 ml (¼ pint/5 fl oz) apple juice
4 tbsp vinegar

2 tbsp soy sauce
2 tbsp cornflour   (Serves 4-6)

1   In a large pan, heat oil and add cabbage, carrots, onion,
    garlic, ginger and cayenne pepper. Cook until vegetables
    are crisp-tender, about 10 minutes.
2   Put the rest of the ingredients into a blender and purée
    until smooth.
3   Add to the cooked vegetables and mix together. Continue
    cooking, stirring frequently until liquid is thickened.

Now for our first swede recipes. In America swede is called rutabaga. According to Darra Goldstein in her book The Winter Vegetarian, "Rutabaga is one of the world's least understood vegetables and may also be the most maligned. Noses turn up at the very word. [Robin is our testament to this fact]. Yet under the rough skin of this unprepossessing tuber a treasure lies hidden: flesh rich and flavourful, the colour of gold. It is not an ancient food, having made its first appearance only in the seventeenth century. We do know that a Swiss botanist Caspar Bauhin first described rutabaga in 1620. Scientists are unsure whether Bauhin himself developed the plant through experimentation or it arose spontaneously in nature". (Was this the first GM vegetable?!)

"As its French name of chou-navet suggests, the rutabaga is a cross between cabbage and white turnip. Its 38 chromosomes represent a hybridization of the turnip's twenty chromosomes and the cabbage's eighteen."

SWEDE IN CIDER

1 tbsp olive oil
1 onion, chopped
450 g (1 lb/2 cups) swede, peeled and diced
1 tsp dried tarragon

½ tsp dried thyme
2 tbsp dried currants
½ tsp ground cinnamon
450 ml (16 fl oz/2 cups) dry cider
Salt and freshly ground black pepper to taste
150 ml (5 fl oz/¼ pint) cream   (Serves 4)

1   Heat the oil in a pan and sauté the onion until soft, about
    5 minutes.
2   Add the swede and sauté for about 5-10 minutes or until
    browned.
3   Add the tarragon, thyme, currants, cinnamon, cider and
    season to taste. Bring to the boil, reduce heat and
    simmer for about 15 minutes or until swede is cooked
    and liquid has reduced.
4   Stir in the cream and serve with rice.

SWEDE AND LEEK SOUP
2 tbsp vegetable or olive oil
700 g (1½ lb/3 cups) swede, peeled and diced
225 g (8 oz/1 cup) potatoes, peeled and diced
450 g (1 lb/2 cups) leeks, sliced and washed well
1 garlic clove, crushed
½ tsp mixed herbs
1.5 L (2 ½ pints/6 cups) vegetable stock
Salt and freshly ground black pepper to taste
150 ml (¼ pint/5 fl oz) milk   (Serves 4-6)

1   Heat the oil in a large pan and sauté the swede, potatoes,
    leeks and garlic for about 5 minutes.
2   Add the mixed herbs, vegetable stock and season to taste.
3   Bring to the boil, reduce heat and simmer for about

    30 minutes or until vegetables are soft.
4   Soup can be left like this, or puréed if you like a
    smooth texture.
5   Stir in the milk, reheat and serve.

In Scotland, swede is traditionally served mashed with butter and pepper and, probably as you know, is called 'neeps'. We found several interesting variations of swede purée.

SWEDE PURÉE WITH CHEESE AND PEARS
450 g (1 lb/2 cups) swede, peeled and sliced
450 g (1 lb/2 cups) pears, peeled and cored
50 g (2 oz) butter or margarine
1 onion, chopped
50 g (2 oz) mature Cheddar cheese
Salt and freshly ground black pepper to taste
¼ tsp nutmeg, grated   (Serves 6-8)

1   Put swede into salted water. Bring to the boil, reduce
    heat and simmer until tender, about 10-15 minutes. Drain
    and set aside.
2   Steam pears over boiling water for about 5-10 minutes,
    or until pears are tender.
3   Melt butter or margarine in a pan and sauté onion until
    tender, about 5 minutes.
4   Transfer onion mixture to food processor. Add the
    swede, pears and cheese. Process until smooth.
    Season to taste.
5   Transfer mixture to a serving bowl and sprinkle with
    nutmeg. Can be served hot or chilled.

SWEDE PUREE WITH CREME FRAICHE, GINGER AND NUTMEG

700g (1 ½ lb/3 cups) swede, peeled and diced
25 g (1 oz) butter or margarine
½ tsp ground ginger
¼ tsp nutmeg, grated
Salt and freshly ground black pepper to taste
2 tbsp crème fraîche
To garnish
Extra crème fraîche
2 tbsp parsley, roughly chopped
Freshly ground black pepper   (Serves 4)

1   Put swede in salted water and bring to the boil. Reduce heat and simmer for about 15 minutes or until very tender. Drain. Purée in a food processor until smooth.
2   Transfer purée into a saucepan. Stir in the butter or margarine, ginger and nutmeg. Season with salt and pepper. Gently heat through.
3   Stir in the crème fraîche and place mixture into a serving dish. Garnish with a swirl of crème fraîche, parsley and freshly ground black pepper.

SWEDE PUREE WITH GROUND ELDER

The Romans introduced ground elder into Britain as a source of vitamin C. You can use any root vegetable in this recipe. It was donated by Phil Read, a local tennis coach.

2 handfuls of ground elder, washed and sliced into
2 cm (¾") lengths
450 g (1 lb) swede, peeled and diced
2-3 tbsp single or double cream
50 g (2 oz) butter or margarine

Salt and freshly ground black pepper to taste   (Serves 4)

1   Put sliced elder into boiling salted water. Bring back to the boil, reduce heat and simmer for about 10 minutes or until tender. Drain.
2   Put swede into salted water, bring to the boil, reduce heat and simmer until tender, about 15 minutes. Drain.
3   Mash swede or blend. Add cream and butter or margarine. Season to taste.
4   Add ground elder, stir and serve.

SPROUT SNIPPET: Jack-jump-about is a folk name for ground elder. It's every gardener's nightmare so we were amazed to discover that it is edible. You can eat it on its own like spinach by heating a knob of butter in a pan, adding some water and cooking the ground elder leaves for about 10 minutes. Drain, add salt, pepper, nutmeg, lemon juice and serve. You can also add it to stews.

SWEDE PUREE WITH WHISKY AND CREAM

900 g (2 lb) swede, peeled and cubed
45 g (1½ oz) butter or margarine
3 tbsp whisky
2 tbsp single cream
Salt and freshly ground black pepper to taste   (Serves 4-6)

1   Put swede in a pan with salted water, bring to the boil, reduce heat and simmer until tender, about 15 minutes. Drain.
2   Transfer swede to a food processor.
3   Add butter or margarine, whisky, cream and season to taste.
4   Process until smooth.

"Above and beyond any other motivation, it is apparently the quality and variety of the produce that lures most people to join a CSA and keep them interested year after year. CSAs offer foods that would never survive being picked at the peak of perfection, being trucked long distances, and then being pawed over by shoppers."

From 'Farms of Tomorrow Revisited'
by Trauger Groh & Steven McFadden

SPROUT SNIPPET: What is the difference between a swede and a turnip? In some areas you ask for a swede and receive a large orange-fleshed vegetable. In other areas you need to ask for a turnip to receive a large orange-fleshed vegetable. On top of this, a swede is called a rutabaga or yellow turnip in the United States. One definition of a turnip, as we understand, is that it is a smaller cousin of the swede or rutabaga. It has white flesh with a purple trimming and green top. It has a sharper taste and is most frequently available during the summer before the new crop of swede or rutabaga. Some people call it a 'white turnip'. Our recipes are written for the orange-fleshed vegetable. Confused? So are we! Be reassured the recipes work with all three, whatever you call it.

NOTES:

FARMING NEWS FOR FEBRUARY

Potato grading or dressing is done weekly.

HARVESTING

Broccoli, Brussels sprouts, green and red cabbage, cauliflower, chicory, curly kale, leeks, parsnip and swede continue to be cropped. In addition, the harvesting of oriental greens from polytunnels at Cullerne commences. Most of the oriental greens come from Northern China and Japan, which have much colder winters than Scotland. These varieties of salad greens always do well in the conditions created within the polytunnels, better than over-wintered lettuce, which is subject to mildew.

PLANTING

Christopher sows the first carrots, lettuce, radish and spinach in modules in the polytunnels at Cullerne, ready for April. The carrots are ready to crop in late May to dovetail with the end of the last season's carrots.

WEATHER

The weather is best described as lousy: windy and too cold to work on machines outside. It beats the canker, root fly and anything else to become the pest this month.

Pak Choi

Christopher Raymont with trailer of EarthShare vegetables

BEETROOT PIE

(Donated by Mathis, EarthShare)

450 g (1 lb/2 cups) cooked and peeled beetroot
125 g (4 oz/½ cup) raw onion
1 egg
50 g (2 oz/½ cup) flour
1 tbsp mustard
8 tbsp cream
Salt and pepper to taste   (Serves 4)

1   Blend beetroot and onion in a food processor until smooth.
2   Add remaining ingredients and blend thoroughly.
3   Place mixture into an oiled baking dish. Set the dish in a shallow baking or roasting tin, with about 2.5 cm (1") of cold water and bake for about 30 minutes at 220°C (425°F/Gas 7).
4   Serve with millet, potatoes or potato cakes with goat's cheese on page 38.

BEETROOT AND WALNUT HOUMOUS

2 medium beetroot, scrubbed but not topped and tailed
1 onion, chopped
400 g (14 oz tin) chickpeas or cooked chickpeas
5 cloves garlic
45 g (1 ½ oz/2 tbsp) tahini
90 g (3 oz/½ cup) roasted walnuts
1 tsp ground cumin
2-4 tbsp olive oil
1 tsp salt
Black pepper to taste
2 tbsp water
2 tsp lemon juice   (Serves 4)

1   Place beetroot in a saucepan with cold, salted water. Bring to the boil, reduce heat and simmer until cooked, about one hour depending on size. Drain, remove skin, and quarter.
2   Put cooked beetroot, onion, drained chickpeas and rest of ingredients into a food processor and blend thoroughly. Adjust seasoning to taste.
3   Serve as a starter or light lunch on pitta bread.

BRUSSELS SPROUTS WITH OLIVE AND RED PEPPER SAUCE

225 g (8 oz/1 cup) Brussels sprouts, trimmed with outer leaves removed
2 tbsp olive oil
1 clove of garlic, crushed
15 black olives, finely chopped
1 red pepper, finely chopped
Salt and freshly ground black pepper to taste
To serve: spaghetti, for 4   (Serves 4)

1   Put Brussels sprouts into boiling salted water. Bring back to the boil, cover, reduce heat and simmer until tender, then finely chop.
2   In a large pan, heat oil and sauté garlic for about 2 minutes.
3   Add Brussels sprouts, olives and red pepper. Season to taste. Sauté until pepper is crisp-tender.
4   Cook enough spaghetti for 4, add to Brussels sprouts mixture and stir well.
5   Serve immediately.

: Many people who do not like Brussels sprouts (Jacqui included) are haunted by childhood memories of smelly, green, mushy globs that had to be eaten before pudding. Fresh Brussels sprouts, properly cooked, are delicate in flavour. Try some of these recipes and give them another chance.

BRUSSELS SPROUTS, ORANGE AND HONEY GLAZED

450 g (1 lb/2 cups) Brussels sprouts, trimmed with
outer leaves removed
½ fresh orange, cut into wedges
25 g (1 oz) butter or margarine
1 tbsp honey
¼ tsp ground cloves   (Serves 4)

1   Put Brussels sprouts into boiling salted water, bring back
    to the boil, cover, reduce heat and simmer until tender,
    about 10 minutes. Drain.
2   Add rest of ingredients to sprouts in the pan and
    stir well.
3   Transfer to serving dish.

SPROUT SNIPPET: To relieve constipation, drink a mixture of one teaspoon each of olive oil and lemon juice before breakfast.

CABBAGE WITH COCONUT

3 tbsp vegetable or olive oil
Pinch of mustard seeds
¼ tsp chilli powder
450 g (1 lb/2 cups) cabbage, finely shredded
¼ tsp turmeric
2½ tsp mustard powder
2 tbsp water

50 g (2 oz) desiccated coconut
Salt and freshly ground black pepper to taste   (Serves 4)

1   Heat oil in pan and fry mustard seeds until they begin to pop.
2   Add chilli powder, cabbage and turmeric and cook gently
    for about 5 minutes, stirring occasionally. Cover and
    simmer until the cabbage is tender.
3   Mix the mustard powder with water to make a paste and
    add to pan.
4   Add coconut, salt and pepper. Cook, stirring occasionally
    until the liquid has almost been absorbed.

Serving suggestions: Serve with boiled rice or bread

CABBAGE, SPICED

2 tbsp olive oil
2 medium onions, sliced in rings
½ tsp cumin seeds
450 g (1 lb/2 cups) cabbage or spring greens, shredded
¼ tsp chilli powder
1 tsp garam masala
Salt and freshly ground black pepper to taste
Lemon wedges to serve   (Serves 4)

1   Heat oil in large pan. Add the onions and fry until golden
    brown, about 10 minutes, stirring from time to time.
2   Add the cumin seeds and cook over a medium heat for
    one minute.
3   Add cabbage and cook until leaves are shiny and tender.
4   Add chilli, garam masala and seasoning. Cook for 3–4
    minutes, stirring constantly.
5   Serve hot with lemon wedges.

CARROT BAKE WITH HORSERADISH AND CHEESE

450 g (1 lb/2 cups) carrots, washed or peeled and cut into
1.25 cm (½") slices
2 tbsp onion, finely chopped
4 tbsp mayonnaise
4 tbsp water
1 tbsp creamed horseradish
Salt and freshly ground black pepper to taste
Topping
125 g (4 oz) fresh breadcrumbs
45 g (1 ½ oz) butter or margarine
125 g (4 oz) Cheddar cheese, grated   (Serves 4)

1 Bring carrots to boil in salted water. Reduce heat and simmer until just tender. Drain and place in a baking dish, set aside.
2 In a bowl combine the onion, mayonnaise, water, horseradish and seasoning. Mix well.
3 Pour over carrots.
4 Mix together the topping ingredients and sprinkle on top of the carrots.
5 Bake in oven 180°C (350°F/Gas 4) for about 25 minutes or until golden.

CARROTS, BUTTERED WITH TARRAGON
(Donated by Pam Bochel of EarthShare)

4 large carrots, cut into batons
50 g (2 oz/½ stick) butter
2 tbsp fresh tarragon, or 1 tsp dried tarragon
Salt and freshly ground black pepper to taste   (Serves 4)

1 Place half the carrots in greased ovenproof dish.
2 Dot with half the butter and sprinkle with half the tarragon.
3 Place the second half of the carrots on top of the first, dot with the rest of the butter and tarragon. Season to taste if required.
4 Cover with lid or foil, and bake for about 30 minutes at 190°C (375°F/Gas 5) or until carrots are tender.

CARROT AND COCONUT SOUP
(Another delicious recipe from Pam Bochel)

125 g (4 oz/½ cup) red lentils
225 g (8 oz/1 cup) carrots, grated
½ medium onion, chopped
2 cloves garlic, chopped
1 tbsp tomato purée
600 ml (1 pint/20 fl oz) water or vegetable stock
1 tbsp creamed coconut, grated from block
Salt and freshly ground black pepper to taste   (Serves 4)

1 Cook lentils, carrots, onion, garlic and tomato purée in the water or stock for about 20 minutes, or until lentils are soft.
2 Add the coconut. Simmer for 2–3 minutes.
3 Liquidise until smooth.
4 Season to taste and reheat gently adding more liquid if necessary.

CAULIFLOWER AND BRUSSELS SPROUTS TOPS, WITH SPICES AND LIME JUICE

2 tbsp olive oil
1 onion, thinly sliced
2 garlic cloves, chopped

1 cauliflower (white or green), broken into florets
1 carrot peeled and finely chopped
3 medium potatoes, peeled and cubed
½ tsp turmeric
1 tsp ground cumin
1 tsp mustard seeds
Salt and freshly ground black pepper to taste
450 g (1 lb/2 cups) Brussels sprouts tops, chopped
Juice and zest of one lime   (Serves 4-6)

1   Heat oil in a large pan and sauté the onion and garlic until
    browned, about 8-10 minutes.
2   Add the cauliflower, carrot and potato and mix well.
3   Add the turmeric, cumin, mustard seeds, salt and pepper.
4   Add the sprout tops with 150 ml (¼ pint/5 fl oz) water.
5   Cover and cook until the sprout tops have wilted, about
    3-5 minutes.
6   Add the lime zest and juice.
7   Mix well and serve with rice.

CURLY KALE AND CHICKPEA BALTI

1 tbsp olive oil
1 medium onion, chopped
2 garlic cloves, crushed
1 tsp cumin seeds
1 tbsp ground coriander
1 tsp turmeric
225 g (8 oz/1 cup) curly kale, cut into fine strips
1 x 400 g (14 oz) tin tomatoes
1 x 400 g (14 oz) tin chickpeas, drained and rinsed
Salt and freshly ground black pepper to taste   (Serves 4)

1   Heat oil in a pan and add onion and garlic. Sauté for

about 3 minutes.
2   Add cumin seeds, coriander, and turmeric and sauté for
    another 2-3 minutes.
3   Add the curly kale, tomatoes and chickpeas. Bring to the
    boil, reduce heat and simmer for 5-10 minutes, or until
    kale is cooked.
4   Season to taste.
5   Serve with rice or chapattis.

CURLY KALE WITH GARLIC AND CINNAMON

1 tbsp olive oil
1 medium onion, chopped
2 cloves garlic
½ tsp ground cinnamon
450 g (1 lb/2 cups) curly kale, finely chopped
225 ml (8 fl oz/1 cup) vegetable stock
1 tsp red wine vinegar
Salt and freshly ground black pepper to taste   (Serves 4)

1   Heat oil in pan and sauté onion for 5 minutes. Add garlic
    and cook for further 2 minutes.
2   Stir in the cinnamon.
3   Add the kale, and mix well.
4   Add the vegetable stock and wine vinegar. Bring to the
    boil, reduce heat, cover and simmer for about 15 minutes
    or until kale is tender. Season to taste.

CURLY KALE WITH RED PEPPERS

2 tbsp olive oil
1 medium onion, chopped
2 garlic cloves, crushed
1 large red pepper, seeded and chopped
450 g (1 lb/2 cups) curly kale, finely chopped

Salt and freshly ground black pepper to taste   (Serves 4)

1 In a pan heat the oil and sauté onion, garlic and red pepper until onions become transparent, about 5 minutes.
2 Add curly kale and mix well so that it gets coated with the oil mixture. Add up to 4 tablespoons of water if kale appears a little dry.
3 Sauté for about 5-10 minutes until kale is cooked.
4 Season to taste.

LEEKS AND GREENS WITH PASTA

3 tbsp olive oil
450 g (1 lb/2 cups) leeks, sliced and washed well
2 garlic cloves, crushed
900 g (2 lb/4 cups) mixed greens, chopped
Salt and freshly ground black pepper to taste
450 g (1 lb) pasta
To garnish: 1 tbsp Parmesan cheese   (Serves 4-6)

Any greens can be used for this recipe such as sprout tops, Chinese cabbage, beet greens, chard, sprouting broccoli.

1 In a large pan, heat the oil and add the leeks and sauté until very soft, about 10 minutes.
2 Add garlic and sauté for about one more minute.
3 Add chopped greens and continue cooking for about another 5-8 minutes or until greens are soft and tender. Season well.
4 Meanwhile, cook pasta, following instructions on packet. Drain and toss with greens and leeks.
5 Add another tablespoon of olive oil to the mixture.
6 Sprinkle with Parmesan cheese.

LEEK AND LEMON SOUP

2 tbsp olive oil
4 medium leeks, washed well and finely sliced
1 medium onion, chopped
6 celery sticks, chopped
2 bay leaves
1 litre (1¾ pints) vegetable stock
Salt and freshly ground black pepper to taste
Juice and grated rind of one lemon
To garnish: celery leaves   (Serves 4)

1 In a large pan, heat olive oil and add leeks, onion, and celery sticks. Stir until they are completely coated with oil. Add bay leaves. Sauté until vegetables are soft.
2 Add vegetable stock, bring to the boil, reduce heat and simmer for about 40 minutes. Adjust seasoning.
3 Stir in juice and grated rind of lemon just before serving.
4 Garnish with celery leaves.

This soup can be liquidised if preferred. Place cooked soup in blender and zap until smooth. Serve with toast or crusty breads.

LEEK AND LENTIL RISOTTO

1 tbsp olive or vegetable oil
4 leeks, washed well and chopped
4 cloves garlic, sliced or crushed
1 red pepper, finely chopped
600 ml (1 pint/2½ cups) vegetable stock or water
225 g (8 oz/1 cup) white rice
225 g (8 oz/1 cup) red lentils
Salt and freshly ground black pepper to taste
½ tsp dried basil

To garnish
1 tbsp chopped fresh parsley
75 g (3oz) finely grated carrots   (Serves 4)

1 Heat oil in a pan and sauté leeks, garlic and red pepper
   until soft.
2 Add vegetable stock or water and stir in rice, lentils,
   seasoning and basil. Bring to boil, then reduce heat and
   simmer covered for about 10–15 minutes or until rice and
   lentils are cooked.
3 Place in serving dish and garnish with fresh parsley and
   grated carrot.

NOTE: Brown rice can be used instead of white rice. Make sure
you cook the brown rice for 25 minutes before adding the lentils,
then cook for a further 15 minutes once lentils have been added
to pan.

LEEKS WITH PEARS AND MASHED POTATO

8 medium potatoes (peeled or not, as you prefer) cut into
1.25 cm (½") cubes
3 ripe pears, peeled, cored and cut into 2.5 cm (1") cubes
50 g (2 oz) butter or margarine
225 g (8 oz/1 cup) leeks, washed well and sliced
Salt and freshly ground black pepper to taste   (Serves 4)

1 Put potatoes and pears into salted water, bring to the boil,
   reduce heat and simmer for 5–10 minutes, until very tender.
2 Melt 25 g (1 oz) of the butter or margarine in pan over a
   medium heat and sauté leeks until lightly browned and
   quite soft. Set aside.
3 When potatoes and pears are cooked, mash well with remaining butter or margarine, adding salt and pepper to taste.
4 Stir in the sautéed leeks and serve.

LEEK AND THREE-CHEESE PÂTÉ
WITH VERMOUTH

2 tbsp olive oil
3–5 cloves garlic, chopped or crushed
2 large leeks, washed and cut into long thin strips
1 tsp soy sauce
2 tbsp dry vermouth
340 g (12 oz) Brie cheese, sliced
225 g (8 oz) blue cheese, sliced
225 g (8 oz) cream cheese
½ tbsp freshly ground black pepper
                            (Makes about 3 x 225 g/½ lb jars)

1 Heat oil in pan over medium heat. Add garlic and leeks.
   Sauté until golden brown.
2 Stir in soy sauce and dry vermouth and sauté until liquid
   is absorbed and evaporated. Allow to cool.
3 Place the three cheeses in a food processor. Add leek
   mixture and pepper. Pulse until combined.
4 Transfer to serving dish.

Serve with flat breads and crusty olive bread. Can store in the
refrigerator in jars.

LEEK AND TOMATO SOUP
WITH BASIL CREAM

1 tbsp vegetable or olive oil
2 medium leeks, washed and chopped
2 x 400 g tins of tomatoes
1 tbsp butter or margarine (optional)
1 tbsp brown sugar
Salt and freshly ground black pepper to taste
4 tbsp single or double cream

1 tbsp fresh basil, chopped   (Serves 4)

1 Heat oil in pan and sauté leeks until tender.
2 Add tomatoes, bring to the boil, reduce heat and simmer
   for 10 minutes. Cool slightly.
3 Place vegetables in blender and purée until smooth.
   Return to pan.
4 Stir in butter or margarine and add sugar and seasoning
   to taste.
5 Mix cream and basil together in a bowl and stir well. Add
   salt to taste, and heat through.
6 Ladle soup into bowls and garnish with basil cream.
7 Serve with hot crusty bread.

LEEK AND WALNUT SOUP

This is an interesting medieval recipe – perfect for a cold
winter evening.

4 medium leeks, washed and coarsely chopped
10 fl oz (½ pint/1¼ cups) vegetable stock
5 fl oz (¼ pint/½ cup) white wine (optional)
¼ tsp salt
1 tbsp sugar
125 g (4 oz/¾ cup) finely chopped walnuts
1 tsp vinegar   (Serves 4)

1 Place leeks, vegetable stock and wine in large saucepan
   with lid. Bring to boil, reduce heat and simmer for about
   12 minutes, or until just cooked.
2 Add salt, sugar, nuts and vinegar. Simmer uncovered for
   7 minutes.
3 Ladle into individual serving bowls.

PARSNIP AND EROTIC BANANA EXPERIENCE

We called this erotic – make it and see why! An ideal dish on
St. Valentine's Day.

4 medium sized parsnips, peeled and left whole
4 cabbage leaves, blanched
25 g (1 oz) butter or margarine
2 spring onions, chopped
1 red pepper, chopped
4 tbsp lemon juice
4 tbsp maple syrup
2 bananas, mashed   (Serves 4)

1 Put whole parsnips into salted water. Bring to the boil,
   reduce heat and simmer until tender, about 15-20
   minutes. Drain and keep warm.
2 Blanch 4 cabbage leaves by putting them into boiling
   water, quickly return to the boil, and simmer for about
   2 minutes. Immediately after blanching, drain and plunge
   the cabbage leaves into cold water to cool and to prevent
   further cooking. Put onto a serving dish.
3 Heat butter or margarine in a pan and sauté the spring
   onions, red pepper, lemon juice and maple syrup until
   sauce gives a glossy coating.
4 Add bananas and heat through gently.
5 Cut parsnips in half lengthwise, almost to the base and
   spread apart and lay on blanched cabbage leaves
6 Spoon the banana mixture into the cut parsnip and serve.

SERVING SUGGESTIONS: Great by itself, or with lightly
cooked fresh greens or a crispy salad.
VARIATION: You can use any other root vegetable instead
of parsnips.

PARSNIPS WITH HONEY AND ORANGE

700 g (1½ lb/3 cups) parsnips, peeled and diagonally sliced
1.25 cm (½") thick
25 g (1 oz) butter or margarine
1 tbsp honey
4 tbsp orange juice
Grated rind of one orange
Salt and freshly ground black pepper to taste   (Serves 4–6)

1   In saucepan, cook sliced parsnips in salted water over a
    medium heat until just tender, about 10 minutes.
2   Drain and remove from pan. In same pan heat butter or
    margarine, honey, juice and orange rind together.
3   Toss with parsnips and season as required.

Variation: You can use swede instead of parsnips.

POTATOES WITH FETA CHEESE AND OLIVES

150 ml (¼ pint/5 fl oz) olive oil
900 g (2 lb) potatoes, peeled
1 tbsp fresh rosemary or 1 tsp dried rosemary
275 g (10 oz) Feta cheese, crumbled
125 g (4 oz) black and green olives, pitted
300 ml (½ pint/10 fl oz) vegetable stock
Salt and freshly ground black pepper to taste   (Serves 6-8)

1   Preheat oven to 200°C (400°F/Gas 6).
2   Grease an ovenproof dish with some of the olive oil.
3   Place potatoes in a pan of salted water, bring to the boil,
    reduce heat and simmer for about 15-20 minutes, or until
    just tender. Drain and cool slightly.
4   Cut the potatoes into thin slices.
5   Layer the potatoes in the ovenproof dish with the

rosemary, Feta cheese a
6   Drizzle over remaining olive o
7   Season to taste.
8   Cover with foil and bake in the oven fo
9   Serve.

PURPLE SPROUTING BROCCOLI
WITH POTATOES AND DILL

700 g (1½ lb/3 cups) potatoes, peeled and cut into 2.5 cm
(1") chunks
1 medium onion, chopped
½ tsp dried dill weed or 4 fresh dill sprigs
225 g (½ lb/1 cup) purple sprouting broccoli
3 tbsp lemon juice
1 tbsp olive oil
Salt and freshly ground black pepper to taste   (Serves 4)

1   Bring potatoes, onion and dill to boil in salted water,
    reduce heat and simmer until tender, about 10-15
    minutes. Drain and remove dill sprigs if using fresh dill.
2   Put broccoli into boiling salted water, return to boil,
    reduce heat and simmer until tender, about 5-10 minutes.
    Drain.
3   Place potatoes, onion and broccoli in a large bowl. Add
    lemon juice, olive oil and pepper. Mix well.
4   Serve warm as a main dish, or chill for 1 hour and serve
    as a salad.

...LI

...lso tells his friends and his
... Joan likes it because there
...you can use all of the broccoli,
...p roughly.

...d cut into 0.6 cm (¼") slices
...e sprouting broccoli, including

22... ...ar cheese, grated
225 g (... ...age cheese
2 eggs, beate...
1 medium onion, ch...ped (optional)
1½ tsp Dijon mustard
Salt and freshly ground black pepper to taste

Topping
50 g (2 oz/¼ cup) Cheddar cheese, grated   (Serves 6)

1 Put potatoes into salted water, bring to the boil, reduce
   heat and simmer for about 5-10 minutes or until potatoes
   are just cooked but holding their shape. Drain.
2 Grease a 24 cm (9½") pie dish. Arrange the sliced, boiled
   potatoes in a single layer over the bottom and sides of the
   dish to form a crust. Brush the sides with oil.
3 Excluding the topping, combine broccoli and the rest of the
   ingredients together in a large bowl and stir to mix well.
4 Pour the broccoli mixture into the crust. Top with grated cheese.
5 Bake at 190°C (375°F/Gas 5) for about 45 minutes, or
   until the top is golden brown and a sharp knife inserted
   into the centre of the quiche comes out clean.
6 Remove the dish from the oven and let sit for 5 minutes
   before slicing and serving.

PURPLE SPROUTING BROCCOLI WITH SESAME SAUCE

This recipe only takes 10 minutes for the cooking stage but you
need to allow an hour for the marinading.

900 g (2 lb/4 cups) purple sprouting broccoli, chopped into
bite-sized pieces
50 g (2 oz/¼ cup) sesame seeds, toasted
4 tbsp soy sauce
½ tsp honey
2 tbsp sesame oil   (Serves 6)

1 Put broccoli into boiling, salted water, return to boil, reduce
   heat and simmer until just tender, about 5 minutes. Cool.
2 Toast the sesame seeds by placing them on a baking tray
   and put under the grill for a couple of minutes until
   browned. Mix toasted sesame seeds with remaining
   ingredients in a large bowl. Add broccoli and marinade
   for at least 1 hour.
3 Serve on a bed of lettuce leaves.

RED CABBAGE CREAMY SOUP

2 tbsp vegetable or olive oil
1 leek, finely sliced and washed well
1 medium onion, finely sliced
900 g (2 lb/4 cups) red cabbage, sliced finely
350 g (12 oz/1½ cups) potatoes, thinly sliced
1 L (1¾ pints) vegetable stock
150 ml (¼ pint/5 fl oz) milk or cream
Salt and freshly ground black pepper to taste   (Serves 4–6)

1 In a medium saucepan, heat oil and sauté leek and onion
   until soft, but not browned.

2 Add red cabbage, potatoes and vegetable stock.
3 Cover, bring to the boil, reduce heat and simmer for about 30 minutes or until vegetables are tender.
4 Purée in a food processor or blender.
5 Pour soup back into saucepan and stir in milk or cream. Season.

SWEDE AND CARROTS WITH CHEESY CELERY SAUCE

450 g (1 lb/2 cups) swede, peeled and diced
350 g (12 oz/1½ cups) carrots, peeled and sliced
¼ tsp ground ginger
150 ml (¼ pint/5 fl oz) water
½ tsp salt
1 medium onion, peeled and chopped
125 g (4 oz/½ cup) celery, diced
45 g (1½ oz) butter or margarine
3 tbsp flour
Salt and freshly ground black pepper to taste
300 ml (½ pint/1¼ cups) milk
120 g (4 oz) Cheddar cheese, grated   (Serves 4–6)

1 In a saucepan combine swede, carrots, ginger, water and salt. Cover and cook over medium heat for 10–15 minutes or until vegetables are tender. Drain and reserve liquid. Set vegetables aside.
2 In a pan, sauté onion and celery in butter or margarine until tender.
3 Stir in flour and seasoning.
4 Gradually add milk and reserved vegetable liquid and cook, stirring continuously until thickened and bubbly.
5 Stir in cheese until melted.
6 Stir in the vegetables and serve.

SWEDE, BAKED WITH GRUYÈRE CHEESE AND CREAM

We found we liked this dish even better when we let the swede slightly overcook and become crisp. It reheats well. Try it with a different cheese, such as goat's cheese.

2 tbsp plain four
Salt and freshly ground black pepper
450 g (1 lb/2 cups) swede, peeled, quartered and thinly sliced
1 clove garlic, crushed
75 g (3 oz) Gruyère cheese, grated
15 g (½ oz) butter or margarine
575 ml (20 fl oz/1 pint/2½ cups) single cream   (Serves 4)

1 Preheat oven to 190°C (375°F/Gas 5).
2 Mix flour, salt and pepper into a mixing bowl. Add the swede slices and toss well to coat the slices in flour.
3 Grease an ovenproof dish with butter or margarine and rub the crushed garlic over the inside of the dish.
4 Layer the flour-coated swede slices in the dish with the grated Gruyère cheese, ending with a layer of cheese.
5 Dot 15 g (½ oz) butter over the surface of the swede and pour over the cream.
6 Bake in oven for about one and a half hours until golden brown and the swede is tender. Cover with foil during cooking if over browning.

SWEDE ROASTED WITH MAPLE SYRUP

Roasting gives the swede a sweet caramelised flavour.

450 g (1 lb/2 cups) swede, peeled and diced
2 tbsp olive oil
15 g (½ oz) butter or margarine

Salt and freshly ground black pepper to taste
2 tbsp maple syrup   (Serves 4)

1   Preheat oven to 190°C (375°F/Gas 5).
2   Place swede on a baking tray. Drizzle over olive oil and
    dot with butter or margarine. Season to taste.
3   Roast in preheated oven for about 10 minutes, stirring
    occasionally.
4   Pour over maple syrup and mix well, and roast for about
    another 10 minutes or until golden brown and tender,
    stirring occasionally.

SPROUT SNIPPET: Indian tribes share various legends about
how maple syrup was first made. One relates to the experience of
an Algonquin chief. He struck a maple tree with his axe one day.
His wife saw the tree wound dripping. She collected the sap in a
wooden bucket and used it to boil the meat for supper. Both the
chief and his wife were amazed at the sweetness of the meat
that night.

SWEDE ROASTED SOUP WITH CREAM
450 g (1 lb/2 cups) swede, peeled and diced
3 tbsp olive oil
Salt and freshly ground pepper to taste
1 medium onion, chopped
2 carrots, finely sliced
2 cloves garlic, crushed
½ tsp dried thyme
1 L (1¾ pints/36 fl oz) vegetable stock
150 ml (5 fl oz/¼ pint) single cream   (Serves 4)

1   Preheat oven to 190°C (375°F/Gas 5).
2   Place the swede on a baking tray. Drizzle over 2
    tablespoons of the olive oil and add seasoning.

3   Roast in the preheated oven for about 20 minutes or
    until golden brown and tender, stirring occasionally.
4   Heat the remaining oil in a pan, stir in the onion, carrots,
    garlic and thyme and cook for 4-5 minutes until softened
    but not browned.
5   Add the roasted swede to the pan with the vegetable
    stock. Bring gently to the boil, reduce heat, cover and
    simmer for about 15-20 minutes, stirring occasionally.
6   Purée the soup in a food processor or blender until smooth.
7   Transfer soup to a saucepan. Stir in most of the cream,
    reserving some for garnishing and gently heat through.
8   Ladle into individual bowls and garnish with a swirl of
    cream and a pinch of dried thyme.

SPROUT SNIPPET: Swede was one of the vegetables that really
plunged Joan in to her then 2 sprouter guilt and drove her into the
depths of despair. So, it really was the darkest hour before dawn
before she and Jacqui got together to conceive this book.

FARMING NEWS FOR MARCH

In the words of Mathis: "Muck spreading and cultivating, tilling and ploughing. The sap is rising and the farmer is getting excited and restless".

One of the EarthShare celebrations takes place near to the time of the Spring Equinox, 21/22 March. Called the Spring Blessing, it is held in the fields where many of the crops are grown. Water collected from the Findhorn River, some EarthShare seed potatoes, broad bean seeds and onion sets are placed together on the ground and subscribers form a large circle around them. They link hands and sing, led by Sheila Pettitt. They ask for blessings for their land and its crops in the coming year, including field land, Cullerne gardens and Rafford. Some subscribers plant the first of the seed potatoes, others put in broad beans and onion sets. While the planting takes place, a group of subscribers walk around the boundaries of the EarthShare fields to view and bless the land.

HARVESTING
Brussels sprouts, carrots, chicory, curly kale, green and red cabbage, purple sprouting broccoli, parsnips, swede, leeks, and potatoes. Rhubarb from Rafford, spinach and exotic salad greens such as Mizuna and Pak Choi from the polytunnels at Cullerne.

MAINTENANCE AND MACHINERY
This is often the month the EarthShare Land Rover gets its spring maintenance and anti-rusting painting of the chassis. This is particularly important because of the corrosive salt on the roads and in the atmosphere from being so close to the sea.

PLANTING
The first onion sets are planted, as are parsnips and the early potatoes in the open fields. The broad beans are also planted using EarthShare's own saved seed. First outdoor sowings at Cullerne of rocket, radish and peas.

WEATHER
Often wetter than we want. Mathis is frequently seen at field gates waiting eagerly for dry days to start the fieldwork.

An abundance of carrots!

BRUSSELS SPROUTS WITH BALSAMIC VINEGAR

700 g (1½ lb/3 cups) Brussels sprouts, washed and trimmed
2 tbsp olive oil
2 cloves garlic, crushed
1 onion, peeled and chopped
4 tbsp balsamic vinegar
25 g (1 oz) butter or margarine
Salt and freshly ground black pepper to taste   (Serves 6)

1   Bring salted water to the boil, add Brussels sprouts,
    cover the pan and quickly return to the boil. Reduce heat
    and simmer until just tender, about 10 minutes. Drain.
2   In a large frying pan, heat the oil and add the garlic and
    onion. Sauté for a few minutes until the onion just
    becomes tender.
3   Add the Brussels sprouts and heat through.
4   Add the vinegar so that all the sprouts are coated with
    the vinegar. Add the butter or margarine, season to
    taste and mix well.
5   Serve immediately.

BRUSSELS SPROUTS IN BEER

450 g (1 lb/2 cups) Brussels sprouts, washed and trimmed
275 ml (½ pint/1¼ cups) beer, any brand, to cover sprouts
25 g (1 oz) butter or margarine
Salt and freshly ground black pepper to taste   (Serves 4)

1   Place sprouts in a medium-sized saucepan and pour over
    enough beer to cover them.

2   Bring the boil, reduce heat, and simmer for about 10
    minutes, or until crisp-tender. Add more beer if needed,
    as liquid evaporates.
3   Drain, add butter or margarine, and season to taste.
4   Serve immediately.

BRUSSELS SPROUTS IN MUSTARD SAUCE

150 ml (¼ pint/5 fl oz) vegetable stock to cook sprouts
450 g (1 lb/2 cups) Brussels sprouts, washed and trimmed
1 tsp vegetable or olive oil
1 medium onion, peeled and chopped
1 tsp Dijon mustard
Salt and freshly ground black pepper to taste
1 tbsp cornflour
150 ml (¼ pint/5 fl oz) evaporated milk   (Serves 4)

1   Bring the vegetable stock to the boil, add the Brussels
    sprouts, cover the pan and quickly return to the boil.
    Reduce heat and simmer until just tender, about
    10 minutes.
2   You will need to reserve the stock, so drain the Brussels
    sprouts over a bowl.
3   Put drained Brussels sprouts into a serving dish
    and keep warm.
4   Heat the oil in a saucepan and sauté the onion until
    transparent. Remove from heat and add the reserved
    vegetable stock. Stir in the mustard and seasoning.
    Return to the heat.
5   Mix cornflour with the evaporated milk and then add to
    the vegetable stock. Cook, stirring continuously until the
    sauce is smooth and thickened. Add more water if needed.
6   Pour the mustard sauce over the Brussels sprouts and
    stir to coat. Serve immediately.

CABBAGE FRIED RICE

450 g (1 lb/2 cups) Basmati rice
50 g (2 oz/½ stick) butter or margarine
650 ml (24 fl oz/3 cups) water or vegetable stock
450 g (1 lb/2 cups) cabbage, cut into fine strips
225 g (8 oz/1 cup) carrots, cut into sticks
1 onion, chopped
1-2 garlic cloves, crushed
2.5 cm (1") piece fresh root ginger, peeled and finely chopped
1 tbsp fresh parsley, chopped
Salt and freshly ground black pepper to taste   (Serves 4-6)

1   Wash the rice.
2   Heat half the butter or margarine in a pan and fry the rice until the water the rice has been washed in has evaporated.
3   Add the water or vegetable stock. Bring to the boil, reduce heat and simmer until rice is cooked, about 8-10 minutes. Do not overcook the rice. Drain and keep warm.
4   Put the cabbage and carrots into boiling water, and cook until the carrots are crisp-tender, about 5-10 minutes. Drain and keep warm.
5   In another pan, melt the remaining butter or margarine and fry the onion, garlic and ginger until the onions are soft, about 4-5 minutes.
6   Add the cooked vegetables and parsley to the onion and garlic mixture. Stir well.
7   Add the cooked rice and mix well.

CABBAGE FRUIT SALAD

Robin: "Fruity cabbage salad? Are you trying to put me off fruit?"
Jacqui: "No, turn you on to cabbage."

1 apple, cored, unpeeled and diced.
1 tbsp fresh lemon juice
450 g (1 lb/2 cups) cabbage, finely sliced or grated
125 g (4 oz/½ cup) raisins
4 tbsp pineapple juice
2 tsp fresh lemon juice
1 tbsp sugar
125 ml (4 fl oz/½ cup) sour cream   (Serves 4)

1   Coat apple in 1 tablespoon of lemon juice to prevent darkening.
2   Place cabbage in a bowl.
3   Add raisins, pineapple juice, lemon juice, sugar and sour cream.
4   Mix well.
5   Refrigerate before serving.

CARROTS WITH APRICOTS AND GINGER

700 g (1½ lb/3 cups) carrots, peeled and sliced
2 tbsp vegetable or olive oil
1 onion, finely chopped
1-2 garlic cloves, crushed
2.5 cm (1") piece of fresh root ginger, peeled and chopped
125 g (4 oz) dried apricots, chopped
2 tbsp brown sugar
1 tbsp balsamic vinegar
Salt and freshly ground black pepper to taste   (Serves 6-8)

1   Put carrots in salted water, bring to the boil, reduce heat and simmer for about 10 minutes or until tender. Drain and keep warm.
2   Melt oil in a pan; add onion, garlic, ginger, apricots, brown sugar, vinegar, and seasoning. Cook over a medium heat

for about 4 minutes, stirring frequently.

3   Pour glaze over carrots, heat through and serve.

CARROTS WITH COUSCOUS AND THYME

2 tbsp olive oil
225 g (8 oz/1 cup) carrots, coarsely grated
2 tsp lemon juice
¼ tsp sugar
300 ml (10 fl oz/½ pint/1¼ cups) water
½ tsp fresh thyme leaves or ¼ tsp dried thyme
Salt and freshly ground black pepper to taste
225 g (8 oz/1 cup) couscous   (Serves 3-4)

1   Heat the oil in a pan and cook the carrots, for about 3
    minutes, stirring frequently.
2   Add the lemon juice, sugar, and one tablespoon of water,
    thyme, and season to taste. Simmer the mixture,
    covered for about 2 minutes.
3   Add the remaining water, bring to the boil and stir in
    the couscous.
4   Remove the pan from the heat, cover and let the
    couscous stand for about 5 minutes. You may need to
    adjust the water slightly.
5   Fluff the couscous with a fork and serve.

CARROT CHOCOLATE CAKE

This cake is made without eggs. It doesn't rise much, but is very
moist, dark and full of chocolate flavour. Seb loved it.

350 g (12 oz/1½ cups) carrots, peeled and grated
150 g (5 oz/¾ cup) granulated sugar
125 ml (4 fl oz/½ cup) vegetable oil

225 ml (8 fl oz/1 cup) boiling water
175 g (6 oz/1½ cups) wholewheat flour
1½ tsp baking powder
125 g (4 oz/½ cup) cocoa powder, unsweetened
1 tsp cinnamon
Pinch of salt

1   Pre-heat oven to 180°C (350°F/Gas 4).
2   Mix together the carrots, sugar and oil in a large bowl.
    Pour the water over the mixture.
3   In another bowl mix together flour, baking powder, cocoa,
    cinnamon and salt. Add to the carrot mixture and stir well.
4   Pour into a lightly greased and floured 20 cm (8") square
    pan and bake for about 35 minutes, or until a knife
    inserted into the centre of the cake comes out clean.
5   Remove from tin and cool on a wire rack.

CHICORY, BRAISED

2 tbsp vegetable or olive oil
900 g (2 lb/4 cups) chicory, washed and separated into spears
1 onion, finely chopped
Juice of ½ lemon
Salt and freshly ground black pepper to taste   (Serves 4)

1   Heat oil in frying pan and fry the chicory on all sides
    until golden.
2   Add chopped onion and lemon juice. Season.
3   Cover the pan and simmer for about 35 minutes, turning
    the chicory occasionally. You may need to add a little water.

NOTE: If chicory is bitter, 1 teaspoon of sugar can be added to
remove bitter taste.
Serve with cheese, Béchamel or tomato sauce.

CHICORY AND CAMEMBERT FLAN

450 g (1 lb/2 cups) shortcrust pastry
1 small onion, finely chopped
2 heads chicory, finely sliced
125 g (4 oz) Camembert, roughly chopped
2 eggs
150 ml (¼ pint/5 fl oz) milk or single cream
1 tbsp parsley
Salt and freshly ground black pepper to taste   (Serves 4)

1   Roll out the pastry and line a 20 cm (8") fluted flan case.
    Chill for 30 minutes.
2   Prick the pastry base and blind bake in a preheated oven
    200°C (400°F/Gas 6) for 15 minutes. Remove and reduce
    oven temperature to 190°C (375°F/Gas 5).
3   Sprinkle onions, chicory and Camembert over the
    pastry base.
4   Beat the eggs, milk or cream together, add parsley and
    seasoning and pour into pastry case.
5   Place on a baking tray and return to the oven for 30–35
    minutes, until filling is set and golden. Can be served hot
    or cold.

CHICORY AND CARROT SALAD

2 tsp white wine vinegar
1 tsp Dijon-style mustard
¼ tsp sugar
1 tsp water
Salt and freshly ground black pepper to taste
3 tbsp olive oil
900 g (2 lb/4 cups) chicory, rinsed and torn into pieces
125 g (4 oz/½ cup) carrot, coarsely grated   (Serves 4)

1   In a bowl mix together the vinegar, mustard, sugar,
    water and salt and pepper to taste.
2   Add the oil in a stream, whisking, until the dressing
    has emulsified.
3   Add the chicory and the carrot and mix well.

CHICORY AND POTATOES

2 tbsp olive oil
3 cloves garlic, crushed
900 g (2 lb/4 cups) potatoes, peeled and sliced
1 celery stick, cut into thin slices
450 g (1 lb/2 cups) chicory, washed, and cut into 5 cm (2")
pieces
Salt and freshly ground black pepper to taste
50 g (2 oz/¼ cup) chopped mint
150 ml (¼ pint/5 fl oz) water
2 tbsp fresh lemon juice   (Serves 6)

1   Heat oil in a large pan over medium-low heat. Add garlic,
    potatoes, celery, chicory, salt, pepper and mint. Stir well
    to coat ingredients with oil.
2   Cover and cook, stirring frequently, for 5–10 minutes,
    until chicory is wilted.
3   Add water, stirring well to mix. Cover and continue
    cooking, stirring frequently, for about 15 minutes, or
    until potatoes are tender. Add more water if needed
    to prevent sticking.
4   Just before serving, stir in lemon juice.

CHICORY WITH RICE AND PARMESAN

125 g (4 oz/½ cup) rice
4 tbsp olive oil

225 g (8 oz/1 cup) onion, chopped
3 cloves garlic, crushed
900 g (2 lb/4 cups) chicory, washed, dried and chopped
125 g (4 oz/½ cup) sorrel leaves (optional)
2 tbsp Parmesan
Salt and freshly ground black pepper to taste
125 g (4 oz/½ cup) fresh breadcrumbs   (Serves 4)

1   Preheat oven to 190°C (375°F/Gas 5).
2   Bring salted water to the boil, add the rice, return to
    boil, and simmer until cooked, about 10 minutes. Drain,
    rinse under hot water and keep warm.
3   In a large saucepan, heat the oil and cook onions until
    soft, about 5 minutes.
4   Add the garlic, stir for about 30 seconds.
5   Add the chicory, a little at a time, stirring to coat with
    the oil. Cook chicory until wilted and add sorrel
    (if used), and cook until tender, about 5 minutes.
6   When the chicory is tender, add the rice with one
    tablespoon of Parmesan. Mix well and season.
7   Put in a greased, deep, baking dish. Mix remaining
    Parmesan with breadcrumbs and sprinkle on the top.
    Drizzle with a little olive oil and bake for 30–40 minutes.
8   Can serve hot or cold.

CURLY KALE FRIED IN BEER BATTER

This recipe is dedicated to all those people who are more likely to
have beer in the fridge than eggs.

For the beer batter
125 g (4 oz) plain flour
225 ml (8 fl oz) beer
Salt and freshly ground black pepper to taste

Vegetable oil for deep-frying
Curly kale leaves, torn into pieces to be dipped in batter
Salt for sprinkling the leaves
Lemon wedges to serve

1   Sift the flour into a bowl and make a hole in the centre.
2   Gradually add the beer to the flour and beat until
    smooth.
3   Season with salt and pepper.
4   Let the batter stand, covered, for one hour, before
    using.
5   Heat the oil in a pan, dip one piece of kale into the
    batter, coating it thoroughly, and fry it in the oil for
    30 seconds on each side, or until golden.
6   Transfer the kale once it is fried onto kitchen paper
    towels to drain, and sprinkle lightly with salt.
7   Repeat until all leaves are cooked.
8   Serve with lemon wedges.

CURLY KALE WITH CURRIED LENTILS

135 g (4 oz/½ cup) brown lentils
2 tbsp olive oil
1 tsp curry powder
1 medium onion, chopped
4 cloves
1 tbsp raisins
125 g (4 oz/½ cup) carrot, peeled and diced
125 g (4 oz/½ cup) potato, peeled and diced
Salt and freshly ground black pepper to taste
350 ml (12 fl oz/1½ cups) water
225 g (8 oz/1 cup) curly kale, chopped finely
For the topping: 2 tbsp plain yoghurt   (Serves 4)

1 Rinse and soak lentils in the water for about 15 minutes. Drain.
2 In a pan heat oil and sauté curry powder, onion and cloves for about 2 minutes.
3 Add raisins, carrot, potato and soaked lentils.
   Season to taste.
4 Add water, bring to boil, reduce heat and simmer until lentils are tender, about 15 minutes.
5 Place kale on top of lentils, and cook until reduced by half, about 5-10 minutes. When done, lentils should be tender but not mushy.
6 Remove from heat. Gently stir to mix kale with lentils. Transfer to a serving dish and top with yoghurt.

CURLY KALE WITH MASHED POTATOES

225 g (8 oz) curly kale, chopped finely
700 g (1 ½ lb/3 cups) potatoes, peeled and quartered
1 garlic clove, peeled
50 g (2 oz/½ stick) butter or margarine
150 ml (¼ pint/5 fl oz) milk or single cream
Salt and freshly ground black pepper to taste   (Serves 4)

1 Bring 2-4 tablespoons salted water to the boil. Add the kale, bring back to the boil, reduce heat and simmer until just tender, about 5-10 minutes stirring occasionally. Drain well and keep warm.
2 Place potatoes and garlic together in a pan, cover with water, bring to the boil, reduce heat and simmer until cooked, about 15 minutes. Drain well and return to the pan.
3 Add the butter or margarine to the potatoes, and mash with a potato masher. Gradually add the milk or cream and season to taste.
4 Add the cooked kale to the potato mixture, stir well and serve.

LEEK, MUSHROOM AND CASHEW NUT CANNELLONI

Filling

2 tbsp olive oil
450 g (1 lb/2 cups) leeks, finely chopped and washed
225 g (8 oz/1 cup) mushrooms, finely chopped
50 g (2 oz/¼ cup) cashew nuts, toasted
Freshly grated nutmeg
½ tsp dried thyme
Salt and freshly ground black pepper to taste
1 x 500 g packet Cannelloni tubes

Sauce

50 g (2 oz/¼ cup) butter or margarine
1 onion, finely chopped
1 garlic clove, crushed
3 tsp plain flour
175 ml (6 fl oz/¾ cup) crème fraîche
Salt and freshly ground black pepper to taste
Freshly grated nutmeg

Topping

25 g (1 oz/½ cup) fresh breadcrumbs
25 g (1 oz/¼ cup) Parmesan or Cheddar cheese, grated
Preheat oven to 180°C (350°F/Gas 4).   (Serves 4)

1 Heat olive oil in a pan and sauté the leeks and mushrooms for about 5 minutes or until soft.
2 Toast the cashew nuts by stir-frying them in a hot, dry, frying pan for a minute or two until golden.
3 Add the toasted cashew nuts to the leeks and mushrooms, and then add nutmeg, thyme and season to taste.
4 Fill 8-12 cannelloni tubes with the leek mixture and arrange in a greased, ovenproof dish.
5 To make the sauce, melt the butter or margarine in a

...rlic and cook until soft, about 5

...en add the crème fraîche to
...th salt, pepper and nutmeg.
...oni, and sprinkle with mixed
...e.
...out 25 minutes or until golden and

50 g (1 oz) butter or margarine
900 g (2 lb/4 cups) leeks, chopped and washed thoroughly
4 eggs
2 tbsp milk
Salt and freshly ground black pepper to taste   (Serves 4)

1   Heat butter or margarine in a pan, add the leeks and
    sauté until leeks have softened, about 3-4 minutes.
2   Break the eggs into a bowl, add the milk, salt and pepper.
    Beat until blended, but not foamy.
3   Pour eggs on top of leeks, making sure that the egg
    mixture thoroughly coats the leeks.
4   Cook until bottom of the omelette is golden, about
    1-2 minutes.
5   Carefully turn the omelette over. Cook other side until
    just set, about one minute. Cut into 4 and serve.

OLIVE CAKE (CAKE AUX OLIVES)

This recipe was given to Jacqui by her friend Michelle Price who
lives in Paris. We thought we would include it in anticipation of
Mathis' delivery of olives and olive oil to subscribers of his
FruitShare when he returns to Scotland from sunny Spain. It can
be served as a starter or as a main course with salad.

150 g (5 oz) self-raising flour
3 eggs
Salt and freshly ground black pepper to taste
120 ml (4 fl oz/½ cup) olive oil
120 ml (4 fl oz/½ cup) full cream milk, warmed
75 g (3 oz) olives (black, green or a mixture), chopped
125 g (4 oz) Gruyère cheese, cut into tiny squares
200 g (7 oz) ham or streaky bacon, cut in squares (optional)

1   Preheat the oven to 180°C (350°F/Gas 4).
2   Mix together flour, eggs, salt and pepper, oil and milk.
3   Add the olives, cheese, and ham or bacon (if used).
4   Put mixture into a greased loaf tin and bake for 35-45
    minutes or until cooked.

PAK CHOI WITH GINGER AND SOY SAUCE

2 tbsp olive oil
1-2 garlic cloves, crushed
1 x 2.5 cm (1") piece root ginger, peeled and finely chopped
450 g (1 lb/2 cups) pak choi, chopped
1 tbsp soy sauce
Freshly ground black pepper   (Serves 2-3)

1   Heat oil in a pan and sauté garlic and root ginger for
    about 1-2 minutes.
2   Add pak choi to the pan and cook for about 3-5 minutes
    or until cooked.
3   Add soy sauce, pepper, stir well, and serve.

SPROUT SNIPPET: Pak choi is native to eastern Asia where it
has been grown for thousands of years. The Celts brought the
vegetable to the British Isles.

PARSNIP AND CARAWAY CAKE

225 g (8 oz) self-raising flour
1 tsp bicarbonate of soda
225 g (8 oz) parsnip, grated
½ tsp caraway seed
180 g (6 oz) soft margarine
125 g (4 oz) caster sugar
2 eggs, beaten
Zest and juice of one lemon
Lemon water icing
125 g (4 oz) icing sugar
1 tbsp warm water
1 tbsp lemon juice

1   Heat oven to 180°C (350°F/Gas 4).
2   Sieve together flour and bicarbonate of soda.
3   Stir in the parsnip and caraway seed.
4   Cream together the margarine and sugar and stir in the eggs gently.
5   Fold in the flour mixture, lemon zest and juice to make a dropping consistency.
6   Place mixture into a greased and floured 20 cm (9") round cake tin and bake for 25–30 minutes.
7   Cool on a wire rack.
8   To make the lemon water icing, sift icing sugar into a bowl.
9   Add water and lemon juice until the mixture is thick enough to coat the back of a wooden spoon. Drizzle over cake.

PARSNIP, CARROT AND POTATO CAKE WITH APPLE

180 g (6 oz) soft margarine
180 g (6 oz) caster sugar
3 eggs, beaten
225 g (8 oz) self raising flour
½ tsp ground nutmeg
125 g (4 oz/½ cup) grated carrot
125 g (4 oz/½ cup) parsnip, grated
125 g (4 oz/½ cup) grated potato
125 g (4 oz/½ cup) grated eating apple
Zest and juice of 1 orange
Orange water icing
125 g (4 oz/½cup) icing sugar
1 tbsp warm water
1 tbsp freshly squeezed orange juice

1   Heat the oven to 180°C (350°F/Gas 4).
2   Cream together the margarine and sugar, and stir in the eggs gently.
3   Sieve together the flour and nutmeg, add the carrot, parsnip, potato and apple. Mix well.
4   Fold the flour mixture into the creamed mixture and stir in the orange zest and juice.
5   Turn into a greased and floured 24 cm (9½") round cake tin and bake for 45–50 minutes or until a skewer comes out clean.
6   Turn on to a wire rack to cool.
7   To make the orange water icing, sift icing sugar into a bowl.
8   Add water and orange juice until the mixture is thick enough to coat the back of a wooden spoon. Drizzle top of cake with orange water icing.

PARSNIP AND CARROTS WITH HONEY AND ALMONDS

75 g (3 oz) almonds, slivered
50 g (2 oz) butter or margarine
450 g (1 lb/2 cups) parsnips, peeled and cut into long strips
450 g (1 lb/2 cups) carrots, peeled and cut into long strips

2 tbsp lemon juice
2 tbsp honey
1 tsp wholegrain mustard
Salt and freshly ground black pepper to taste   (Serves 4)

1   Toast almonds on a baking tray in oven 180°C (350°F/Gas 4)
    until golden, about 5-10 minutes. Keep checking them so
    that they do not burn.
2   Melt butter or margarine in a pan, add parsnips and carrots
    and cook gently until tender, about 5-10 minutes.
3   Add toasted almonds, lemon juice, honey, mustard and
    heat through. Season and serve.

PARSNIP, LEEK AND GINGER SOUP

1 tbsp olive oil
450 g (1 lb/2 cups) leeks, sliced into rings and washed well
2 tbsp fresh ginger root, finely chopped or grated
700 g (1½ lb/3 cups) parsnips, peeled and roughly chopped
150 ml (¼ pint/5 fl oz) dry white wine
1.5 L (2¾ pints/5½ cups) vegetable stock
To garnish
2 tbsp cream
½ tsp paprika   (Serves 4-6)

1   Heat oil in a large pan and add the leek and ginger. Cook
    for about 2-3 minutes, until the leeks begin to soften.
2   Add the parsnips and cook for about another 10 minutes.
3   Pour in the wine and vegetable stock and bring to the boil.
4   Reduce heat and simmer for about 20 minutes or until
    the parsnips are tender.
5   Purée in a blender until smooth. Check seasoning.
6   Reheat and serve with a swirl of cream and a light
    dusting of paprika.

POTATOES WITH BLUE CHEESE AND WALNUTS

450 g (1 lb) potatoes, cut into wedges
1 onion, sliced
125 g (4 oz) blue cheese, mashed
150 ml (¼ pint/5 fl oz) single cream
Salt and freshly ground black pepper to taste
50 g (2 oz) walnut pieces   (Serves 4)

1   Put the potatoes into salted water, bring to the boil, reduce
    heat and simmer until tender, about 15 minutes. Add the
    onion to the pan for the last 5 minutes or so of cooking.
2   Drain the potatoes and onion, put into a shallow serving
    dish and keep warm.
3   In a small pan, gently melt the cheese and cream, stirring
    occasionally. Do not allow the mixture to boil, but heat
    until it scalds. Season to taste.
4   Pour the sauce evenly over the potatoes and onion and
    sprinkle over the walnut pieces. Serve.

PURPLE SPROUTING BROCCOLI WITH HORSERADISH AND WALNUTS

1 tbsp vegetable or olive oil
2 cloves garlic, crushed
700 g (1½ lb/3 cups) purple sprouting broccoli, chopped
4 tbsp water
150 ml (¼ pint/5 fl oz) sour cream
1 tsp creamed horseradish
¼ tsp dried thyme
½ tsp dried marjoram
Salt and freshly ground black pepper to taste
125 g (4 oz/½ cup) walnuts, roasted and chopped   (Serves 4)

1   Heat oil in a pan and sauté the garlic for about 1 minute.

2   Add broccoli and water. Cover and steam until crisp-tender over a medium heat, or until most of the liquid has gone.
3   Add sour cream, horseradish, thyme, marjoram and seasoning.
4   Add nuts, toss and serve.

PURPLE SPROUTING BROCCOLI WITH LENTILS, BULGAR AND YOGHURT

1 tbsp vegetable or olive oil
1 medium onion, chopped
125 g (4 oz/½ cup) bulgar
125 g (4 oz/½ cup) red lentils
425 ml (¾ pint/15 fl oz) water
225 g (8 oz/1 cup) purple sprouting broccoli, chopped
Salt and freshly ground black pepper to taste
225 ml (8 fl oz/1 cup) plain yoghurt   (Serves 4)

1   Heat oil in a pan and sauté onion and bulgar until onion is soft.
2   Stir lentils and water into onion and bulgar mixture, and bring to the boil.
3   Sprinkle broccoli over mixture, cover and simmer for about 15 minutes or until water is absorbed and broccoli is tender. Season to taste. Stir well.
4   Transfer to serving bowl and top with yoghurt.

PURPLE SPROUTING BROCCOLI AND MUSHROOM DIP

450 g (1 lb/2 cups) purple sprouting broccoli, chopped
1 tbsp vegetable or olive oil
2 garlic cloves

½ medium onion, chopped
125 g (4 oz/½ cup) mushrooms, chopped
175 g (6 oz/¾ cup) cottage cheese
4 tbsp plain yoghurt
Salt and freshly ground black pepper to taste   (Serves 4)

1   Cook broccoli in boiling salted water until crisp-tender, about 3-5 minutes. Drain and rinse under cold water.
2   In a pan, heat oil over medium heat. Add garlic, onion and mushrooms and cook until onion is tender and transfer to a blender.
3   Add broccoli, cottage cheese, yoghurt and seasoning to the blender and process until smooth. Taste to check seasonings and adjust if necessary.
4   Transfer to a bowl and serve.

RED CABBAGE WITH PEARS AND BROWN SUGAR

50 g (2 oz) butter or margarine
2 tsp vegetable oil
1 onion, finely chopped
1 large clove of garlic, crushed
3 tbsp brown sugar
1 tbsp tomato purée
2 tbsp red wine vinegar
Freshly ground black pepper
450 g (1 lb/2 cups) red cabbage, quartered, cored, and finely shredded
2 ripe medium pears, peeled, cored and cut into thin strips
Parsley, chopped to garnish (optional)   (Serves 6)

1   Melt butter or margarine in a large saucepan, add oil,

onion and garlic. Cook for one minute without browning.

2   Add sugar, tomato purée, red wine vinegar and pepper. Mix well and cook for one minute.
3   Increase heat to medium high. Add cabbage and pears, cook, stirring frequently until crisp-tender. Put into serving dish.
4   Garnish with chopped parsley if desired.

RED CABBAGE SALAD WITH RAISINS AND GINGER
125 g (4 oz/½ cup) raisins
450 g (1 lb/2 cups) red cabbage, grated
1 tbsp root ginger, finely chopped
Juice of 1 lemon
1 tsp olive oil
¾ tsp ground coriander
¼ tsp cayenne pepper
Salt and freshly ground black pepper to taste   (Serves 4)

1   Soak raisins in water until softened.
2   Put red cabbage in a bowl and add the softened raisins and ginger.
3   Mix the lemon juice, olive oil, coriander and cayenne pepper together to make the dressing. Season.
4   Pour the dressing over the red cabbage just before serving.

RHUBARB WITH LENTILS AND POTATOES
225 g (8 oz) red lentils
2 medium potatoes, peeled and sliced
1 tbsp olive oil
2 garlic cloves, crushed
2 tsp ground coriander
2 tsp ground cumin

1 tsp chilli powder
1 tsp fresh ginger root, grated
225 g (8 oz) rhubarb, sliced, and 150 ml (¼ pint) water
50 g (2 oz) sugar
50 g (2 oz) desiccated coconut
Salt and freshly ground black pepper to taste   (Serves 4)

1   Cover lentils with water in a pan. Bring to the boil, reduce heat and simmer.
2   Once lentils are simmering, add potatoes, and simmer until tender, about 10-15 minutes.
3   Remove from heat, drain and set aside.
4   Heat oil in a pan and fry garlic, coriander, cumin, chilli, and ginger for about 1-2 minutes.
5   Add the rhubarb and water, bring to the boil, reduce heat and simmer until just cooked, about 10 minutes.
6   Add the sugar, coconut, salt and pepper to taste.
7   Stir in the potatoes and lentils, and heat through gently.
8   Put into bowls, garnish with coconut and serve with rice or crusty bread and chutney.

RHUBARB STICKY CAKE
180 g (6 oz) butter or soft margarine
180 g (6 oz) caster sugar
3 eggs, beaten
180 g (6 oz) self-raising flour
Pinch of salt
About 2 tbsp milk
450 g (1 lb/2 cups) rhubarb, sliced into 2.5 cm (1") pieces
1 tbsp Demerara sugar
Topping
50 g (2 oz) butter or soft margarine
90 g (3 oz) plain flour

25 g (1 oz) caster sugar

1   Heat the oven to 190°C (375°F/Gas 5).
2   Grease and line a 24 cm (9½") round cake tin.
3   Cream together the butter or margarine and sugar, stir
    in the eggs and fold in the flour and salt. Add enough
    milk to give a dropping consistency.
4   Turn the cake mix into the tin.
5   Toss sliced rhubarb with Demerara sugar.
6   Arrange rhubarb on top of the cake mix.
7   Make the topping by rubbing the butter or margarine
    into the flour and stirring in the sugar. Sprinkle the
    topping mixture on top of the rhubarb and bake in the
    oven for 40–45 minutes or until skewer comes out clean.
8   Cool on a wire rack.

SPINACH WITH FETA AND CHICKPEAS

450 g (1 lb) chickpeas, cooked or tinned
150 ml (¼ pint/5 fl oz) water
1 tbsp olive oil
450 g (1 lb/2 cups) fresh spinach, washed and chopped
1 tsp ground cumin
1 tbsp lemon juice
225 g (8 oz) Feta cheese, crumbled
Salt and freshly ground black pepper to taste   (Serves 4)

1   Combine cooked chickpeas, water, oil, spinach and cumin
    in a large pot.
2   Bring to the boil, reduce heat, cover and simmer until
    spinach is just tender, about 5–10 minutes.
3   Stir in lemon juice, Feta, salt and pepper.
4   Serve immediately.

SPINACH WITH LENTILS AND COCONUT MILK

125 g (4 oz/½ cup) red lentils
450 g (1 lb/2 cups) fresh spinach, washed, trimmed
and chopped
2 tbsp vegetable or olive oil
2 cloves garlic, crushed
1 onion, chopped
1 green pepper, deseeded and diced
1 tbsp mustard
2 tsp curry powder
2 tsp turmeric
Pinch of cinnamon
225 ml (8 fl oz/1 cup) water
150 ml (¼ pint/5 fl oz) coconut milk
Salt and freshly ground black pepper to taste   (Serves 4)

1   Wash the lentils, and mix with spinach.
2   Heat oil in a pan, add garlic, onion, green pepper,
    mustard, curry powder, turmeric and cinnamon. Sauté for
    about 5 minutes, stirring frequently or until onion is soft.
3   Add the lentils and spinach and stir well.
4   Add water and coconut milk, bring to the boil, reduce
    heat and simmer for about 10-15 minutes, or until lentils
    are cooked.
5   Season to taste and serve.

SPINACH WITH ORANGE AND WALNUTS

900 g (2 lb/4 cups) fresh spinach, washed and chopped
Zest and juice of one orange
50 g (2 oz/½ cup) walnuts
Salt and freshly ground black pepper to taste.   (Serves 4)

1   Place spinach, orange zest and juice in a wok or frying pan over a high heat. Cook, stirring frequently until spinach has wilted and just cooked, about 3–5 minutes.
2   Add walnuts and stir well.
3   Season and serve immediately.

SPINACH WITH PINE NUTS AND RAISINS

50 g (2 oz) butter or margarine
2 tbsp olive oil
3 cloves of garlic, crushed
4 tbsp seedless raisins
4 tbsp pine nuts
900 g (2 lb/4 cups) fresh spinach, washed and roughly chopped
2 tbsp Parmesan   (Serves 4)

1   Heat butter or margarine and olive oil in pan. Add garlic, raisins and pine nuts and cook over moderate heat for 2 minutes.
2   Add spinach and stir well. Cook over low heat until spinach is just cooked, about 5 minutes.
3   Transfer to serving dish and sprinkle Parmesan over the top. Serve immediately.

SPINACH WITH SESAME SEEDS

900 g (2 lb/4 cups) fresh spinach, washed and chopped roughly
50 g (2 oz/¼ cup) sesame seeds
2 tbsp light soy sauce
Juice of ½ lemon
Salt and freshly ground black pepper to taste   (Serves 4)

1   Place spinach in a saucepan with only the water that clings to the leaves after washing. Do not season.
2   Cover, bring to the boil, reduce heat and cook just until leaves wilt, stirring once or twice, about 3–5 minutes.
3   Drain well and keep warm.
4   Heat frying pan and add the sesame seeds and toast for about 2 minutes, or until brown, stirring frequently. Remove from heat.
5   Transfer spinach to serving dish. Mix soy sauce with lemon juice, season and pour over spinach. Sprinkle toasted sesame seeds on top and serve.

SPINACH SPICY FRIED

2 tbsp vegetable or olive oil
2 medium onions, finely sliced
2 cloves garlic, crushed
1 tsp fresh root ginger, finely grated or ½ tsp ground ginger
1 tsp cumin seeds or ground cumin
½ tsp ground coriander
½ tsp ground turmeric
½ tsp chilli powder (optional)
900 g (2 lb/4 cups) fresh spinach, well washed and roughly chopped
Salt and freshly ground black pepper to taste   (Serves 4)

1   Heat oil in pan and fry the onion until golden.
2   Add garlic and ginger and fry for a further minute.
3   Add cumin, coriander, turmeric and chilli (if used).
4   Add spinach, stir well and cook uncovered on low heat until spinach has wilted and just cooked. It may be necessary to add a little water to prevent spinach sticking to the pan. Season.
5   Serve with rice, chapattis or other Indian breads.

SPINACH AND PURPLE SPROUTING BROCCOLI CURRY

2 tbsp vegetable oil or butter
2 onions, chopped
3 cloves garlic, crushed
½ tsp chilli powder (more if you like a hot curry)
2 tbsp fresh ginger, chopped finely, or 1 tsp ground ginger
2 tsp ground cumin
2 tsp ground coriander
4 fresh tomatoes (or 1 x 400 g (14 oz) tin)
450 g (1 lb/2 cups) purple sprouting broccoli,
washed and trimmed
450 g (1 lb/2 cups) fresh spinach
Salt and freshly ground black pepper to taste   (Serves 4-6)

1   Heat vegetable oil or butter in large pan and sauté onions until just tender but not brown.
2   Add garlic, chilli, ginger, cumin and coriander. Mix until spices are coated in oil.
3   Add tomatoes and sprouting broccoli. Cover and cook until broccoli is just tender, about 10–15 minutes.
4   Add spinach and cook for about another 5 minutes or until spinach is tender. Season to taste.

SPINACH, STIR FRIED WITH GINGER AND ALMONDS

1 tbsp miso
2 tbsp soy sauce
1 tsp wine vinegar
2 tbsp almonds, chopped
1 tbsp sesame oil
900 g (2 lb/4 cups) fresh spinach, well washed and chopped

2 tsp fresh root ginger, finely grated, or ½ tsp
ground ginger   (Serves 4)

1   Mix miso, soy sauce and wine vinegar together. Set aside.
2   Heat wok or frying pan over high heat. Add almonds and stir-fry until edges turn golden. Transfer to plate.
3   Heat sesame oil in wok or frying pan, add the spinach and ginger, and stir-fry until just tender, about 3 minutes.
4   Add miso, soy sauce and wine vinegar mixture to spinach. Add almonds. Stir well and serve immediately.

SWEDE BRUSCHETTA

4 tbsp extra virgin olive oil
2 garlic cloves, crushed
1 medium onion, chopped
225 g (8 oz) swede, peeled and cut into small cubes
1 tsp fresh rosemary leaves, chopped
1 tbsp balsamic vinegar
8 slices thickly sliced bread (sourdough or ciabatta)
2 garlic cloves lightly crushed for rubbing over toast
Salt and freshly ground black pepper to taste   (Serves 4)

1   Heat 2 tablespoons of the olive oil in a pan and add the garlic, onion and swede. Sauté, stirring regularly, until the swede has softened and is golden brown, about 10 minutes.
2   Transfer to a mixing bowl and add the rosemary and balsamic vinegar. Keep warm.
3   Toast the bread until golden on both sides but still soft in the centre.
4   Rub the cloves of garlic over the surface of the toast.
5   Pile the swede mixture on top of the toast, drizzle on the rest of the olive oil, salt and freshly ground black pepper.
6   Serve.

SWEDE AND LEEK FRITTERS WITH LEMON, OREGANO AND TOMATO SAUCE

For the sauce
1 x 420 g (15 oz) tin of Italian plum tomatoes, mashed
150 ml (¼ pint/5 fl oz) vegetable stock
Juice of 1 lemon
1 tsp dried oregano
Salt and freshly ground black pepper to taste
For the fritters
700 g (1½ lb/3 cups) swede, peeled and grated
1 medium leek, washed and finely chopped
3 eggs, lightly beaten
4 tbsp plain flour
Salt and freshly ground black pepper to taste
4 tbsp vegetable oil for frying   (Makes about 12)

1   To make the sauce, in a pan, combine the tomatoes, stock, lemon juice, oregano, salt and pepper. Mix well. Bring to the boil, reduce heat, and simmer for about 15 minutes, stirring occasionally.
2   To make the fritters, place the swede, leek, eggs, flour, salt and pepper in a large bowl, and mix well. This will make a batter.
3   Heat the oil over a high heat. Spoon 1 tablespoon of the batter into the pan at a time, putting in as many as you can but ensuring that the pan is not too crowded.
4   Cook until lightly browned on one side, about 2-3 minutes, turn and brown on the other side.
5   Drain on kitchen paper towels.
6   Repeat until all the fritters are cooked.
7   To serve, put fritters on a plate and top with the sauce.

SWEDE WITH SPINACH AND CORIANDER

50 g (2 oz) butter or margarine
1 medium onion, chopped
1 tsp coriander seed, crushed
½ tsp turmeric
¼ tsp cayenne pepper
Salt and freshly ground black pepper to taste
4 tbsp plain yoghurt
450 g (1 lb/2 cups) fresh spinach, washed and roughly chopped
450g (1 lb/2 cups) swede, peeled and diced
1 garlic clove, crushed
150 ml (¼ pint/5 fl oz) water   (Serves 4-6)

1   Heat butter or margarine in a pan and sauté onion until golden, about 5 minutes.
2   Add coriander, turmeric, cayenne pepper, salt, pepper and yoghurt. Cook for about 5 minutes, stirring frequently.
3   Add half the spinach to the spice mixture, along with the swede and garlic.
4   Cook, covered, over medium heat for about 3 minutes.
5   Stir in rest of spinach and water.
6   Cook, covered, for about 15-20 minutes or until swede is tender.

FARMING NEWS FOR APRIL

Potato grading or dressing is carried out weekly.

HARVESTING

Brussels sprouts, carrots, parsnips, spring cabbage, spring cauliflower, swedes, purple sprouting broccoli. Rhubarb from Rafford, herbs such as coriander and parsley from Cullerne, as well as chicory, lettuce, radish and rocket salad.

MAINTENANCE AND MACHINERY

The onion planting machine, which is used to plant onion sets, is another example of Mathis' ingenuity. He modified a precision drill to plant the onion sets onto ridges. He saved the frame and the roller from the drill and fitted a seat on the back of the tractor. Someone sits on the seat and feeds the onions sets into a tube so that they get planted on top of the ridge and the furrows get closed again. EarthShare is able to plant one acre of land, about 100,000 onions sets, in six hours.

PESTS AND DISEASES

Woodpigeons are a big pest this month, as they seem to think the vegetables are being grown solely for them. Using a bird-scarer with a wide repertoire of sounds keeps them at bay.

PLANTING

This is the month for planting potatoes, the two varieties being Remarka for the main crop and Aminka for the earlies. Mathis chose Remarka because they grow into big potatoes. One of the differences between subscribers in Germany and in Scotland was that Scottish subscribers wanted bigger potatoes.

It is also the month for planting onion sets. Further south in the UK onions grow easily from seed, but that is not possible up here because of the shorter growing season. The season is just about long enough for onion sets that were sown as seeds in the middle of the previous year.

Originally from Mediterranean countries, onions have gradually crept further north into Scotland as varieties have been developed that will cope better with the colder climate. The same applies to garlic.

Chicory is sown during this month, and Christopher sows the first batch of lettuce destined for planting outside. These are sown in modules within the Cullerne propagation tunnel.

Julie Adams and Nicky Molnar potato grading

BEETROOT CASSEROLE WITH ORANGE AND HONEY

4 tbsp olive oil
225 g (8 oz) onions, chopped
450 g (1 lb) beetroot, peeled and diced
1 tbsp tomato purée
1 tbsp honey
Salt and freshly ground black pepper to taste
½ tbsp cornflour
300 ml (½ pint/10 fl oz) orange juice   (Serves 4)

1   Heat the oil in a pan and add the onions. Sauté for about 5 minutes until onions are soft.
2   Add the beetroot and cook for another 5 minutes.
3   Add the tomato purée and honey and transfer to a baking dish. Season to taste.
4   Mix the cornflour with the orange juice and pour over the beetroot and bake for about 35-40 minutes or until beetroot is cooked.

BEETROOT AND CHOCOLATE LOAF

225 g (8 oz) self-raising flour
25 g (1 oz) cocoa powder
Pinch of salt
1 tsp baking powder
125 g (4 oz) caster sugar
125 g (4 oz) raw beetroot, peeled and grated
75 g (3 oz) dark chocolate, melted
75 g (3 oz) butter, melted
2 eggs, beaten

1   Heat oven to 180°C (350°F/Gas 4).
2   Grease and line a 900 g (2 lb) loaf tin.
3   Sift together the flour, cocoa powder, salt and baking powder.
4   Stir in the sugar, beetroot, melted chocolate and butter, and the eggs.
5   Turn into the greased tin and bake for 45–50 minutes until firm on top and an inserted skewer comes out clean.
6   Cool on a wire rack.

BEETROOT LEAF, STIR FRIED WITH COCONUT AND RAISINS

2 tbsp olive oil
2 garlic cloves, chopped
450 g (1 lb) beetroot leaf, washed and chopped
2 tbsp desiccated coconut
2 tbsp raisins
4 tbsp orange juice
Salt and freshly ground black pepper to taste   (Serves 4)

1   Heat the olive oil and sauté the garlic for about 2 minutes.
2   Add the beetroot leaf and cook for about another 2-3 minutes, or until wilted.
3   Add the coconut, raisins and orange juice. Season.
4   Cook for about another 5 minutes and serve.

BEETROOT IN A TANGY MUSTARD SAUCE

700 g (1½ lb/3 cups) beetroot, scrubbed but not topped and tailed
50 g (2 oz) butter or margarine
50 g (2oz/¼ cup) onions, chopped finely
1 tbsp flour

120 ml (4 fl oz) vegetable stock
3 tbsp Dijon mustard
4 tbsp cream or fromage frais
Salt and freshly ground black pepper to taste
To garnish: chopped parsley   (Serves 4-6)

1   Place beetroot in a saucepan with salted water. Bring to
    the boil, cover the pan and quickly return to the boil.
    Reduce heat and simmer until cooked, about one hour
    depending on size. Drain under cold water, peel and
    slice into 5 mm (¼") pieces.
2   Melt butter or margarine in a pan, add onions and cook
    for 4 minutes over medium heat.
3   Turn heat down, stir in flour and cook for 2 minutes,
    stirring continuously.
4   Gradually add the stock, mustard and cream or fromage
    frais. Cook for a few minutes until thick.
5   Add the cooked beetroot and heat for a few minutes
    until warm. Add salt and pepper to taste.
6   Put into a serving dish, and garnish with parsley.

BRUSSELS SPROUTS IN PECAN SAUCE
450 g (1 lb/2 cups) Brussels sprouts, washed and trimmed
45 g (1½ oz) butter or margarine
50 g (2 oz/¼ cup) Pecan nuts, chopped
Salt and freshly ground pepper to taste   (Serves 4)

1   Bring salted water to the boil, add Brussels sprouts,
    cover the pan and quickly return to the boil. Reduce
    heat and simmer until just tender, about 10 minutes.
    Drain, transfer to a serving dish and keep warm.
2   Heat the butter or margarine in a small saucepan and
    brown the Pecans, stirring frequently, about 2 minutes.

Do not let them burn. Season to taste.
3   Pour the Pecans over the Brussels sprouts, mix well and serve.

BRUSSELS SPROUTS WITH RICE
450 g (1 lb/2 cups) Brussels sprouts, washed and trimmed
1 tin 425 g (15 oz) condensed cream of mushroom soup
225 ml (8 fl oz/1 cup) milk
300 ml (½ pint/1¼ cups/10 fl oz) water
25 g (1 oz) butter or margarine
Salt and freshly ground black pepper to taste
¾ tsp caraway seeds
150 g (5 oz/¾ cup) Basmati rice   (Serves 6)

1   Bring salted water to the boil, add Brussels sprouts,
    cover the pan and quickly return to the boil. Reduce
    heat and simmer until just tender, about 10 minutes.
    Drain and keep warm.
2   In a saucepan, gently heat undiluted soup, milk, water,
    butter or margarine, salt, pepper and caraway seeds to
    boiling, stirring occasionally.
3   Stir in rice, reduce heat to low, cover and simmer for
    about 10 minutes or until rice is cooked.
4   Stir in Brussels sprouts and mix well.
5   Transfer to serving dish.

BRUSSELS SPROUTS SATAY
When considering Brussels sprouts recipes, Jacqui thought that
CSA should stand for Chuck Sprouts Away (rather than Robin's
version of Chuck Swedes Away). So surprisingly, she quite
enjoyed this recipe. So don't give up you sprout haters out there!

450 g (1 lb/2 cups) Brussels sprouts
1 tbsp smooth peanut butter

5 tbsp tamari or soy sauce
2 tbsp vegetable oil
4 tbsp toasted pine nuts, roughly chopped   (Serves 4)

1   Put Brussels sprouts into boiling salted water. Return to boil, reduce heat and simmer for about 5-6 minutes until crisp tender. Drain well.
2   Mix together peanut butter and 4 tablespoonfuls of tamari or soy sauce to a smooth paste.
3   Heat oil in a pan, quickly stir fry the sprouts for about 2 minutes.
4   Remove from heat and stir half the peanut soy paste into the pan.
5   Transfer to a serving dish.
6   Drizzle with the remaining paste and the remaining one tablespoon of tamari or soy sauce.
7   Sprinkle with the pine nuts.
8   This dish can be served warm or cold.

SPROUT SNIPPET: The difference between soy sauce or shoyu and tamari is that tamari is wheat free and is popular with those who have wheat allergies.

CABBAGE AND BARLEY SOUP WITH TAHINI
75 g (3 oz) pearl barley
1 tbsp vegetable or olive oil
1 onion, thinly sliced
1 garlic clove, crushed
450 g (1 lb/2 cups) cabbage, cut into fine strips
Vegetable stock – enough to make up 1 L (1¾ pints/36 fl oz) with barley water
1 bay leaf
1-2 tbsp tahini

Salt and freshly ground black pepper to taste   (Serves 4)

1   Cook the pearl barley according to the instructions on the packet. Reserve the liquid.
2   Heat the oil and sauté the onion and garlic for about 5 minutes or until onion is soft.
3   Add the cabbage and the cooked barley, with the cooking water and make it up to 1 L (1¾ pints/36 fl oz) with vegetable stock.
4   Bring to the boil, add the bay leaf and simmer for about 3-5 minutes until cabbage is just cooked, but still crunchy.
5   Remove from heat and stir in tahini.
6   Season to taste and serve.

CABBAGE CHOWDER WITH CORIANDER AND WHISKY
900 g (2 lb/4 cups) cabbage, cut into fine strips or grated
450 g (1 lb/2 cups) carrots, peeled and cut into strips
700 g (1½ lb/3 cups) potatoes, peeled and diced
450 ml (16 fl oz/2 cups) vegetable stock
1 tbsp fresh coriander, chopped
1-2 tbsp whisky
450 ml (16 fl oz/2 cups) milk
2 tbsp cream (optional)
Salt and freshly ground black pepper to taste   (Serves 8)

1   In a large pan place cabbage, carrots, potatoes and stock.
2   Bring to the boil, reduce heat and simmer until vegetables are cooked, about 15-20 minutes.
3   Add the coriander, whisky, milk and cream (if used). Heat through. Season to taste and serve.

CABBAGE WITH HONEY AND WINE

Now that the bottle of wine is opened, you have a good excuse to finish it off.

50 g (2 oz/½ stick) butter or margarine
1 onion, finely chopped
4 tbsp cider vinegar
2 tsp honey
125 ml (4 fl oz) white wine
125 ml (4 fl oz) vegetable stock
450 g (1 lb/2 cups) cabbage, cut into fine strips
Salt and freshly ground black pepper to taste   (Serves 4)

1   Heat butter or margarine in a large pan and sauté the onion for about 4 minutes or until soft.
2   Add the cider vinegar, honey, white wine and vegetable stock. Bring to the boil.
3   Reduce heat, add the cabbage and mix well.
4   Cover and allow the cabbage to simmer until it is crisp-tender, about 10-15 minutes. Season to taste.
5   Serve with rice or an omelette.

CARROTS WITH NOODLES

45 g (1½ oz) butter or margarine
1 medium onion, chopped
225 g (8 oz) carrots, grated
150 ml (¼ pint/5 fl oz) orange juice
1 tbsp cider vinegar
Salt and freshly ground black pepper to taste
175 g (6 oz) egg noodles, cooked   (Serves 4-6)

1   In a pan melt butter or margarine and add onion and carrots. Sauté for about 3 minutes.

2   Add the orange juice, vinegar and season to taste.
3   Bring to the boil and cook for about 2-3 minutes.
4   Cook the egg noodles following instructions on packet.
5   Stir the cooked noodles into the carrot mixture and serve.

CARROT AND PEANUT BUTTER BISCUITS

125 g (4 oz) peanut butter
50 g (2 oz) margarine
90 g (3½ oz) brown sugar
50 g (2 oz) granulated sugar
1 egg
½ tsp vanilla essence
125 g (4 oz/1 cup) plain flour
1 tsp bicarbonate of soda
½ tsp salt
125 g (4 oz/1 cup) 100% bran cereal
225 g (8 oz/1 cup) carrots, grated
100 g (3½ oz) chopped peanuts or sunflower seeds

Preheat oven to 180°C (350°F/Gas 4)

1   Cream peanut butter, margarine, brown sugar, granulated sugar, egg and vanilla essence until light and fluffy.
2   Mix together flour, bicarbonate of soda and salt and fold into creamed mixture.
3   Stir in cereal, carrots and peanuts or sunflower seeds.
4   Form into 2.5 cm (1") balls and place on a greased baking sheet, about 5 cm (2") apart. Flatten with a fork.
5   Bake for 10-12 minutes or until lightly browned.
6   Cool on a wire rack.

CHICORY AND BEETROOT SALAD WITH WALNUTS

450 g (1 lb/2 cups) beetroot, scrubbed, but not topped and tailed
225 g (8 oz/1 cup) walnuts
2 tsp Dijon mustard
2 tsp chopped tarragon or ½ tsp dried tarragon
2 cloves garlic, crushed
Salt and freshly ground black pepper to taste
4 tbsp white wine vinegar
175 ml (6 fl oz/¾ cup) olive oil
450 g (1 lb/2 cups) chicory, trimmed washed and
chopped roughly   (Serves 4-6)

1   Place the scrubbed beetroot in boiling salted water,
    reduce heat and simmer until tender, about 1 hour.
    Drain, peel and slice. Allow to cool.
2   Toast walnuts in oven for about 10 minutes,
    180°C (350°F/Gas 4). Allow to cool, and break into
    smaller pieces. Reserve.
3   In a jar with a lid, combine mustard, tarragon, garlic,
    salt, pepper, vinegar and olive oil. Put on lid and shake
    vigorously until ingredients are blended well.
4   Arrange beetroot in a serving bowl. Place chicory on top,
    pour dressing over chicory and sprinkle with walnuts.

CHICORY AND RED LEICESTER SALAD WITH HONEY

Dressing
150 ml (¼ pint/5 fl oz) natural yoghurt
2 tsp honey
2 tsp lemon juice
1 tsp French mustard
Zest of one orange, grated
Salad
225 g (8 oz) red Leicester cheese, cubed
2 chicory heads, sliced
2 sweet apples, peeled, cored and chopped
2 oranges, peeled and segmented
To garnish: chopped parsley

1   Mix yoghurt, honey, lemon juice, mustard and orange
    zest together for dressing.
2   Put cheese, chicory, apples and oranges in a bowl.
    Add dressing and mix well.
3   Sprinkle with chopped parsley and serve.

CHICORY WITH WARM APPLE AND CIDER THYME DRESSING

450 g (1 lb/2 cups) chicory, trimmed, washed and
roughly chopped
Dressing
150 ml (¼ pint/5 fl oz) cider
1 apple, finely chopped
2 tbsp lemon juice
1 tbsp olive oil
½ tsp dried or fresh oregano
½ tsp dried or fresh thyme   (Serves 4)

1   Put chicory into serving bowl.
2   Combine all of the dressing ingredients together in a
    small saucepan and boil for 3–5 minutes, until the juices
    are slightly thickened and apple is soft, but not

broken down.

3 Allow the dressing to cool slightly, pour over the chicory and serve immediately.

The dressing will keep in a jar in the refrigerator for 3 days.

PARSNIP AND APPLE BAKE WITH CORIANDER AND PARSLEY

450 g (1 lb/2 cups) parsnips, peeled and grated
1 medium apple, grated and mixed with 2 tsp lemon juice
1 onion, finely chopped
1 tbsp fresh coriander, chopped
1 tbsp fresh parsley, chopped
2 eggs, beaten
Salt and freshly ground black pepper to taste   (Serves 4)

1 Preheat oven to 180°C (350°F/Gas 4).
2 Mix the parsnips, apple, onion, coriander and parsley together.
3 Add the egg to bind the mixture. Season to taste.
4 Put mixture into a greased baking dish and bake for about 25 minutes or until browned.

PARSNIP, CARROT AND SPROUTING BROCCOLI CURRY

2 tbsp vegetable or olive oil
1 onion, finely chopped
1 tbsp ground cumin
2 tsp ground coriander
½-1 tsp cinnamon
1 tsp turmeric
3 garlic cloves, crushed
1 tbsp fresh root ginger, finely chopped
1 fresh green chilli, seeded and finely chopped (optional)
300 ml (10 fl oz/½ pint/1¼ cups) plain yoghurt
300 ml (10 fl oz/½ pint/1¼ cups) water
Salt and freshly ground black pepper to taste
350 g (12 oz/1½ cups) parsnips, peeled and diced
350 g (12 oz/1½ cups) carrots, peeled and cut into sticks
225 g (8 oz) sprouting broccoli, chopped
To garnish: fresh coriander, chopped   (Serves 4)

1 In a large pan, heat the oil and sauté the onion until golden brown.
2 Stir in the cumin, coriander, cinnamon and turmeric. Cook for about one minute.
3 Add the garlic and ginger. Add the chilli if you like a hot curry. Cook for about another minute, stirring continuously.
4 Stir in the yoghurt, a little at a time. Cook, stirring continuously for about 2 more minutes.
5 Stir in the water and season to taste.
6 Add the parsnips, carrots and sprouting broccoli. Bring to the boil, reduce heat, cover and simmer for about 15-20 minutes or until the vegetables are tender.
7 To garnish, sprinkle with chopped coriander.

PARSNIPS WITH MAPLE SYRUP AND DIJON MUSTARD SAUCE

450 g (1 lb/2 cups) parsnips, peeled and cut into diagonal slices, 0.6 cm (¼") thick
1 tbsp maple syrup
1 tsp Dijon mustard
50 g (2 oz) butter or margarine
Salt and freshly ground black pepper to taste   (Serves 4)

1. Place the parsnips in a pan with salted water. Bring to the boil, reduce heat and simmer until tender, about 15 minutes. Drain and keep warm.
2. Whilst parsnips are cooking, in a small pan combine maple syrup, mustard, butter or margarine, salt and pepper. Heat gently and stir until the butter or margarine has melted.
3. Pour sauce over parsnips. Stir to coat them well.
4. Serve with potatoes with lemon tahini sauce on page 94.

Another maple syrup legend is the Legend of Nokomis (the land), which tells about Nokomis' granddaughter, Manabush, tasting the drips after Nokomis had tapped the maple tree to collect syrup. Manabush felt that men would get lazy if all they had to do was to tap the tree, so she grabbed a bucket of water, climbed the maple tree and poured water into the centre of the tree, diluting the sweet sap to between 1% and 2% sugar. So it was that she made it necessary for men to work hard to get the syrup.

POTATO CURRY, THAI STYLE
2 tbsp vegetable oil
1 onion, chopped
2.5 cm (1") piece root ginger, peeled and chopped or grated
3 garlic cloves, crushed
1 - 2 fresh green chillies, seeded and chopped (optional)
900 g (2 lb) potatoes, peeled and diced
1 x 440 ml (14 fl oz) can coconut milk
Juice of 2 limes or lemons, salt and pepper to taste
1 x 2.5 cm (1") piece fresh lemon grass, (optional)

1. Heat the oil in a pan, add the onion and fry until golden brown.
2. Add the ginger, garlic and chilli (if used) and fry for another 2 minutes, stirring constantly.
3. Add the potatoes, coconut milk, lime or lemon juice and lemon grass (if used). Season to taste.
4. Bring to the boil, reduce heat and simmer for about 35 minutes.
5. Remove lemon grass before serving with jasmine rice.

PURPLE SPROUTING BROCCOLI WITH MACARONI AND BLUE CHEESE SAUCE
450 g (16 oz/2 cups) macaroni
450 g (1 lb/2 cups) purple sprouting broccoli, chopped
25 g (1 oz) butter or margarine
35 g (1 oz/¼ cup) flour
½ tsp dried mustard
Salt and freshly ground black pepper to taste
175 ml (6 fl oz) milk
150 ml (¼ pint/5 fl oz) yoghurt
225 g (8 oz) Stilton or other blue cheese, crumbled

(Serves 4-6)

1. Cook macaroni in boiling water until just cooked. Drain.
2. Cook broccoli in boiling salted water for about 3 minutes or until crisp-tender. Drain.
3. In a pan, melt butter or margarine, add flour, mustard, salt and pepper and cook for 2 minutes, stirring continuously with a wooden spoon.
4. Gradually add the milk using a whisk. Whisk briskly until smooth. Remove from the heat.
5. Stir in the yoghurt and blue cheese.
6. Add the sauce to the macaroni and mix well.
7. Gently fold in the broccoli.
8. Grease an ovenproof dish and fill with the mixture.
9. Bake for about 20 minutes at 180°C (350°F/Gas 4) or until browned.

NOTE: Can top with breadcrumbs or extra cheese before baking.

PURPLE SPROUTING BROCCOLI WITH BAKED POTATOES

5 potatoes, baked
700 g (1½ lb/3 cups) purple sprouting broccoli
25 g (1 oz) butter or margarine
2 tbsp plain flour
225 ml (8 fl oz/1 cup) milk
¼ tsp powdered mustard
120 g (4 oz/½ cup) Cheddar cheese, grated
Salt and freshly ground black pepper to taste   (Serves 5)

1   Put broccoli into pan of boiling, salted water, return to boil, reduce heat and simmer for about 10-15 minutes or until cooked.
2   In another pan, melt butter or margarine. Add flour and stir to make a smooth paste.
3   Stir in milk a little at a time and cook over a low heat, stirring continuously, until thickened.
4   Add the mustard.
5   Stir in cheese and cook until melted.
6   Fold in broccoli and season to taste.
7   Serve over hot baked potatoes.

PURPLE SPROUTING BROCCOLI AND CARROTS WITH LIME DRESSING

2 carrots, thinly sliced on the diagonal
450 g (1 lb/2 cups) purple sprouting broccoli, chopped
Dressing
1 tbsp dark sesame oil
1 tbsp soy sauce
2 tsp honey
3 tbsp fresh lime juice (about 1 lime)
Salt and freshly ground black pepper to taste   (Serves 4-6)

1   Bring 5 cm (2") of water to a rapid boil in a covered pot. Add the vegetables, cover and simmer for about 5 minutes or until crisp-tender.
2   While the vegetables cook, mix together all of the dressing ingredients.
3   Drain the vegetables and plunge them into cold water, drain again and chill until ready to serve.
4   Mix the vegetables with the dressing just before serving.

PURPLE SPROUTING BROCCOLI AND CREAMY CARROT SLAW

3 tbsp mayonnaise
1½ tbsp fresh lemon juice
1½ tsp onion, grated
1½ tsp Dijon mustard, coarse grained
350 g (12 oz/1½ cups) purple sprouting broccoli, finely chopped
225 g (8 oz/ 1 cup) carrots, peeled and grated
Salt and freshly ground black pepper to taste   (Serves 4)

1   Combine mayonnaise, lemon juice, onion and mustard in a medium bowl and whisk to blend.
2   Add broccoli and carrots. Mix well.
3   Season to taste and refrigerate to blend flavours before serving.

PURPLE SPROUTING BROCCOLI PESTO (RECIPE I)

Jacqui and Joan have surprisingly similar tastes, but this recipe Jacqui loved and Joan didn't. In addition to the flavour, Jacqui particularly liked it because the stalks of the broccoli can be used and no cooking is involved. More olive oil may be needed, adjust until you get a smooth consistency.

450 g (1 lb/2 cups) purple sprouting broccoli, with stalks,
roughly chopped
175 g (6 oz/1 cup) walnuts
175 g (6 oz) fresh Parmesan cheese, cut into small chunks, or
1 x 80g tub of grated Parmesan cheese
225 ml (8 fl oz/1 cup) olive oil
3 cloves garlic (can add more if you like a strong garlic taste)
Salt and freshly ground black pepper to taste.
(Makes about 3 x 450g jars)

1   Combine all ingredients in a food processor.
    Adjust seasonings to taste.
2   Serve with pasta or use as a dip.
3   Stores well in a jar in the refrigerator for up to 3 days.

PURPLE SPROUTING BROCCOLI PESTO (RECIPE II)

450 g (1 lb/2 cups) purple sprouting broccoli, chopped
175 ml (6 fl oz/¾ cup) olive oil
175 g (6 oz) Parmesan cheese, grated
8 sun-dried tomatoes
125 g (4 oz) unsalted cashew nuts
3 cloves garlic (can adjust to taste)
Salt and freshly ground black pepper to taste.
(Makes about 3 x 500 g jars)

1   Immerse broccoli into boiling salted water, bring back to
    the boil, reduce heat and simmer until just tender, about
    5 minutes. Drain and cool.
2   In a blender or food processor, purée cooled broccoli,
    plus rest of the ingredients until smooth.
3   Serve over hot pasta.

4   Stores well in a jar in the refrigerator for up to 3 days.

PURPLE SPROUTING BROCCOLI WITH TAGLIATELLE, FETA CHEESE AND OLIVES

350 g (12 oz/1½ cups) tagliatelle
450 g (1 lb/2 cups) purple sprouting broccoli
4 tbsp olive oil
3 tbsp pine nuts
175 g (6 oz) Feta cheese, crumbled
175 g (6 oz) black olives, pitted and halved
125 g (4 oz/½ cup) Parmesan cheese, grated
2 tbsp fresh basil, chopped
Salt and freshly ground black pepper to taste   (Serves 4–6)

1   Cook tagliatelli in boiling salted water until tender but
    firm, following instructions on packet, about 5 minutes.
2   Add broccoli to tagliatelle and continue boiling until
    broccoli is crisp-tender, about 2 minutes.
    Remove from heat.
3   Heat oil in pan over medium heat and add the pine nuts
    and stir until golden brown, about 2 minutes.
    Remove from heat.
4   Drain tagliatelle and broccoli and transfer to a large bowl.
5   Pour pine nuts with oil over tagliatelle and broccoli, and
    toss to coat.
6   Add Feta, olives, Parmesan and basil and stir well.
    Season to taste.

RADISH AND POTATO SPREAD

225 g (8 oz/1 cup), potatoes peeled and quartered
225 g (8 oz/1 cup) radishes, washed and grated finely
1 small onion, finely chopped or grated
Bunch of parsley, finely chopped

4 tbsp sour cream
Salt and freshly ground black pepper to taste

1 Put potatoes into salted water, bring to the boil, reduce heat and simmer until tender, about 10-15 minutes. Drain and cool.
2 Chop cooked potatoes finely
3 Add rest of the ingredients to the potatoes and mix well.
4 Serve.

RHUBARB, GINGER AND ORANGE MOUSSE

450 g (1 lb) rhubarb, washed and cut into chunks
125 g (4 oz) brown sugar
1 tbsp orange juice
½ tsp ground ginger
300 ml (½ pint/10 fl oz) whipping cream   (Serves 4)

1 Put the rhubarb, sugar, orange juice and ginger in a pan, bring to the boil, reduce heat and simmer until tender, about 10-15 minutes.
2 Allow to cool.
3 Whip the cream until it is stiff and fold in the rhubarb mixture.
4 Chill before serving.

ROCKET STIR-FRY WITH RADISH AND PARSLEY

2 tbsp olive oil
2 garlic cloves, chopped
A good handful of rocket, washed and chopped
6-8 radishes, washed and quartered
1 tbsp fresh parsley, chopped
Salt and freshly ground black pepper to taste   (Serves 2)

1 Heat oil in a pan and fry the garlic for about 2 minutes.
2 Add the rocket, radishes and parsley and stir-fry for about 5 minutes.
3 Season to taste and serve.

SWEDE WITH CORIANDER, PARSLEY AND PARMESAN

50 g (2 oz) butter or margarine
1 onion, chopped
450 g (1lb) swede, peeled and cut into small cubes
1 tbsp fresh coriander
1 tbsp fresh parsley
2 tbsp Parmesan cheese
Salt and freshly ground black pepper to taste   (Serves 4)

1 Heat the butter or margarine in a pan and fry the onion for about 2-3 minutes, or until soft.
2 Add the swede and fry gently until golden brown, about 10-15 minutes.
3 Add the coriander, parsley and Parmesan. Season to taste.
4 Serve.

FARMING NEWS FOR MAY

Sowing, ploughing and planting remain the major activities this month.

HARVESTING

May is when the last of the sprouting broccoli and the carrots are harvested, and the time when the new carrots are coming through in the polytunnels at Cullerne. Spinach from Cullerne is picked. This is a crop that would have been sown the previous summer and already yielded a harvest that season. Over the winter the spinach plants are kept covered with straw so that they will not be eaten by the deer, which are very much part of the food chain in Scotland. Often in both directions, so to speak. Just before it goes to seed in the spring it is possible to get one more crop off these leafy greens. Rhubarb grown at Cullerne is a wonderfully reliable harbinger of spring.

PLANTING

May is the month for planting beetroot and carrots. Mathis plants *Phacelia*, a blue flower that keeps away the carrot fly and attracts bees amongst the crops. It is pretty too. Pioneering educator, Rudolf Steiner, believed that bees have a healing effect on the land because they leave behind a trail of silica in the atmosphere that is good for the health of the land and the plants.

This is also the month to sow all the brassicas, including purple sprouting broccoli and cauliflowers. Brassicas like manure, so it means shifting something approaching 100 tons of muck onto three acres. Cauliflowers go in this month, and they need the most manure of all the brassicas. They are particularly difficult to grow in our part of Scotland because they are sensitive to cold weather. Pigeons and cabbage root fly enjoy them as much as we do, adding to the workload, but Mathis perseveres because the subscribers really like them.

This is also the period when the summer crops are planted in the polytunnels at Cullerne. Tomatoes, French beans, and cucumber go in. Christopher tries to do this without clearing away the old crops completely so that he can continue to reduce 'the hungry gap' until the outdoor beds are ready. The hungry gap is that period before the new season's vegetables are ready, and the winter crops are tailing off.

MAINTENANCE AND MACHINERY

Mathis flame-weeds the beetroot, carrots and parsnips with a machine he has designed himself. It is a blow torch fitted with a gas bottle, which is mounted on the front of the tractor and burns off the weeds before the crops emerge.

EarthShare has invested in a stone buryer – like a rotovator that works backwards and buries the stones to a depth of five inches. It was initially bought to bury stones deep enough so that when harvesting potatoes, the stones would not be mixed up with the potatoes. This has not worked as well as Mathis had hoped but it has proved to be a stunning ground working tool when planting the brassicas because there are no stones on the surface which makes the use of planting machines easier. It leaves a good tilth, which allows delicate seedlings to get a good start.

At Cullerne, the polytunnels need to be reskinned every 5-7 years and this has to be done in warm weather. If it is done in the winter, when the warm weather comes, the polythene expands and in high winds the loose polythene would whip, split and blow away. May is when this job would be done, after early spring crops are harvested and before the summer crops are planted.

PESTS AND DISEASES

May and September are usually the months when the carrot fly flies and lays its eggs. The carrot fly is probably the most challenging pest here. The flies deposit their eggs in the soil and then the maggots feed on the carrots.

Over the years Mathis has employed various methods to stay one step ahead. Tactics employed include: moving from field to field; covering the carrots with 'Environmesh' netting; using a complicated, homeopathic biodynamic preparation. The modern method is to zap them with organo-phosphates. This is not an option for an organic farmer, and evidence is building up to suggest it is not a healthy option for anyone.

Mathis' latest weapon against the carrot fly is pigs. The pigs forage on recently-cropped land, digging it up with their snouts. As they snuffle around looking for food in the shape of roots, birds clean the ground by picking off the insects, grubs and weeds that are driven to the surface by the action of the pigs.

WEATHER
May is usually the driest, warmest and prettiest month of the year in Scotland.

May vegetable box

RECIPES FOR MAY

CARROTS WITH GINGER, COCONUT AND SPINACH

2 tbsp vegetable or olive oil
1 medium onion, chopped
2 garlic cloves, crushed
½ tsp turmeric
700 g (1½ lb/3 cups) carrots, roughly grated or cut into thin strips
1.25 cm (½") fresh root ginger, peeled and finely chopped or grated
½ tsp ground coriander
125 g (4 oz) desiccated coconut
350 g (12 oz) fresh spinach, chopped
Salt and freshly ground black pepper to taste   (Serves 6)

1   Heat oil in a pan and sauté the onion, garlic and turmeric until onions are soft.
2   Add the carrots, ginger, coriander, coconut, spinach, salt and pepper. Stir well.
3   Simmer for 10 minutes or until the carrots are cooked.

CARROTS WITH WHITE WINE AND HERBS

450 g (1 lb/2 cups) carrots, peeled or scrubbed and cut into chunks
450 ml (16 fl oz/2 cups) water
350 ml (12 fl oz/1½ cups) dry, white wine
225 ml (8 fl oz/1 cup) white wine vinegar
3 sprigs parsley
1 sprig rosemary
3 mint leaves
3 basil leaves
1 bay leaf
1-2 garlic cloves, peeled
1 tbsp sugar
4 tbsp olive oil
Salt and freshly ground black pepper to taste   (Serves 4)

1   Place carrots into a pan and cover with the water, wine and vinegar.
2   Add the herbs, garlic, sugar, olive oil, salt and pepper.
3   Bring to the boil and simmer, uncovered, for 30 minutes.
4   Remove the carrots and place in a serving dish. Strain the liquid and pour over the carrots.
5   The carrots can be eaten straight away, but they taste better if stored in the refrigerator for 1-2 days before eating to allow the flavours to fuse. Just re-heat before serving. You can also keep the wine in the fridge for 1-2 days, but why bother – its flavours have already fused!

PURPLE SPROUTING BROCCOLI WITH GARLIC AND MACARONI

450 g (1 lb/2 cups) macaroni
450 g (1 lb/2 cups) purple sprouting broccoli, chopped
2-4 tbsp olive oil
6 cloves garlic, chopped (adjust to taste)
120 g (4 oz/½ cup) Cheddar cheese, grated
Salt and freshly ground black pepper to taste   (Serves 4)

1   Cook the macaroni following instructions on the packet. Drain, transfer to a serving dish and keep warm.
2   Put the broccoli into boiling, salted water and quickly return to the boil. Reduce heat and simmer until crisp-tender. Drain.
3   Heat oil in pan and add the garlic. Cook for about

2 minutes. Add the cooked broccoli to the pan.

4 Add the cheese and season to taste. Mix well and cook gently until cheese has melted.

5 Pour broccoli, cheese and oil mixture over the macaroni and stir well.

6 Sprinkle more cheese on top and serve.

PURPLE SPROUTING BROCCOLI, POTATO AND CHEESE SOUP

25 g (1 oz) butter or margarine
225 g (8 oz/1 cup) onion, chopped
700 g (1½ lb/3 cups) potatoes, peeled and cut into
1.25 cm (½") cubes
20 fl oz (1 pint/2½ cups) boiling water
1 tbsp bouillon or vegetable stock
450 g (1 lb/2 cups) purple sprouting broccoli, chopped
175 g (6 oz) Cheddar cheese, grated
Salt and freshly ground black pepper to taste   (Serves 4)

1 Melt butter or margarine in pan. Add the onion and sauté for 5 minutes.

2 Add potatoes, water, stock and broccoli. Cover and bring to boil. Reduce heat and cook until vegetables are tender, about 15 minutes.

3 Pour the contents of the saucepan into a blender and process until smooth.

4 Return to the saucepan, and gradually add the cheese, stirring until heated through and the cheese has completely melted. Season to taste.

PURPLE SPROUTING BROCCOLI AND ROASTED GARLIC CHEESE SPREAD

2 bulbs garlic, separated into individual cloves, unpeeled

2-3 tbsp olive oil
225 g (8 oz/1 cup) purple sprouting broccoli, roughly chopped
225 g (8 oz) cream cheese
2 tsp chives
Salt and freshly ground black pepper to taste

1 Coat garlic cloves liberally with olive oil. Place on foil and roast for about 30 minutes in oven 190°C (375°F/Gas 5) or until soft.

2 Allow to cool, remove pulp from roasted cloves and discard skins. Set aside.

3 Immerse broccoli into boiling salted water, return to boil, reduce heat and simmer until crisp-tender, about 8 minutes. Set aside and allow to cool.

4 Combine broccoli, garlic, cream cheese and chives in a food processor. Process until mixture is smooth. Season to taste.

5 Remove from food processor and chill for about 2 hours before serving.

A delicious dip for a party served with crackers or fresh vegetables.

PURPLE SPROUTING BROCCOLI SLAW

450 g (1 lb/2 cups) purple sprouting broccoli, chopped
225 g (8 oz/1 cup) celery, finely chopped
1 medium onion, finely chopped
225 g (8 oz/1 cup) black olives, pitted and halved
3 hard boiled eggs, chopped
225 g (8 oz) mayonnaise   (Serves 8)

1 Put broccoli into boiling, salted water, return to boil, reduce heat and simmer until just tender, about 5 minutes. Drain and allow to cool.

2 Combine cooled broccoli, celery, onion, olives and

eggs together.

3   Mix in mayonnaise. Refrigerate before serving.

PURPLE SPROUTING BROCCOLI WITH SPICY CHICKPEA SAUCE

450 g (1 lb/2 cups) purple sprouting broccoli
1 x 400 g (14 oz) can chickpeas, drained
150 ml (¼ pint/5 fl oz) plain yoghurt
2 garlic cloves, peeled
2 tbsp water
2 tsp olive oil
2 tsp lemon juice
¼ tsp ground cumin
¼ tsp cayenne pepper
Salt and freshly ground black pepper to taste   (Serves 4)

1   Put broccoli into boiling, salted water, return to boil,
    reduce heat and cook until tender, about 10-15 minutes.
    Drain and keep warm.
2   In a food processor or blender, add drained chickpeas,
    yoghurt, garlic, water, olive oil, lemon juice, cumin,
    cayenne pepper and seasoning and blend until smooth.
    Taste and adjust seasoning if necessary.
    Heat sauce in a pan.
3   Transfer cooked broccoli to a serving dish, spoon the
    sauce over the broccoli and stir well.

PURPLE SPROUTING BROCCOLI WITH TOFU AND JASMINE RICE

225 g (8 oz/1 cup) Jasmine rice
2 tsp brown sugar
4 tsp tamari
2 tbsp vegetable oil
1 tsp dried ginger or 1.25 cm (½") fresh root ginger peeled
and chopped
2 garlic cloves, crushed
1 small onion, chopped
225 g (8 oz/1 cup) firm tofu, cubed
4 tbsp water
450 g (1 lb/2 cups) purple sprouting broccoli, chopped
                                                (Serves 4)

1   Cook rice following instructions on packet.
2   Dissolve sugar in tamari and set aside.
3   Heat oil in pan over medium-high heat.
    Stir-fry ginger and garlic for one minute.
4   Add onion and cook for 2 minutes
5   Add tofu and water, and cook for 2 minutes.
6   Add broccoli and cook until crisp-tender. Add sugar and tamari.
7   Serve hot with the Jasmine rice.

SPROUT SNIPPET: Jasmine rice is the favoured grain of
Thailand in the heart of Southeast Asia, where the story of rice
began more than 10,000 years ago. Of all the many strains of rice
born in the world's Rice Bowl, this is the one the locals kept for
their own. Infused with a subtle floral essence, Jasmine rice is a
beautiful, long-grain white rice. Its tenderness and mild flavour
are a perfect balance to the fiery tastes of Thai cuisine.

RADISH AND BEETROOT SLAW

2 medium beetroot, peeled and grated
10-15 radishes, grated or finely chopped
1 tsp sesame oil
2 tsp vegetable oil
1 tsp white wine vinegar
Salt and freshly ground black pepper to taste   (Serves 2-4)

1 Put grated beetroot and radish in a bowl.
2 Add rest of ingredients and stir well.
3 Refrigerate before serving.

RADISH, CARROT AND ORANGE SALAD

175 g (6 oz/¾ cup) radishes, thinly sliced
450 g (1 lb/2 cups) carrots, peeled and grated
1 large onion, chopped
3 tbsp olive oil
2 tbsp lemon juice
2 tbsp orange juice
Pinch of cinnamon
Bunch parsley, chopped
Salt and freshly ground black pepper to taste   (Serves 4)

1 Combine radishes, carrots and onion in a large bowl.
2 Whisk together olive oil, lemon juice, orange juice,
   cinnamon, parsley, salt and pepper. Pour over salad.
3 Cover and chill.
4 Serve with warm pitta bread.

RADISH AND FETA SALAD WITH GARLIC VINAIGRETTE

For the vinaigrette
150 ml (¼ pint/5 fl oz) olive oil
150 ml (¼ pint/5 fl oz) white wine vinegar
1 tsp Dijon mustard
¼ - ½ tsp herbs, such as dill or basil, can be dried or fresh
2 cloves garlic, crushed
Juice of ½ lemon
Salt and freshly ground black pepper to taste
For the salad
225 g (8 oz/1 cup) radishes, thinly sliced

225 g (8 oz/1 cup) Feta cheese, crumbled
225 g (8 oz/1 cup) black olives, pitted
3 spring onions, or one small onion, finely chopped (Serves 4)

1 Place all ingredients for the vinaigrette in a jar with a lid
   and shake vigorously to mix well.
2 Place salad ingredients in a bowl, mix well.
3 Add vinaigrette and refrigerate before serving.

RHUBARB BREAD FOR BREAD MAKING MACHINE

225 g (8 oz/1 cup) rhubarb, chopped
225 ml (8 fl oz/1 cup) water
½ tsp orange peel, finely grated
225 g (8 oz/2 cups) wholemeal flour
125 g (4 oz/1 cup) white bread flour
25 g (1 oz) butter or margarine
3 tbsp brown sugar
¾ tsp salt
½ tsp ground cinnamon
1 tsp active dry yeast   (Makes 1½ lb loaf)

1 Combine rhubarb and water in a medium saucepan. Bring
   to boil and reduce heat. Simmer, uncovered for 5 minutes
   or until rhubarb is tender.
2 Measure rhubarb-water mixture and add water, if
   necessary, to equal 350 ml (12 fl oz). Cool slightly.
3 Add ingredients to bread machine according to
   manufacturer's direction.

SPROUT SNIPPET: Six rhubarb plants will provide enough
rhubarb for a family of four. According to folklore, Chinese
doctors recommended rhubarb for its medicinal qualities as a lax-
ative, to reduce fever, and cleanse the body.

RHUBARB AND OATMEAL BARS

Great for picnics and lunches. We noticed that the bars held together better when we refrigerated them.

Crumble mixture for base and top
175 g (6 oz/1 ½ cups) plain flour
225 g (8 oz/2 cups) oatmeal
90 g (3 oz) brown sugar
175 g (6 oz) butter or margarine, melted

Filling
450 g (1 lb/2 cups) rhubarb, cut into 1.25 cm (½") pieces
150 g (5 oz/¾ cup) brown sugar
1½ tbsp plain flour
¼ tsp ground nutmeg
25 g (1 oz) butter or margarine, softened
1 egg, beaten   (Makes about 12 bars)

1   For the base and top, mix flour, oatmeal, brown sugar and butter or margarine together until crumbly.
2   Press half of the crumble mixture into a greased 24 cm (9½") square baking tin.
3   Add rhubarb.
4   Mix sugar, flour, nutmeg and butter or margarine together and add egg. Beat until smooth.
5   Pour over the rhubarb.
6   Top with the other half of the crumble mixture, and press down lightly.
7   Bake in oven 180°C (350°F/Gas 4) for about 35–40 minutes.
8   Refrigerate and cut into bars.

RHUBARB TART

Crumble mixture for the base
125 g (4 oz/1 cup) plain flour
90 g (3 oz/½ cup) icing sugar
90 g (3 oz) butter or margarine

Filling
225 g (8 oz/1 cup) brown sugar
4 tbsp plain flour
1 tsp vanilla essence or ½ tsp ground cinnamon
2 eggs, lightly beaten
700 g (1½ lb/3 cups) rhubarb, finely chopped   (Serves 6-8)

1   In a bowl combine flour and icing sugar. Rub in the butter or margarine until the mixture resembles fine breadcrumbs.
2   Put the crumble mixture into the bottom of a square 24 cm (9½") baking tin. Press down firmly and bake in oven 180°C (350°F/Gas 4) for about 10 minutes until lightly baked. Do not brown.
3   In a bowl mix together sugar, flour and vanilla or cinnamon. Beat in the eggs until smooth.
4   Stir in rhubarb.
5   Pour over warm crumble mixture in baking tin.
6   Return to oven and bake for about 35 minutes.
7   Cool or refrigerate before slicing.

SPINACH WITH CORIANDER AND YOGHURT
2 tsp ground cumin
2 tbsp fresh coriander or 2 tsp ground coriander
900 g (2 lb/4 cups) fresh spinach, washed and roughly chopped
2 cloves garlic, crushed

150 ml (¼ pint/5 fl oz) yoghurt
Pinch ground nutmeg
Salt and freshly ground black pepper to taste   (Serves 4)

1   Heat frying pan and toast the cumin and ground
    coriander for about one minute. If using fresh coriander,
    do not toast.
2   Add spinach, fresh coriander (if used) and garlic.
    Stir continuously until spinach has wilted.
3   Transfer to a serving bowl and stir in the yoghurt
    and nutmeg. Season. Serve immediately.

SPINACH BAKE WITH CREAM CHEESE, BASIL AND PARSLEY

900 g (2 lb/4 cups) fresh spinach, well washed
2 medium onions, finely chopped
120 g (4 oz) cream cheese
1 tbsp basil, chopped
2 tbsp parsley, chopped
1 egg
Salt and freshly ground black pepper to taste   (Serves 4)

1   Place washed spinach in a pan with no extra water,
    sprinkle with a little salt, cover and cook gently, shaking
    the pan occasionally for about 10 minutes. Drain well.
2   Combine spinach, onion, cream cheese, basil, parsley and
    egg together. Season.
3   Put mixture into a greased baking dish and bake for
    about 30 minutes or until cooked.

SPINACH WITH GREEN PEPPER AND PEANUT BUTTER

1 tbsp vegetable or olive oil
1 medium onion, chopped
1 medium green pepper, deseeded and chopped
1 medium tomato, chopped
450 g (1 lb/2 cups) fresh spinach, washed and roughly chopped
50 g (2 oz/¼ cup) peanut butter
Salt and freshly ground black pepper to taste   (Serves 4)

1   Heat oil in pan and cook onion and green pepper until
    onion is tender.
2   Add tomato and spinach, cover and simmer until spinach
    is tender, about 5 minutes.
3   Stir in peanut butter, season, and heat gently.
4   Serve immediately.

FARMING NEWS FOR JUNE

More Brassica planting, planting, planting! Subscribers also join Mathis to weed the beetroot, carrots, chicory, leeks, onions, and parsnips, getting together for what turns out to be a social event as well. These work shifts and the regular festivals that EarthShare arranges are great opportunities for the subscribers to get together and network. The diverse backgrounds and skills of subscribers often lead to useful contacts being made.

At around the time of almost continuous daylight of the Summer Solstice, 21/22 June, all subscribers are invited to the Summer Tea Party which celebrates the crops of summer. It is a chance to view the gardens of Cullerne and see the salad crops and delicacies growing. Garden staff conduct tours, musicians play, there is singing, and the children play games. Teas of cucumber sandwiches with strawberries and cream follow to complete an enjoyable afternoon.

EarthShare has the use of two big Clydesdale horses, owned by Nicky Molnar. The horses assist in preparing and manuring the land before brassica planting as part of the rotation process. They are used for inter-row cultivation of potatoes and then heaping up again ie tattie row ridging. They work all times of the year doing general harrowing of bare land – when new land is broken to fight the couch grass – and for the springtime harvesting. Nicky is a farming assistant, and is Mathis' right hand man. He will be in charge of the fields from November to February, when Mathis is farming his olive groves in Spain.

HARVESTING

What harvesting? Slim pickings. Subscribers live on salad crops from Cullerne: parsley, basil, new carrots, lettuce and spinach, with rhubarb from Rafford for puddings. Pick elderflowers to make fritters, cordial and champagne.

MAINTENANCE AND MACHINERY

Machines take a back seat as the land gets maintained – by hand weeding.

PEST AND DISEASES

The cabbage root fly tries – and often succeeds – to lay eggs on brassica seedlings. Mathis' battle with the bug begins in earnest.

PLANTING

In Cullerne Garden, fortnightly planting of lettuces continues.

WEATHER

June often catches us out with a cold snap, even a light frost on occasion. At least the month is usually dry, allowing access to the weeding.

A 'hungry gap' box.

CARROTS WITH CASHEW NUTS

700 g (1½ lb/3 cups) carrots, scrubbed and grated
2 tbsp cashew nuts, toasted and chopped
1 tbsp fresh basil, chopped
2 tbsp lime juice
½ tbsp maple syrup   (Serves 4-6)

1   Place carrots in a bowl.
2   To toast cashew nuts, place them on a baking tray and
    put under the grill until just browned, about 1-2 minutes.
    Keep an eye on them to make sure they do not burn.
3   Add cashew nuts and basil to carrots. Mix well.
4   Blend together the lime juice and maple syrup.
5   Pour over carrots and mix well.

CARROTS IN A MUSTARD AND LEMON DRESSING

Juice of one lemon
2 tsp Dijon mustard
1 tsp sugar
1 medium onion, finely chopped
5 tbsp olive oil
1 tbsp fresh basil, chopped
Salt and freshly ground black pepper to taste
450 g (1 lb/2 cups) carrots, scrubbed and cut into
thin strips, or grated   (Serves 4)

1   In a jar with a lid, combine lemon juice, mustard, sugar,
    onion, olive oil, basil, salt and pepper. Shake vigorously
    until blended.
2   Put carrots into a salad bowl. Pour dressing over and mix well.

3   Chill before serving.

ELDERFLOWER CHAMPAGNE

Joan has been making this recipe since her oldest boys Ben and
Joe (29 and 27 respectively) were small. Everyone loves this
champagne and can't get enough of it. Joan also likes it because
elderflowers are free and readily available all over Britain. Once
Joan gets her act together she makes it in London from May and
carries on until the end of July in Scotland. Sometimes it fizzes and
sometimes it doesn't. Don't ask her why, but she always means to
make more that she finds the time to do. Her Earth Mother side
is still developing (don't rush her, she's only 57 going on 7!).

4 litres (7¼ pints) water
450 g (1 lb) granulated sugar
2 lemons, sliced
2 tbsp white wine vinegar
7 large elderflower heads

1   Boil the water.
2   Put sugar in a large container and pour the boiled water
    over the sugar. Stir to dissolve. Leave to cool.
3   Add the lemons, white wine vinegar and flower heads.
4   Leave for 24-36 hours.
5   Sterilise 4-5 one-litre glass bottles with screw tops.
    To sterilise the bottles, wash them in soapy water.
    Then rinse in hot clean water. Put the glass bottles
    into an oven at 120°C for 20 minutes.
6   Strain the liquid through muslin, or fine sieve, and bottle.
7   Leave for 7-10 days until fizzy. The time varies,
    depending on the weather.

ELDERFLOWER CORDIAL

Janet Banks gave this recipe to Jacqui. Janet lives in a small family-based community in Scotland. The community grow most of their own organic vegetables. Children as well as adults like this drink. Citric acid is readily available in chemists.

25 good elderflower heads, stalks removed
3 large lemons, thinly sliced
1.5 L (2¾ pints) boiling water
1.4 Kg (3 lbs) granulated sugar
50 gm (2 oz) citric acid

1   Place elderflowers and lemons in a stainless steel, pottery, or plastic container.
2   In another pan, pour boiling water over the sugar and stir over heat until the sugar is dissolved. Add the citric acid.
3   Leave to cool until luke warm and pour liquid over elderflowers and lemon.
4   Leave to stand for 48 hours, stirring occasionally.
5   Strain through muslin or a fine sieve.
6   Pour into sterilised bottles. To sterilise the bottles wash them in soapy water. Then rinse in hot clean water. Put the glass bottles into an oven at 120°C for 20 minutes.

ELDERFLOWER FRITTERS

Once in another incarnation Robin and Joan ran Minton House, a one-time spiritual retreat and bed and breakfast in Findhorn for 2 years. Joan wowed some American guests with this recipe who considered it a delicacy despite the fact that elderflowers are common, even in cities.

For the batter
125 g (4 oz) plain flour

Pinch of salt
1 tbsp vegetable oil
150 ml (¼ pint/5 fl oz) water
1 egg white

Oil for frying
8 elderflower heads
Sugar for coating cooked fritters   (Serves 4)

1   Sift the flour and salt together into a bowl.
2   Make a well in the centre and add the oil and water, beating until smooth. Allow the batter to rest for about one hour.
3   Whisk the egg white until stiff, then fold evenly into the batter with a metal spoon.
4   Heat the oil in a pan.
5   Dip one elderflower head into the batter and add to hot oil. Deep fry for about 2 minutes or until the batter is cooked.
6   Remove and place on a kitchen towel to drain.
7   Dredge in sugar before serving.
8   Repeat until all elderflower heads are used.

LETTUCE AND WALNUT LOAF

You can make this recipe without the lettuce, but we found that it added colour and moistness to the loaf. It tastes much better than it sounds!

350 g (12 oz/1½ cups) sugar
175 ml (6 fl oz/¾ cup) vegetable oil
1½ tbsp lemon juice, freshly squeezed
4 eggs
350 g (12 oz/3 cups) plain flour

2 tsp baking powder
1½ tsp bicarbonate of soda
½ tsp cinnamon
1 tsp salt
450 g (1 lb/2 cups) lettuce, finely chopped
125 g (4 oz/¾ cup) walnuts, chopped

1 Whisk sugar and oil together.
2 Add the lemon juice and eggs and beat well.
3 Fold in the flour, baking powder, bicarbonate of soda, cinnamon and salt.
4 Stir in the lettuce and walnuts.
5 Pour into a greased loaf tin.
6 Bake in a preheated oven, 180°C (350°F/Gas 4) for about 50 minutes, or until knife inserted into the centre of the bread comes out clean.

LETTUCE AND COCONUT CHUTNEY

425 ml (¾ pint/15 fl oz) hot water
175 g (6 oz/¾ cup) desiccated coconut
1 large lettuce, washed and chopped roughly
¼-½ tsp of dried chilli powder (according to taste)
1 tsp tamarind paste
½ tsp salt
½ tsp ground cumin

1 Pour half the water and all of the coconut into a pan. Bring to the boil and simmer for about 1 minute.
2 Stir and add the remaining water.
3 Spread the lettuce leaves on top of the liquid evenly, put a lid on the pan, bring back to the boil and then cook gently for about 3 minutes.

4 Remove from the heat, stir i
   and let stand for 5 minutes w
5 Uncover and allow to cool for
6 Put the mixture into a food
   blend roughly.
7 Put into jars.

LETTUCE, FRIED

1 large lettuce, washed and trir
1 tbsp vegetable or olive oil
2 garlic cloves, crushed
1 tsp soy sauce
Salt and freshly ground black pepper to taste   (Serves 4)

1 Cut lettuce into four.
2 Heat oil in a pan and fry the lettuce for about one minute.
3 Add the garlic, soy sauce and mix well. Cook for another minute.
4 Season to taste.

LETTUCE AND HAZELNUT SOUP

1 tbsp olive oil
1 medium onion, finely chopped
50 g (2 oz) hazelnuts
2 medium potatoes, peeled and finely diced
725 ml (1¼ pint/27 fl oz) vegetable stock
2 large or 4 small-medium lettuce, roughly chopped
75 ml (3 fl oz) double cream
¼ tsp nutmeg, finely grated
Salt and freshly ground black pepper to taste   (Serves 4)

1 Heat oil in a large pan and fry the onion and three quarters of the hazelnuts until the onions are tender,

...tato and stock, bring to the boil and
...e potato is cooked, about 5 minutes.
...ttuce and cook for a further 2 minutes.
...soup into a food processor or blender and
...until it is smooth.
...4 tablespoons of cream and adjust with a little
...ater if the soup is too thick. Add the nutmeg and
season to taste.

6   Can be served hot or cold with rest of cream drizzled
    over the soup and rest of hazelnuts.

LETTUCE RISOTTO

1 L (1¾ pints/4½ cups) vegetable stock
3 tbsp olive oil
1 onion or 1-2 shallots, finely chopped
2 cloves garlic, chopped
350 g (12 oz) Arborio rice
2–4 mixed lettuce, depending on size, washed
and roughly shredded
125 g (4 oz) fresh garden peas, shelled
12 spring onions, cut diagonally into 1 cm (½") pieces
To finish:
Knob of butter or margarine,
25 g (1 oz) fresh Parmesan, grated   (Serves 5-6)

1   Bring the stock to the boil, then turn down the heat to
    simmering point.
2   Heat the olive oil in a large pan and add the onion or
    shallots for about 2 minutes, without browning, then add
    the garlic and cook for a further 1-2 minutes.
3   Add the Arborio rice to the pan and stir well to coat rice
    with oil.

4   Pour in the first ladleful of hot stock. Stir risotto until
    stock has been absorbed, and continue to add stock in
    this way until all has been used.
5   When rice is almost done, about 15 minutes into the
    cooking time, add shredded lettuce, peas and sliced
    spring onions. Stir gently to mix vegetables through the
    rice. At first it will seem that you have added too much
    lettuce, but it will soon wilt and the rice will absorb its
    juices.
6   The risotto is ready when all the liquid has been
    absorbed, the peas are tender and the rice is cooked,
    about 3 minutes after adding the lettuce. The texture
    should be creamy rather than dry.
7   Stir in a knob of butter or margarine and sprinkle with
    Parmesan just before serving.

POTATOES WITH LEMON TAHINI SAUCE

1 tsp vegetable or olive oil
¼ tsp toasted sesame oil
1 onion, chopped
1-2 gloves garlic, crushed
700 g (1½ lb/3 cups) potatoes, peeled and diced
1 tsp fresh basil, chopped
For the lemon tahini sauce
1-2 garlic cloves, crushed
2 tbsp tahini
Juice of one lemon
1 tbsp fresh parsley, chopped
Water
Salt and freshly ground black pepper to taste   (Serves 4)

1   Heat oil in a pan and sauté onions and garlic until the
    onion is soft.

2   Add potatoes and basil to the pan and stir well. Sauté for about another 2-3 minutes.
3   Pour in 225 ml (8 fl oz/1 cup) boiling water. Bring to the boil, reduce heat and simmer for about 15 minutes or until the potatoes are cooked and most of the liquid has been absorbed.
4   To make the sauce, mix together the garlic, tahini and lemon juice. Slowly add water until the mixture becomes the texture of mayonnaise. Add the parsley and season to taste.
5   Pour sauce over the potatoes, and heat gently until warmed through. Serve.

SPROUT SNIPPET: Tahini is a sesame seed paste readily available in health food stores.

SALAD DRESSINGS
Try some of these dressings to make greens more interesting and palatable

BASIL AND SESAME DRESSING
1 clove garlic, crushed
3 tsp white wine vinegar
1 tbsp lemon juice
2 tbsp Parmesan or mature cheddar cheese, grated
½ tsp dried basil
2-4 leaves fresh basil
2 tbsp parsley, chopped
150 ml (¼ pint/5 fl oz) olive oil
½ tsp sesame oil
Salt and freshly ground black pepper to taste

1   Combine all ingredients in a blender and blend until smooth.
2   Chill and serve with a green salad.

BLUE CHEESE DRESSING
175 ml (6 fl oz/¾cup) sour cream
½ tsp powdered mustard
2 cloves garlic, crushed
1 tsp Worcestershire sauce
8 tbsp mayonnaise
125 g (4 oz) blue cheese, crumbled
Salt and freshly ground black pepper to taste

1   Place sour cream, mustard, garlic, Worcestershire sauce and mayonnaise into a blender or food processor and mix for 2 minutes at low speed.
2   Add crumbled cheese and blend again at low speed until well blended. Season.

FRUITY DRESSING
150 ml (¼ pint/5 fl oz) orange juice
½ tsp orange peel, grated
75 g (3 oz) cream cheese
3 tbsp mayonnaise
1 tsp sugar
¼ tsp cayenne pepper

Put all ingredients into a blender and blend until smooth.

GARLIC, OLIVE OIL AND HERB DRESSING
Seb loves this recipe and will eat any greens when this dressing is used. He also pours it over pasta.

8 tbsp olive oil
4 tbsp white wine vinegar
2 tsp English, French or Dijon mustard
2-3 garlic cloves, crushed

½ tsp salt
½ tsp freshly ground black pepper
1 tbsp of any herbs or 1 tsp any dried herbs

Place all ingredients in a jar with a lid and shake vigorously until blended.

GARLIC MAYONNAISE AND CUCUMBER DRESSING

This is a thick dressing, and could be used as a dip as well.

2 garlic cloves, crushed
4 tbsp mayonnaise
½ cucumber, peeled and chopped
4 tbsp plain yoghurt
2 tbsp fresh parsley, chopped
1 tbsp fresh chives or spring onions, chopped

1   Mix together all ingredients.
2   Chill before serving.

GINGER AND LEMON DRESSING

1 tbsp fresh ginger root, chopped
Juice of ½ lemon
1 small onion, chopped
4 tbsp olive oil
2 tbsp rice wine vinegar or white wine vinegar
2 tbsp water
1 tbsp tomato purée
1 tbsp soy sauce
Salt and freshly ground black pepper to taste

Put all ingredients into a blender and blend until smooth.

HERBY VINAIGRETTE

150 ml (¼ pint/5 fl oz) olive oil
4 tbsp white wine vinegar
1 tbsp lemon juice
1 tsp mustard powder
½ tsp dried oregano
¼ tsp dried sage or coriander
¼ tsp ground cumin
1 clove garlic, crushed
Salt and freshly ground black pepper to taste

1   Place all ingredients in a jar with a lid.
2   Shake vigorously until blended.
3   Chill before serving.

MAYONNAISE AND PARMESAN CHEESE DRESSING

Can be used as a salad dressing or dip for vegetable crudités or chips.

8 tbsp mayonnaise
1 tbsp lemon juice
1 clove garlic, crushed
1 tbsp onion, finely chopped
4 tbsp Parmesan cheese
Salt and freshly ground black pepper to taste

1   Combine all ingredients together and mix well.
2   Cover and refrigerate.

MUSTARD AND HONEY DRESSING

6 tbsp vegetable oil
2 tbsp cider vinegar

2 tbsp honey
2 tbsp Dijon mustard
2 tbsp toasted sesame seeds
2 cloves garlic, crushed
Salt and freshly ground black pepper to taste

(Makes about 225 ml/1 cup)

1   Combine all ingredients in blender and process until smooth.
2   Taste and adjust seasoning.
3   Store in the refrigerator.

PEANUT AND LIME DRESSING

This can be a little thick, so add more olive oil if necessary.

Juice of 2 limes
2 tsp sugar
2 tbsp unsalted roasted peanuts, finely chopped
1 tbsp fresh ginger, chopped finely or grated
4 cloves garlic, crushed
3 tbsp olive oil
Salt and freshly ground black pepper to taste

1   Place all ingredients in a blender and process until smooth.
2   Refrigerate.

TAHINI

While tahini is readily available in health food stores, it is very easy to make your own.

450 g (1 lb/2 cups) sesame seeds
4-8 tbsp vegetable oil

1   Preheat oven to 180°C (350°F/Gas 4).
2   Spread sesame seeds on a shallow baking tray and bake,

shaking frequently until fragrant, about 8-10 minutes. Do not brown. Cool.

3   Put sesame seeds in a blender or food processor and gradually add the vegetable oil. Use enough oil to make a smooth paste of a thick pouring consistency.
4   The tahini will keep well in a covered jar in the refrigerator for several months.

TAHINI DRESSING

2 tbsp tahini
4 tbsp water, or more
1 tbsp freshly squeezed lemon juice
2-4 cloves garlic to taste, crushed
Salt and freshly ground black pepper to taste

1   Put all of the ingredients in a jar with a lid and shake vigorously until blended. The dressing should be the consistency of a creamy salad dressing.
2   Add more water if necessary.

TOMATO, HONEY AND HORSERADISH DRESSING

225 ml (8 fl oz/1 cup) tinned tomatoes, mashed or thick tomato juice
150 ml (¼ pint/5 fl oz) olive oil
150 ml (¼ pint/5 fl oz) lemon juice
1 tbsp honey
1 tsp paprika
1 small onion, chopped
1 tsp creamed horseradish
1-2 cloves garlic
Salt and freshly ground black pepper to taste.

(Makes about 16 fl oz)

1   Put all ingredients into a blender and blend until smooth.
2   Store in a sealed jar in the refrigerator.

VINEGAR AND HONEY DRESSING WITH HERBS

150 ml (¼ pint/5 fl oz) balsamic vinegar
2 tsp honey
1 tsp Dijon mustard
4 tsp cold water
6–8 tsp olive oil
½ tsp dried dill or basil
Salt and freshly ground black pepper to taste

1   Warm vinegar and honey in a small saucepan until honey dissolves in vinegar.
2   Transfer to a jar with a lid.
3   Add remaining ingredients and shake vigorously until blended.

WALNUT AND TARRAGON DRESSING

½ tsp mustard
2 tbsp white wine vinegar
3 tbsp walnut oil
3 tbsp olive oil
1 tbsp fresh tarragon, chopped finely
Salt and freshly ground black pepper to taste
                                    (Makes about ¼ pint/5 fl oz)

1   Place all ingredients in a jar with a lid.
2   Shake vigorously until well blended.

SPINACH DIP

700 g (1½ lb/3 cups) fresh spinach, washed
350 g (12 oz) mozzarella cheese, grated
150 ml (¼ pint/5 fl oz) sour cream
1-2 garlic cloves, crushed
Salt and freshly ground black pepper to taste   (Serves 6-8)

1   Preheat oven to 180°C (350°F/Gas 4).
2   Place washed spinach in a pan with no extra water, sprinkle with a little salt, cover and cook gently, shaking the pan occasionally for about 10 minutes. Drain well.
3   Transfer spinach to a bowl.
4   Stir in mozzarella cheese, sour cream and garlic. Season to taste.
5   Pour mixture into a greased baking dish and bake for about 15 minutes, or until bubbly.
6   Serve with tortilla crisps or hot crusty French bread.

SPINACH WITH LEMON, YOGHURT AND BLACK PEPPER

2 tsp vegetable oil
2 garlic cloves, crushed
1 tsp cumin seeds
900 g (2 lb/4 cups) fresh spinach, washed
Zest and juice of one lemon
½ tsp sugar
4 tbsp plain yoghurt
¼ tsp black pepper, coarsely ground
Salt to taste   (Serves 4)

1   Heat oil in pan and add the garlic and cumin seeds and fry for one minute.
2   Add spinach, and mix well with the garlic and cumin.

3   Add the lemon zest and juice, and cook until the spinach has wilted.
4   Stir in the sugar, yoghurt, black pepper and salt.
5   Serve immediately.

SPINACH AND PEAR SALAD WITH STILTON
125 g (4 oz/¾ cup) walnuts, hazelnuts, almonds or pistachios
Dressing
150 ml (¼ pint/5 fl oz) sherry or cider vinegar
150 ml (¼ pint/5 fl oz) olive oil
1 tbsp Dijon mustard
Salad
3 ripe pears
450 g (1 lb/2 cups) fresh spinach, washed and chopped
225 g (8 oz/1 cup) Stilton or Gorgonzola cheese, crumbled
125 g (4 oz/½ cup) raisins
Salt and freshly ground black pepper to taste   (Serves 6)

1   Cook nuts in a frying pan, over a medium heat, until golden, stirring often, about 5–10 minutes. Pour onto a towel and let stand until cool. Rub in towel to remove any loose skins. Discard skins and roughly chop nuts.
2   Put dressing ingredients in a jar with a lid, and shake vigorously until blended.
3   Cut pears lengthwise into quarters and core. Cut quarters lengthwise into thin slices.
4   In a large salad bowl, place pear slices, spinach and dressing. Stir well.
5   Sprinkle with cheese, raisins, nuts, seasoning, and mix gently.

SPINACH AND SAGE PESTO
2 tbsp pine nuts, toasted
2 large garlic cloves, peeled

450 g (1 lb/2 cups) spinach, torn
225 g (8 oz/1 cup) fresh flat leaf parsley
125 g (4 oz/½ cup) fresh sage leaves
2 tbsp fresh Parmesan, grated
4 tsp lemon juice
Salt and freshly ground black pepper to taste
3 tbsp extra virgin olive oil   (Makes 1 cup)

1   To toast pine nuts, put them on a baking sheet and place under a hot grill until just browned. Keep an eye on them so that they do not burn.
2   Put pine nuts and garlic into a food processor and blend until finely chopped.
3   Add remaining ingredients, except olive oil. Process until finely chopped.
4   With processor on slow speed, add oil and process until well blended. You may need to add more olive oil. Adjust seasoning to taste.
5   Keeps well in the refrigerator in a jar for up to 3 days.

FARMING NEWS FOR JULY

HARVESTING

Fruit picking at Rafford begins this month. Blackcurrants, raspberries and strawberries appear in boxes, confirming that summer is here even if the weather isn't. It is also the time to begin picking the new potatoes and broad beans and from Cullerne: coriander, cucumber, lettuce, mange tout, parsley, peas and new carrots.

MAINTENANCE AND MACHINERY

Any machinery that has broken is fixed. It is a well-known fact that machines always break when you need them most.

PESTS AND DISEASES

Big fat woodpigeons feed on berry crops and anything else they fancy.

WEATHER

Statistically the wettest month. Rain during this period can have a bad effect on the strawberries as they begin to rot before they can be picked. We are also prone to fog this month.

Broad beans

BLACKCURRANT PANCAKES

125 g (4 oz) plain flour
Pinch of salt
¼ tsp nutmeg, grated
1 egg, lightly beaten
350 ml (12 fl oz) milk
175 g (6 oz) blackcurrants
Oil for frying
Caster sugar for dredging   (Serves 4)

1 Sift the flour, salt and nutmeg into a bowl.
2 Using a wooden spoon, make a hollow in the centre of the flour and drop in the egg.
3 Slowly pour in half the milk and gradually work the flour into the milk. When all the flour is incorporated, beat the mixture with a wooden spoon until smooth.
4 Mix in the rest of the milk, beating continuously until the batter is bubbly and the consistency of double cream.
5 Add the blackcurrants to the batter.
6 Heat a pan with oil and drop 2 tablespoons of the batter into the pan.
7 Cook for 2-3 minutes, or until browned, turn the pancake over and cook for a further 2-3 minutes on the other side.
8 Dredge in sugar.
9 Repeat until all the mixture is used.
10 Serve with yoghurt, fromage frais, fresh cream or ice cream.

BROAD BEAN AND CAULIFLOWER CURRY

350 g (12 oz/1½ cups) broad beans, shelled weight
2 garlic cloves, chopped
2 tbsp fresh ginger, chopped
1 fresh green chilli, chopped
1 tbsp vegetable oil
1 medium onion, sliced
1 large potato, diced
25 g (1 oz) butter or margarine
1 tsp curry powder
1 medium cauliflower, broken into florets
600 ml (1 pint/2½ cups/20 fl oz) vegetable stock
2 tbsp creamed coconut
Juice of ½ lemon
Salt and freshly ground black pepper to taste
To garnish: fresh coriander or parsley.   (Serves 4)

1 Put broad beans into boiling salted water, bring back to boil, reduce heat and simmer until tender, about 5-10 minutes. Drain.
2 Blend garlic, ginger, chilli and oil in a food processor until smooth.
3 In a large pan, fry onion and potato in butter or margarine for 5 minutes.
4 Stir in garlic, ginger, chilli and oil paste, curry powder and cook for one minute.
5 Add cauliflower and stir well.
6 Pour in stock. Bring to the boil and mix in coconut, stirring until melted. Season well and cook, uncovered for about 10 minutes or until cauliflower is just tender.
7 Add cooked broad beans and heat through.
8 Add lemon juice and season to taste.
9 Garnish with fresh coriander or parsley.
10 Serve with rice.

BROAD BEAN GUACAMOLE

Joan used a dried red chilli and the recipe worked well.

450 g (1 lb/2 cups) broad beans, shelled weight
A small bunch of fresh coriander or fresh flat leaf parsley, roughly chopped
3 garlic cloves, crushed
½ tsp ground cumin
1 small onion, roughly chopped
1 small green or red chilli, de-seeded and chopped finely
Juice of ½ lemon
Salt and freshly ground black pepper to taste   (Serves 4)

1   Put the beans in boiling salted water, bring back to the boil, reduce heat and simmer until tender, about 5-10 minutes. Drain.
2   Put all ingredients in a food processor and purée to a rough paste.

CARROTS IN TARRAGON VINEGAR

450 g (1 lb/2 cups) new carrots, scrubbed
1 tbsp butter or margarine
1 tbsp lemon juice
2 tbsp tarragon vinegar   (Serves 4)

1   Put carrots in salted water, bring to the boil, reduce heat and simmer until tender, about 10 minutes. Drain and put in a serving dish.
2   Add butter to the pan and stir until melted.
3   Add lemon juice and tarragon vinegar. Pour over carrots and serve.

CARROTS GLAZED WITH CINNAMON AND CLOVES

450 g (1 lb/2 cups) new carrots, scrubbed
25 g (1 oz) butter or margarine
1 tbsp brown sugar
¼ tsp cinnamon
1/8 tsp ground cloves
Salt and freshly ground black pepper to taste   (Serves 4)

1   Put carrots in salted water, bring to the boil, reduce heat and simmer until tender, about 10 minutes. Drain and keep warm.
2   In a small pan, melt butter and add brown sugar, cinnamon, cloves and seasoning. Stir over heat until sugar has dissolved.
3   Pour glaze over carrots and stir well. Serve.

CORIANDER FETA DIP

225 ml (8 fl oz/1 cup) plain yoghurt
450 g (1 lb/2 cups) Feta cheese
2-3 garlic cloves, chopped
3 tbsp fresh coriander, chopped
Salt and freshly ground black pepper to taste

1   Place yoghurt, Feta cheese, garlic and coriander in a food processor or blender and blend until smooth.
2   Season to taste.
3   Use as a dip for fresh vegetables, such as mange tout, cucumber and new carrots.

CORIANDER, PARSLEY AND LIME PESTO

225 g (8 oz/1 cup) fresh coriander, roughly chopped
125 g 4 oz/½ cup) fresh parsley, roughly chopped
50 g (2 oz/¼ cup) walnuts, toasted and cooled
125 ml (4 fl oz/½ cup) olive oil
3 tbsp grated Parmesan cheese
½ tsp freshly grated lime zest
Salt and freshly ground black pepper to taste

1   Place all ingredients in a food processor or blender and blend until smooth. You may need to add a little more olive oil.
2   Garlic cloves can also be added.
3   Keeps for about one week in a jar in the refrigerator.

CORIANDER AND PARSLEY POTATOES

4 tbsp olive oil
700 g (1½ lb/3 cups) potatoes, peeled and diced into 1.25 cm (½") cubes
1 red chilli, seeds removed and chopped finely (optional)
2 garlic cloves, crushed
Salt and freshly ground black pepper to taste
1 bunch fresh coriander, finely chopped
1 bunch fresh parsley, finely chopped   (Serves 4-6)

1   Heat the oil in a pan and add the potatoes.
    Fry until they are cooked and brown on all sides.
2   Add the chilli and the garlic and season to taste.
3   Continue to cook for about another 2-3 minutes.
4   Stir in the coriander and parsley and cook for about another 2-3 minutes.

CORIANDER RISOTTO OR NEXT DAY PATTIES

You can make two meals in one with this recipe. Just double up on the quantity. The only downside is that there is less wine left over to drink!

50 g (2 oz) butter or margarine
1 onion, finely chopped
2 garlic cloves, crushed
450 g (1 lb) Arborio rice
150 ml (¼ pint/5 fl oz) white wine
1 L (1¾ pints) vegetable stock
1 large bunch fresh coriander, roughly chopped
Salt and freshly ground black pepper to taste   (Serves 4-6)

1   Melt the butter or margarine in a large pan and sauté the onion and garlic until onion is soft, about 4 minutes.
2   Add the rice and stir to coat with the butter or margarine.
3   Add the wine and let it reduce by half.
4   Add the stock a little at a time, allowing the risotto to cook and the stock to be absorbed gradually.
5   Stir frequently until the rice is just cooked and the risotto is very thick.
6   Remove from heat and stir in the coriander. Season to taste. Serve as risotto.

Next day patties

7   Let the risotto cool. Refrigerate. This makes the patties easier to shape.
8   Shape the risotto into patties and fry in vegetable oil until golden brown on both sides.
9   Serve with roasted potatoes or vegetables.

CORIANDER SAUCE WITH COCONUT AND DRY ROASTED PEANUTS

2 tbsp desiccated coconut
1 onion, chopped
25 g (1 oz) butter or margarine
2 tbsp dry roasted peanuts, roughly chopped
1 tsp coriander seeds
1 tsp ground turmeric
3 tbsp fresh coriander leaves, chopped   (Serves 4)

1   Infuse the coconut in 300 ml (10 fl oz/½ pint) of boiling water for 20 minutes.
2   Sauté the onion in butter or margarine until soft.
3   In a food processor, blend the coconut in the liquid, sautéed onions, peanuts, coriander seeds, turmeric, and fresh coriander.
4   Put into a pan and heat gently.
5   Pour sauce over cooked vegetables or baked tomatoes.

COUSCOUS MOROCCAN STYLE

175 g (6 oz/¾ cup) couscous
50 g (2 oz) raisins or currants
300 ml (10 fl oz/½ pint/1¼ cups) vegetable stock, boiling
3 tbsp olive oil
450 g (1 lb/2 cups) onions, chopped
2 garlic cloves, crushed
4 tomatoes, chopped
2 tsp orange peel, grated
Salt and freshly ground black pepper to taste
1 bunch parsley, finely chopped
3 tbsp fresh orange juice
3 tbsp fresh lemon juice   (Serves 4-6)

1   Place couscous and raisins, or currants, in a bowl, and cover with boiling stock. Cover and let stand for 15 minutes.
2   Meanwhile, heat 2 tablespoons of olive oil in a pan and sauté onions and garlic, until onions are golden.
3   Add the tomatoes and orange peel, and cook for about 3-4 minutes, or until heated through. Season well.
4   Uncover the couscous and stir with a fork to fluff up.
5   Add to the pan with the vegetables and stir well. Add the parsley.
6   In a bowl whisk together the remaining oil, orange juice and lemon juice until blended. Add to the pan and stir well.
7   Spoon into a serving bowl and garnish with chopped parsley.

SPROUT SNIPPET: Couscous is for the North Africans what pasta and rice are for the Italians and Chinese. It is made with durum wheat semolina, water and possibly some salt and flour, either hand or factory made. Some think that the name comes from an onomatopoeia referring to the breath and rattling of the semolina grains when they are being hand rolled.

In many North African families, the week could not end without the Friday afternoon's bowl of couscous, served after prayer. During the Ramadan, the 'mesofouf' (sweetened couscous with cinnamon and raisins) is served before sunrise just before the fast, to enable all to 'make it' through the day until sunset.

It is also difficult to talk about couscous without mentioning the numerous virtues people ascribe to it:
➤ It brings God's blessing upon all those who have it
➤ It brings "barak" (good luck)
➤ Superstitious women make sure of their husband's fidelity for the year to come if they serve them with a couscous in which they will have hidden the most tender parts of the mutton tail.

CUCUMBER AND ONION BAKE WITH HERB CRUST

In our boxes we do not usually have an excess of cucumbers but for those who do, the following three recipes offer some other ways of preparing them.

2 cucumbers, sliced into medium slices
2 medium onions, thinly sliced and separated into rings
4 tbsp plain flour
Salt and freshly ground black pepper to taste
150 ml (¼ pint/5 fl oz) vegetable stock
1 tbsp tomato purée or ketchup
Crust
125 g (4 oz) breadcrumbs
25 g (1 oz) butter or margarine
1 tbsp mixed chopped fresh herbs such as coriander,
parsley, chervil   (Serves 4)

Preheat oven to 180°C (350°F/Gas 4)

1 Alternate layers of cucumber and onions in a deep greased casserole dish.
2 Sprinkle each layer with flour, salt and pepper.
3 Mix together the vegetable stock and tomato purée or ketchup and pour over cucumber and onions.
4 Make the crust by mixing together breadcrumbs, butter or margarine and mixed herbs.
5 Sprinkle over the cucumber and onion and bake in oven for about 20 minutes or until brown.

SPROUT SNIPPET: The phrase 'cool as a cucumber' is an apt one. Growing in a polytunnel on a hot summer day, the interior flesh is 20 degrees (F) cooler than the outside air temperature.

CUCUMBER SALSA

1 cucumber, chopped
50 g (2 oz) onion, chopped
2 tbsp fresh parsley, chopped
2 tbsp fresh coriander, chopped
1 chilli, seeded and chopped
1 garlic clove, crushed
2 tbsp lime juice
1 tbsp water
Salt and freshly ground black pepper to taste

1 Combine cucumber, onion, parsley, coriander, chilli, garlic, lime juice and water together.
2 Season to taste.
3 Serve with tortilla chips

SPROUT SNIPPET: Chilli peppers are hot because the burning sensation is attributed to chemical compounds called capsaicinoids, which are stored in the light-coloured veins, on the walls and surrounding the seeds. Capsaicin acts on the pain receptors in the mouth, not the taste buds.

CUCUMBER IN YOGHURT

1 medium-large cucumber
Salt
5 fl oz (¼ pint/150 ml) plain yoghurt
3 tbsp fresh basil, chopped
2 tbsp fresh mint, chopped
1 small onion, chopped
1 clove garlic, crushed
Salt and freshly ground black pepper to taste   (Serves 4)

1. Cut cucumber into medium slices, place in a colander and sprinkle with salt. Leave for about 30 minutes.
2. Rinse cucumber and pat dry.
3. Combine yoghurt, basil, mint, onion, and garlic in a medium bowl.
4. Stir cucumber into yoghurt mixture and season to taste.

LETTUCE AND POTATO SOUP

450 g (1 lb/2 cups) potatoes, peeled and chopped
1 onion, chopped
2 lettuce, chopped
1 litre (35 fl oz/1¾ pints/4 cups) vegetable stock
2 egg yolks
150 ml (¼ pint/5 fl oz) double cream
Salt and freshly ground black pepper to taste   (Serves 4)

1. Place the potatoes, onion, lettuce and vegetable stock into a large pan.
2. Bring to the boil, reduce heat and simmer for about 15 minutes, or until potatoes are cooked.
3. Liquidise and return to the pan.
4. Mix the egg yolks and cream in a bowl. Whisk in about 8 fl oz/1 cup of the hot soup.
5. Gently whisk the egg mixture into the soup.
6. Season to taste and serve.

SPROUT SNIPPET: Make a meringue shell from the two egg whites. This recipe was given to us by Jacqui's mum, Joan, who says it never fails. Put the egg whites in a bowl, add 175 g (6 oz) caster sugar, 2 tablespoons warm water, 2 teaspoons cornflour, ½ teaspoon vanilla essence and ½ teaspoon of any vinegar. Use an electric whisk and whisk for about 10 minutes until stiff. (We know this sounds a long time, but it is really worth it.) Shape meringue into a circle with a well in the middle, on a baking tray lined with greaseproof paper. Bake at 120ºC (250ºF/Gas ½) for about an hour or until firm to the touch. Once cooked switch the oven off and leave in overnight, or cool on wire rack. Fill with fruit and cream.

MANGE TOUT WITH CARROTS AND SOY SAUCE

450 g (1 lb/2 cups) baby carrots, scrubbed
350 g (12 oz/1½ cups) mange tout, trimmed
2 tbsp soy sauce
1 garlic clove, crushed
1.25 (½") fresh root ginger, peeled and finely chopped
Freshly ground black pepper
To garnish: 25 g (1 oz) toasted sunflower seeds   (Serves 4)

1. Put carrots into boiling, salted water, return to boil, reduce heat and simmer until just tender, about 10 minutes. Drain and keep warm.
2. Put mange tout into boiling, salted water, return to boil, reduce heat and simmer until just tender, about 2-3 minutes. Drain and keep warm.
3. Blend the soy sauce, garlic, ginger and pepper together.
4. Place vegetables and soy sauce mixture in a pan and stir for one minute over a low heat until thoroughly mixed.
5. Transfer to a serving dish and sprinkle with toasted sunflower seeds.

MANGE TOUT WITH GARLIC AND PARMESAN

225 g (8 oz/1 cup) mange tout, cut into bite-size pieces
2 tbsp olive oil
1 small onion, sliced
2 garlic cloves, crushed
Salt and freshly ground pepper to taste

5 tbsp single cream
225 g (8 oz) pasta
1 tbsp Parmesan, grated   (Serves 4)

1   Put mange tout into boiling, salted water, return to boil,
    reduce heat and simmer until tender, but still crisp,
    about 2-3 minutes. Drain and set aside.
2   Heat the oil in a pan and sauté the onion and garlic until
    transparent.
3   Stir in the cooked mange tout, and season to taste.
4   Add the cream and heat through gently, without boiling.
5   Cook pasta following instructions on the packet. Serve
    mange tout on top of pasta and sprinkle with Parmesan.

PARSLEY AND GRUYERE CHEESE OMELETTE
4 large eggs
3 tbsp fresh parsley, chopped
2 tsp water
Salt and freshly ground black pepper to taste
25 g (1 oz/¼ stick) butter or margarine
125 g (4 oz) Gruyère cheese, grated   (Makes 2 omelettes)

1   In a bowl beat eggs, 2 tablespoons parsley, water,
    and seasoning.
2   Melt half the butter in a pan and add half the egg
    mixture. Cook until the eggs are just set in the centre.
    Lift the edge of the omelette with a spatula and tilt
    the pan so that uncooked mixture flows underneath,
    about 2 minutes.
3   Add half the cheese. Using spatula, fold other half of
    omelette over cheese. Slide out onto plate.
4   Repeat 2 and 3 above to make the second omelette.
5   Garnish omelettes with remaining parsley.

PARSLEY AND POTATO SOUP
1 onion, chopped
1 tsp olive oil
450 g (1 lb/2 cups) potatoes, peeled and chopped
950 ml (32 fl oz/1¾ pints) vegetable stock
Salt and freshly ground black pepper to taste
2 tbsp fresh parsley, chopped   (Serves 4)

1   In a large pan sauté the onion in the oil until onion is
    soft. Add potatoes, and vegetable stock.
2   Bring to the boil, reduce heat and simmer for about 20
    minutes or until potatoes are cooked.
3   Liquidise. Season with salt and pepper.
4   Stir in the parsley and serve.

POTATOES WITH CARDAMOM AND YOGHURT
450 g (1 lb) new potatoes, washed
150 ml (¼ pint/5 fl oz) plain yoghurt
3 cardamom pods, seeded
Salt and freshly ground black pepper to taste
To garnish: parsley, or coriander, chopped   (Serves 4)

1   Put new potatoes in a pan with salted water, bring to the
    boil, reduce heat and simmer until tender, 15-20 minutes.
    Drain.
2   Mix together the yoghurt, seeds from the cardamom
    pods and seasoning.
3   Combine with the hot potatoes.
4   Transfer to a serving dish, sprinkle with parsley or
    coriander and serve.

RHUBARB AND STRAWBERRY FOOL

Hugh Andrews gave this recipe to Jacqui. He lives in a small family-based community in Scotland, where they grow most of their own organic vegetables. This recipe has been handed down through his family for generations. Hugh says that strawberries and rhubarb taste very good combined, but you can use either fruit individually, or many other fruits. Blackcurrants, gooseberries and plums work particularly well.

450 g (1 lb) rhubarb, chopped
450 g (1 lb) strawberries
125 g (4 oz) sugar (to taste)
36 g (2 tbsp) custard powder
18 g (1 tbsp) sugar
20 fl oz (1 pint/2½ cups) milk
¼ - ½ pint fresh single cream (to taste)

1   Stew the rhubarb by putting it into a pan with 2 tablespoons of water. Bring to the boil reduce heat and simmer until just tender, about 5-10 minutes.
2   Add strawberries and reheat until fruit is soft.
3   Add sugar to taste and allow to cool a little.
4   Meanwhile, put the custard powder and sugar into a bowl. Mix to form a paste with a little of the milk.
5   Heat remaining milk to just under boiling point and pour onto the custard mix, stirring continuously.
6   Return to the pan, bring to the boil over a gentle heat stirring continuously until thick. Cool the custard for a few minutes, stirring if necessary to prevent a skin forming.
7   Blend the custard with the stewed fruit and most of the cream.
8   Pour into a serving dish, or individual bowls, and cool in the fridge.

9   Serve with a swirl of cream on the top.

STRAWBERRIES WITH RASPBERRY SAUCE

900 g (2 lb) strawberries
225 g (8 oz) raspberries
1 tbsp orange juice
1 tbsp maple syrup

1   Wash the strawberries and put them in a serving bowl.
2   In a separate bowl, press the raspberries 2-3 times with the back of a fork to mash them. Stir in the orange juice and maple syrup.
3   Pour the raspberry mixture over the strawberries, mix gently.
4   Serve with fresh cream or ice cream.

STRAWBERRY AND YOGHURT PARFAIT WITH GRANOLA

225 g (8 oz) granola
225 g plain yoghurt
450 g (1 lb) strawberries, stemmed and sliced
4 tsp runny honey
4 tall parfait or sundae glasses

1   You will need to layer the ingredients. Start by placing a tablespoon of granola at the bottom of each glass.
2   Next add a tablespoon of yoghurt.
3   Now place a layer of strawberries over the yoghurt.
4   Repeat the process until layers reach the top of the glass.
5   Top with a dollop of yoghurt, honey and a whole strawberry.

SPROUT SNIPPET: Granola is rolled oats, wheat germ, sunflower seeds, cashews, brown sugar and coconut mixed with oil, honey and baked in the oven. You can buy it in healthfood shops.

FARMING NEWS FOR AUGUST

HARVESTING

Delicious early potatoes and broad beans, and the first onions with green tops. Calabrese and cauliflowers are picked, beetroot cropped. Garlic harvest also starts at Rafford this month, where the picking of blackcurrants and raspberries continue. At Cullerne new carrots, lettuce, courgettes, cucumbers, French beans, parsley, peas and tomatoes are picked.

MAINTENANCE AND MACHINERY

General maintenance of machinery.

PLANTING

The new strawberry plants go in for next year's crop. Spring cabbage sown for next year.

WEATHER

Temperate rather than sweltering.

Garlic ready for hanging-up

BEETROOT AND CABBAGE SALAD WITH GINGER AND CHERRIES

450 g (1 lb/2 cups) beetroot, trimmed and peeled
450 g (1 lb/2 cups) cabbage
1 onion, diced
450 g (1 lb/2 cups) sweet red cherries, pitted
60g (2 oz/¼ cup) crystallized ginger, chopped finely
4 tbsp olive oil
5 tbsp red wine vinegar
2 tbsp parsley, chopped
Salt and freshly ground black pepper to taste.
Garnish: parsley sprigs   (Serves 6–8)

1 Using a food processor, or a hand grater, finely grate beetroot and cabbage and transfer to a large mixing bowl.
2 Add onion, cherries, ginger, oil, red wine vinegar and parsley. Mix well. Season.
3 Garnish with parsley sprigs and serve.

BEETROOT, COCONUT AND LIME SALAD WITH CORIANDER

450 g (1 lb/2 cups) beetroot, scrubbed, but not topped or tailed
175 g (6 oz) yoghurt
50 g (2 oz/¼ cup) desiccated coconut
Finely grated peel and juice of one lime
½ tsp ground coriander
Salt and freshly ground black pepper to taste
4 large lettuce leaves   (Serves 4)

1 Cook beetroot in boiling, salted water for about one hour or until tender. Drain and peel. Cool and cut into 1.25 cm (½") cubes.
2 Put beetroot into mixing bowl.
3 Stir in yoghurt, coconut, lime peel, juice and coriander. Season.
4 Wash and dry lettuce and place on a serving dish.
5 Spoon beetroot mixture over lettuce.

BEETROOT DIP

450 g (1 lb/2 cups) beetroot, scrubbed
125 g (4 oz) soft tofu, drained
1–2 tbsp cider vinegar
2 tbsp shallots or 1 medium onion, chopped
½ tsp powdered mustard
½ tsp dried thyme
½ tsp dried tarragon

Salt and freshly ground black pepper to taste   (Serves 4)

1 Cook beetroot in boiling, salted water until tender, about 1 hour, or until tender. Drain, allow to cool, peel and cut into chunks.
2 Put beetroot, rest of ingredients (with 1 tablespoon of the cider vinegar) in a food processor and blend until smooth. Adjust seasonings, adding more vinegar and salt to taste. Serve immediately or refrigerate in a tightly sealed container for up to 3 days.

BEETROOT TANGY SALAD

700 g (1½ lb/3 cups) beetroot, trimmed and peeled
1 onion, chopped finely
Salt and freshly ground black pepper to taste

Dressing
150 ml (¼ pint/5 fl oz) olive oil
150 ml (¼ pint/5 fl oz) cider vinegar
1 tsp Dijon mustard
1 tsp celery seeds
Salt and freshly ground black pepper to taste   (Serves 4–6)

1   Using a food processor with a fine shredding disc, or a hand grater, finely grate beetroot and transfer to a large mixing bowl.
2   Add onion and combine well. Season and set aside.
3   Mix dressing ingredients together and shake or whisk lightly to blend.
4   Pour dressing over beetroot and toss to coat. Cover and refrigerate for several hours – up to 24 before serving.

BROAD BEAN AND COURGETTE PASTA SAUCE
250 g (8 oz/1 cup) broad beans, shelled
2 garlic cloves, crushed
1 medium onion, chopped
3 tbsp olive oil
2 medium courgettes cut into 1 cm (½") slices
300 ml (½ pint) single cream
1 x 400 g can tomatoes or 400 g (14 oz) fresh tomatoes
100 g (4 oz) mozzarella cheese
1 tsp dried oregano
Salt and freshly ground black pepper to taste   (Serves 4)

1   Put broad beans in boiling salted water, bring back to the boil, reduce heat and simmer for about 5-10 minutes until just tender. Drain and set aside.
2   Sauté garlic and onion in the olive oil until the onion is transparent.

3   Add sliced courgettes to the pan and cook for a further 5 minutes.
4   Stir in the cream and broad beans.
5   Add the tomatoes, sliced mozzarella, oregano and heat gently. Season and serve with freshly cooked penne pasta.

BROAD BEAN PÂTÉ I
900 g (2 lb/4 cups) broad beans (shelled)
2 tsp ground coriander
2 tsp ground cumin
2 tsp turmeric
Juice of one lemon
2 cloves garlic, crushed
4 tbsp olive oil
Salt and freshly ground black pepper to taste   (Serves 4-6)

1   Cook the beans in boiling, salted water until tender, about 5-10 minutes. Drain and reserve the liquid.
2   Place the beans, coriander, cumin, and turmeric in a liquidiser and blend until smooth.
3   Add lemon juice and garlic, plus some of the reserved liquid to form a thick purée.
4   Gradually add the olive oil a little at a time until the desired thickness of pâté is reached.
5   Season to taste.
6   Put into a serving bowl and sprinkle a little turmeric over the top.

BROAD BEAN PÂTÉ II
This is another broad bean pâté recipe and a good way to use up cooked broad beans. Joan served them to her children who usually bypassed broad beans when served whole but when she served them as the pâté the next evening everyone had seconds.

2 tbsp olive oil
1 onion, chopped
225g (8 oz) broad beans (shelled weight)
Grated rind and juice of 1 large orange
4 tbsp Greek style yoghurt
3 tbsp chopped fresh mint
Salt and freshly ground black pepper to taste   (Serves 4-6)

1   If using frozen beans, allow to defrost. If using fresh
    pod them.
2   Heat the oil in a frying pan, add the onion and cook for
    3-4 minutes until softened.
3   Add the beans, orange juice, most of the rind and
    6 tbsp water.
4   Cover and simmer gently for about 20 minutes until the
    beans are tender
5   Transfer the mixture to a food processor or blender and
    add the yoghurt and mint.
6   Process until smooth, season, then chill.

It can be eaten straight away but is better for chilling – less
sloppy on your bread. Can be served with different breads or
crudités or in sandwiches if you like. Whatever!

BROAD BEANS WITH SWEET AND SOUR SAUCE
450 g (1 lb/2 cups) broad beans, shelled
Sweet and sour sauce
1 tbsp soy sauce
3 tbsp pineapple juice
2 tbsp tomato purée
2 tbsp white wine vinegar
2 tbsp vegetable oil
2 tbsp brown sugar

Sauté
1 tbsp olive oil or vegetable oil
2 cloves garlic, crushed
1 tsp fresh, grated ginger
1 bunch spring onions, chopped
1 red pepper, seeded and chopped
Thickening
1 tbsp cornflour
1 tbsp water   (Serves 4)

1   Put the broad beans in boiling salted water, bring back to
    the boil, reduce heat and simmer until tender, about 5-10
    minutes. Drain.
2   Place all the sauce ingredients in a saucepan and heat
    gently until the sugar has dissolved.
3   Heat the oil in a pan and add the garlic, ginger, spring
    onions and red pepper, and sauté for 2 minutes.
4   Add the sauce to the pan and bring to the boil.
5   Make a paste with cornflour and water and stir into the
    saucepan to thicken the sauce.
6   Add broad beans and serve.

CALABRESE AND GREEN PEPPERS WITH CHEESE
2 green peppers, de-seeded and quartered
450 g (1 lb) calabrese, roughly chopped
225 g (8 oz) Cheddar cheese, grated
4 tbsp plain flour
½ tsp powdered mustard
350 ml (12 fl oz/1½ cups) milk
2 eggs, beaten
Salt and freshly ground black pepper to taste   (Serves 4-6)

1   Preheat oven to 180°C (350°F/Gas 4).

2   Place peppers on bottom of a lightly greased baking dish.
3   Put calabrese into boiling salted water. Return to the boil, reduce heat and simmer until crisp tender, about 8-10 minutes. Drain.
4   Place calabrese on top of peppers and top with the grated cheese.
5   Beat flour, mustard, milk and eggs together until smooth. Season.
6   Pour over vegetables and bake for about 30 minutes or until cheese is bubbly and top is brown.

CARROT AND COCONUT SALAD

4 carrots, peeled and grated
2 tbsp desiccated coconut
2 tbsp onion, finely grated
1 tbsp lemon juice
2 tbsp fresh coriander or parsley, chopped
1 fresh green chilli pepper, seeded and chopped (optional)
Salt and freshly ground black pepper to taste   (Serves 4)

1   Mix all ingredients together in a bowl.
2   Refrigerate before serving.

CARROT AND COCONUT RELISH

5 carrots, peeled and diced
2 medium cucumbers, chopped
2 green peppers, de-seeded and chopped
350 ml (12 fl oz/1½ cups) malt vinegar
225 ml (8 fl oz) water
575 g (1¼ lb/1½ cups) granulated sugar
1½ tsp salt
1 tbsp celery seed
2 tbsp flour

½ tbsp powdered English mustard
½ tbsp turmeric

1   Put carrots in salted water, bring to the boil, reduce heat and simmer until just tender, about 10 minutes. Drain.
2   Add cucumbers and peppers.
3   Combine vinegar, water, sugar, salt, celery seed, flour, mustard and turmeric.
4   Add vegetables to liquid and cook until slightly thick.
5   Put into sterilised jars and seal.

CARROT AND SWEDE SALAD

450 g (1 lb/2 cups) carrots, peeled and grated
125 g (4 oz) swede, peeled and finely grated
50 g (2 oz) raisins
Dressing
150 ml (¼ pint/5 fl oz) plain yoghurt
3 tbsp mayonnaise
2 level tsp English ready-made mustard
2-3 level tbsp mango chutney
25 g (1 oz) flaked almonds, toasted   (Serves 4)

1   Put carrots, swede and raisins in a large bowl.
2   Mix the yoghurt, mayonnaise, mustard, and chutney together and add to the grated vegetables and raisins.
3   Transfer to serving dish and sprinkle over flaked almonds before serving.

CAULIFLOWER, APPLE AND COCONUT SOUP

2 tbsp vegetable oil
1 onion, chopped
1 large carrot, diced

225 g (8 oz/1 cup) cauliflower florets
1 cooking apple, peeled, cored and diced
½ tsp ground cumin
½ tsp coriander
½ tsp ginger
½ tsp turmeric
¼ tsp chilli powder
1 L (1¾ pints) vegetable stock
1 x 400 g (14 oz) can butter beans (optional)
50 g (2 oz) creamed coconut
Salt and freshly ground black pepper to taste   (Serves 6)

1   Heat the oil in a pan and sauté the onion and carrot for
    about 5 minutes, or until the onion is soft.
2   Add the cauliflower, apple, cumin, coriander, ginger,
    turmeric and chilli powder and cook for 1–2 minutes,
    stirring continuously.
3   Add the stock, bring to the boil, cover and simmer for
    about 20 minutes or until the vegetables are cooked.
4   Add the butter beans and creamed coconut. Simmer
    gently until beans are heated through and the coconut
    has melted. Season well.
5   Serve with fresh crusty bread.

This soup can also be made using broccoli instead of cauliflower.

CAULIFLOWER, CALABRESE AND CARROT FLAN WITH CORNFLAKE CRUMB

1 small-medium cauliflower, broken into florets
1 head calabrese, chopped
3 medium carrots, sliced
1 tbsp vegetable or olive oil
1 onion, chopped

1 clove garlic
Salt and freshly ground black pepper to taste
2 eggs, beaten
125 g (4 oz) cornflakes, broken into crumbs   (Serves 4)

1   Preheat the oven to 180°C (350°F/Gas 4).
2   Put the cauliflower, calabrese and carrots into boiling
    salted water. Bring back to the boil, reduce heat and
    simmer until carrots are crisp-tender, about 10 minutes.
    Drain and place in a mixing bowl.
3   Heat the oil and sauté the onion and garlic for about
    5 minutes until onion is soft. Add to the vegetables.
    Season to taste.
4   Add the eggs and mix well.
5   Grease a baking dish and coat with half the
    cornflake crumbs.
6   Spoon vegetable mixture onto this layer, and top with
    remaining cornflake crumbs.
7   Bake in oven until heated through and cornflakes are
    browned.

COURGETTE AND BLUE CHEESE SOUP

50 g (2 oz) butter or margarine
1 medium onion, peeled and chopped
2 cloves garlic, peeled and chopped
900 g (2 lb/4 cups) courgettes, roughly chopped
425 ml (15 fl oz/¾ pint) vegetable stock
425 ml (15 fl oz/¾ pint) milk
250 g (9 oz) blue cheese, Stilton or Roquefort, crumbled
Salt and freshly ground black pepper to taste
5 tbsp (3 fl oz/75 ml) single cream   (Serves 4)

1 Melt the butter or margarine in a saucepan.
2 Sauté onion and garlic until softened.
3 Add the courgettes and cook over a low heat for about 10 minutes.
4 Add the stock and milk and bring to the boil.
5 Simmer for 10–15 minutes.
6 Remove from the heat and allow to cool.
7 Pour into a food processor and blend until smooth.
8 Return to the heat. Crumble the cheese into the soup and gently heat until melted.
9 Season to taste.
10 Stir in the cream just before serving.

COURGETTES WITH FRESH MINT, GARLIC, PINE NUTS, AND CURRANTS

2 tbsp olive oil
2 garlic cloves, chopped
4 medium courgettes, sliced
Sprig of fresh mint, chopped
2 tbsp pine nuts
50 g (2 oz) currants
Salt and freshly ground black pepper to taste
To garnish: 1-2 spring onions, chopped   (Serves 4)

1 Heat oil in a pan and sauté garlic for about 1 minute.
2 Add courgettes and mint, and cook until courgettes are just starting to brown, about 10 minutes.
3 Add pine nuts and currants. Cook for about another minute. Season to taste.
4 Put into serving dish and garnish with chopped spring onions.

COURGETTE PANCAKES
(Donated by Mathis, our redoubtable farmer!)

2 eggs, separate yolk from white
450 g (1 lb/2 cups) courgettes, grated
1 tsp baking powder
1 tbsp plain flour
1 small onion or onion top, chopped
125 g (4 oz) Feta cheese, diced
Salt and freshly ground black pepper to taste
One tbsp oil for frying   (Serves 4)

1 Beat the white of the 2 eggs until stiff and set aside.
2 Mix rest of the ingredients together.
3 Fold in the beaten egg white.
4 Heat oil in frying pan and fry mixture until browned on one side, turn and brown on other side. Cut into 4.

COURGETTE PASTY
Donated by Helen Trussell, who worked for EarthShare for several years. She now manages a local bookshop.

1 medium onion, finely chopped
1 tbsp vegetable oil
450 g (1 lb/2 cups) courgettes, grated
Salt and freshly ground black pepper to taste
450 g (1 lb) shortcrust pastry
50 g (2 oz) pine kernels
175 g (6 oz) Feta cheese
2 tbsp milk for brushing   (Serves 4)

1 Sauté the onions in the oil until just browned.
2 Add the grated courgettes and mix well. Season to taste.
3 Roll out pastry into a rectangle.

4   Cover the central one-third with pine kernels.
5   Place mixture of onions and courgettes on top of the pine kernels.
6   Put Feta cheese on top of onions and courgettes.
7   Brush the edges of the pastry with milk.
8   Bring two sides of pastry up into the middle and pinch together, pinch together the sides, sealing the pastry.
9   Brush with milk and bake in oven 190°C (375°F/Gas 5) or until pastry is browned.
10   Serve with a tossed salad.

COURGETTE PIZZA
(Another Mathis speciality)

For the base
450 g (1 lb/2 cups) courgettes, grated
450 g (1 lb/2 cups) potatoes, grated raw
Salt and freshly ground black pepper to taste   (Serves 4)

1   Mix courgettes, potatoes and salt and pepper together.
2   Press into a pizza tin or baking tray to form the base of your pizza. Thickness according to taste.
3   Add topping of your choice and bake pizza in oven 180°C (350°F/Gas 4) for about 20 minutes or until nicely browned.

Topping suggestion
To make use of your vegetable box, cover base with freshly sliced tomatoes, sliced green pepper, grated cheese and chopped parsley.

COURGETTE, POTATO AND CORIANDER PIE
Donated by Shelagh Boughton, an EarthShare subscriber who organises one of the local box pick-up points.

Make sure that you slice the potatoes thinly or they may not cook.

3 tbsp fresh coriander, chopped
1 clove garlic, peeled and chopped
1 cm (½") fresh root ginger, peeled and chopped
150 g (5 oz) Cheddar cheese
350 g (12 oz/1½ cups) potatoes, peeled and thinly sliced
175 g (6 oz) courgettes, thinly sliced
1 large onion, peeled and thinly sliced
5 tbsp white wine or cider, beer or vegetable stock (Serves 4)

1   Mix the coriander, garlic, ginger and cheese in a bowl.
2   Line a dish with half the potatoes and cover with half the courgettes and then half the sliced onion.
3   Spoon on half the coriander, garlic, ginger and cheese mixture.
4   Continue with a second layer of the remaining potato, courgette and onion. Reserve the remaining cheese mixture until later.
5   Pour on the white wine, cider, beer or stock and cover with foil.
6   Bake in the oven 190°C (375°F/Gas 5) for about one hour or until tender.
7   Top with remaining cheese mixture and finish off under the grill.

COURGETTE PURÉE
3 tbsp olive oil
225 g (8 oz/1 cup) onion, chopped
3 cloves garlic, chopped

¼ tsp ground turmeric

1.25 Kg (2¾ lb) courgettes, diced

1 tsp salt

1 tsp ground cumin

¼ tsp cayenne pepper

¼ tsp black pepper

1½ tsp tomato purée   (Serves 4)

1   Heat oil in pan and sauté onion and garlic until softened.
2   Add turmeric and stir. Remove one third of the onions and set aside.
3   Add courgettes and salt to the pan. Cook for 1–2 minutes or until the courgettes begin to release a little liquid. Cover, turn heat to low and cook until courgettes are soft.
4   Add the cumin, cayenne pepper, black pepper and tomato purée.
5   Mash the courgette mixture with a potato masher while they are still cooking gently. Keep cooking and mashing for 1–2 minutes or until the purée is coarse but well mixed.
6   Add the reserved onions and stir.
7   Serve hot, warm or chilled.

Serve with breads, dishes of beans, split peas and yoghurt.

COURGETTE AND TOMATO BAKE

1 tbsp olive oil

1 medium onion, thinly sliced

3 cloves garlic, crushed

450 g (1 lb/2 cups) courgettes, thinly sliced

450 g (1 lb/2 cups) tomatoes, roughly chopped

Salt and freshly ground black pepper to taste

Topping

125 g (4 oz) breadcrumbs

1 tbsp fresh parsley, chopped

2 tbsp grated Parmesan   (Serves 4)

1   Heat oil in a pan and sauté onion until transparent.
2   Add garlic, courgettes and tomatoes and cook until the courgettes are just cooked, about 5 minutes. Season to taste.
3   Transfer to a greased casserole dish.
4   Mix together the breadcrumbs, parsley, and Parmesan and sprinkle over the vegetable mixture.
5   Bake in oven 190°C (375°F/Gas 5) for about 30 minutes or until golden.

GARLIC BAGUETTE WITH LEMON BUTTER

50 g (2 oz/½ stick) butter or margarine

2 tbsp fresh parsley, chopped

3 garlic cloves, crushed

1 tsp lemon peel, grated

Salt and freshly ground black pepper to taste

1 French baguette, cut diagonally into 2.5 cm (1") pieces

                                                           (Serves 6)

1   Mix butter or margarine, parsley, garlic and lemon peel together in a small bowl.
2   Season to taste.
3   Spread evenly over one side of each bread slice.
4   Reassemble the bread slices, wrap in foil and place on a baking sheet.
5   Preheat oven to 160°C (325°F/Gas 3), and bake bread until heated through, about 20 minutes.

GARLIC DIP

125 ml (4 fl oz) mayonnaise
225 ml (8 fl oz) sour cream
4-5 garlic cloves, crushed
1½ tsp fresh parsley, finely chopped
1 tsp dried dill
2 tbsp white vinegar
Milk to thin if necessary
Salt and freshly ground black pepper to taste

1   Mix mayonnaise, sour cream, garlic, parsley, dill and white vinegar together. Thin to desired consistency with milk.
2   Season to taste.
3   Use as a vegetable dip or on salad.

GARLIC PUREE

4 large whole heads of garlic
4 tbsp olive oil
Salt and freshly ground black pepper to taste
1 tbsp fresh lemon juice

1   Chop off bottom of garlic heads and separate whole cloves, leaving outer covering intact.
2   Place cloves in a shallow baking dish, and drizzle with olive oil.
3   Bake at 180°C (350°F/Gas 4) for about 20 minutes or until garlic is cooked.
4   Cool and remove skins.
5   In a food processor or blender add garlic, seasoning and lemon juice and blend until almost smooth, scraping sides of bowl occasionally.
6   Use as a spread for buttered, toasted bread.

GARLIC WITH ROSEMARY, PARSLEY, WINE AND ROQUEFORT

6 whole heads of garlic
45 g (1½ oz) butter or margarine
4 tbsp olive oil
425 ml (15 fl oz/¾ pint) vegetable stock
4 tbsp dry white wine
2 tsp fresh rosemary, chopped
1 tsp fresh parsley, chopped
Freshly ground black pepper to taste
225g (8 oz) Roquefort cheese, crumbled   (Serves 6)

1   Preheat oven to 190°C (375°/Gas 5).
2   Cut 1.25 cm (½") off top end (opposite root end) of each garlic head, so that top of garlic cloves are exposed. Remove any loose papery outer skin.
3   Place garlic, root side down on a greased baking dish. Top each head with a little butter or margarine. Pour olive oil over.
4   Mix vegetable stock and wine together and add to the dish. Sprinkle chopped rosemary and parsley over the garlic. Season with pepper to taste.
5   Bake uncovered for about 1 hour or until garlic is cooked, basting regularly with pan juices. You may need to add more vegetable stock.
6   Sprinkle on the Roquefort and put back in the oven for about another 10 minutes or until cheese is melted.
7   Serve with hot, crusty bread.

LAVENDER AND ORANGE SORBET

1.2 L (2 pints/40 fl oz) orange juice
125 g (4 oz) granulated sugar
1 tbsp lavender flowers

1 Put orange juice, sugar and lavender flowers in a pan.
2 Bring to the boil, reduce heat and simmer for 15 minutes.
3 Cool and put in a plastic freezer container.
4 Freeze until almost solid and serve with a lavender sprig on top.

SPROUT SNIPPET: If you burn yourself on the oven, or iron and the skin is not broken, put 2 drops of neat lavender oil directly on to the burn. This will remove the pain and will clear the burn up in no time. In many cases, it can prevent blistering and scarring.

LETTUCE AND COURGETTE SOUP
2 tsp vegetable or olive oil
2 garlic cloves, crushed
1 medium onion, chopped
450 g (1 lb/2 cups) courgettes, trimmed and sliced
600 ml (1 pint/20 fl oz) vegetable stock
1 large lettuce, washed and chopped
2 sprigs fresh parsley, chopped
300 ml (½ pint/10 fl oz) skimmed milk
1 tbsp cornflour, blended with a little water
¼ tsp nutmeg
Salt and freshly ground black pepper to taste   (Serves 4)

1 Heat oil in large pan and sauté the garlic and onion for about 3-4 minutes until softened.
2 Add courgettes and cook, stirring for about 2 more minutes.
3 Add the stock to the pan and bring to the boil.
4 Lower the heat and add the lettuce and parsley.
5 Cover and simmer for about 20 minutes.
6 Blend the soup in a liquidiser until smooth. Return to pan and add the milk, blended cornflour, nutmeg, salt and pepper. Heat gently until the soup has thickened slightly.

This soup can be served hot or chilled.

ONION, APPLE AND TOMATO SAUCE WITH PASTA
2 tbsp olive oil
2 onions, chopped
1 apple, finely sliced or chopped
1 bay leaf
450 g (1 lb/2 cups) fresh tomatoes, chopped
Salt and freshly ground black pepper to taste
To serve: pasta   (Serves 4)

1 In a pan heat oil and add onions, apple and bay leaf. Cover and simmer over a low heat until apple and onion are dissolved, about 45-60 minutes.
2 Add tomatoes, salt and pepper. Simmer for another 30 minutes. Remove bay leaf.
3 Cook pasta following instructions on packet and pour sauce over the pasta.

PASTA WITH ROASTED VEGETABLES AND GOAT'S CHEESE
Pam Rodway from Wester Lawrenceton Farm gave us this recipe. She says, "When I'm really busy and want a quick and delicious supper, this is what I do".

Enough good quality pasta for 4 portions
4 medium carrots, cut into lengthways slices
4 medium courgettes, cut into lengthways slices
2 onions, chopped into lengthways slices
2-4 tbsp olive oil
1 tsp fresh thyme
2-4 garlic cloves, chopped
Salt and freshly ground black pepper to taste
125 g (4 oz) mange tout (optional)

125 g (4 oz) French beans (optional)
2 Wester Lawrenceton goat's cheese crottins   (Serves 4)

1 Boil pasta in plenty of salted water until tender.
   Drain and put in a fire-proof dish.
2 Put carrots, courgettes and onions in a roasting tin and
   coat with olive oil, fresh thyme, garlic, salt and pepper.
3 Roast in a hot oven 200°C (400°F/Gas 6) until browned,
   about 20 minutes.
4 Steam the mange tout and French beans lightly.
5 Toss all the vegetables into the fire-proof dish with the
   pasta, making sure the olive oil is coating them well.
6 Add the goat's cheese, cut into cubes.
7 Heat through in a hot oven and cook until the goat's cheese
   begins to soften, but do not let it go crisp or brown.
8 Serve with a good crisp green salad – and a glass of good
   red wine. Guaranteed to revive you after a hard day!

POTATOES WITH COCONUT MILK AND BASIL

1 tbsp vegetable oil
2 onions, chopped
2 garlic cloves, crushed
2 tsp coriander seeds, ground
1 green pepper, de-seeded and chopped
1 tbsp tamari
700 g (1½ lb/3 cups) new potatoes, washed
225 ml (8 fl oz/1 cup) coconut milk
2 tsp fresh basil, chopped   (Serves 4-6)

1 Heat oil in a pan and sauté the onions, garlic, and
   coriander seeds until onions are soft, about 5 minutes.
2 Add the green pepper and tamari and cook for about a
   further 2 minutes.

3 Add the potatoes and stir well.
4 Add the coconut milk and basil. Cover and simmer for
   about 10-15 minutes, or until the potatoes are tender.
   Stir occasionally.
5 Serve.

POTATOES IN TANGY YOGHURT SAUCE

700 g (1½ lb) new potatoes, washed
275 g (10 oz/1¼ cups) natural yoghurt
300 ml (½ pint/10 fl oz) water
1 tsp turmeric
½ tsp chilli powder
1 tsp ground coriander
½ tsp ground cumin
½ tsp salt
1 tsp brown sugar
2 tbsp olive oil
1 tbsp fresh coriander or parsley

1 Cook the potatoes in their skins in boiling salted water
   until tender, about 15-20 minutes. Drain and set aside.
2 Mix together the yoghurt, water, turmeric, chilli powder,
   ground coriander, ground cumin, salt and sugar.
3 Heat the oil in a pan and add the yoghurt mixture.
   Cook, stirring continuously for about 3 minutes.
4 Add the cooked potatoes, and coriander or parsley and
   heat through.
5 Serve.

SWEDE WITH PLUMS

450 g (1 lb/2 cups) swede, peeled and diced
225 g (8 oz/1 cup) plums
1 tbsp Dijon mustard

Salt and freshly ground black pepper to taste
75 g (3 oz) sugar
150 ml (¼ pint/5 fl oz) vegetable stock
4 tbsp white wine vinegar
2 tbsp parsley, chopped   (Serves 4)

1 Put swede in salted water, bring to the boil, reduce heat
   and simmer until tender, about 15 minutes. Drain.
2 Remove stones from plums and discard, chop the flesh.
   Place flesh into a bowl and add the mustard, salt
   and pepper.
3 In a pan, over a medium heat, caramelise the sugar
   by melting it until it reaches a light brown, syrupy
   consistency.
4 Add the vegetable stock and vinegar and simmer
   for about 5 minutes.
5 Add the swede and plums and let simmer for about
   another 5 minutes. Add the parsley and serve.

TOMATO BRUSCHETTA
4 large ripe tomatoes
Extra virgin olive oil
4 slices bread thickly sliced (sourdough or ciabatta)
2 large garlic cloves, lightly crushed
Salt and freshly ground black pepper to taste   (Serves 2)

1 Preheat oven to 220°C (425°F/Gas 7).
2 Put the tomatoes in a baking dish and pour a little olive
   oil over them.
3 Roast in the oven until the skins start to blacken slightly
   in places.
4 Toast bread until golden on both sides, but still soft in
   the centre.

5 Rub the garlic cloves over the surface of the toast.
6 Pile the tomatoes on top of the toast and drizzle with
   more oil, salt and freshly ground black pepper.
7 Serve.

FARMING NEWS FOR SEPTEMBER

HARVESTING

Beetroot, calabrese, cabbage, carrots, cauliflower and remaining garlic are harvested. Cullerne provides courgette, cucumber. French beans, lettuce, small leaf greens and tomatoes.

It is also the month to lift the onions; a major job and, if it is wet one, that proves very difficult. Onions last better if they are harvested in dry weather and stored in dry, airy conditions. Any damp leads to rot and mildew, and an early composting for the onion.

Mathis has used various methods to meet these exacting demands over the years. One year he used a fan trained on them to dry them, but it remained a problem to store them properly in bulk. One solution has been to pass the complete year's supply to the subscribers between September and Christmas.

Subscribers are advised on stringing methods to dry them but some simply put them on windowsills. It seems to work. One of the best methods is that of subscriber, John Scott. He strings the onions and puts them in a fir tree for three or four weeks, after which they are stored in a wooden shed. The fir tree environment appears to have sufficient wind and at the same time shelter from the rain to dry them out. As most people do not have fir trees, we look forward to any suggestions!

MAINTENANCE AND MACHINERY

Ongoing maintenance. The tattie harvester serviced and repaired ready for the big event next month.

PLANTING

Strawberries planted out this month, and sowing of oriental greens and winter lettuce in polytunnels.

WEATHER

Can be a little cold and wet, but generally mild and sunny.

Success! Marianne Rosenbusch with a fresh string of onions

Cucumbers growing in Cullerne polytunnel

BEETROOT AND HORSERADISH SALSA

3 beetroot, peeled and grated
3 spring onions or 1 small onion, finely sliced
1 apple, peeled, cored and grated
Juice of 1 lemon
6 tbsp olive oil
1 tbsp creamed horseradish
Salt and freshly ground black pepper to taste
4 dill sprigs or 2 tsp dill weed   (Serves 4)

1   Mix the beetroot and onion together in a bowl.
2   In another bowl, stir the apple into the lemon juice.
    Add the oil, creamed horseradish and seasoning.
    Whisk to blend.
3   Add to the beetroot and onion and stir well.
4   Stir the dill into the mixture.
5   Cover and chill for 30 minutes before serving.

BEETROOT AND TOMATO ROGAN JOSH

2 tbsp vegetable oil
2 onions, sliced
2 garlic cloves, crushed
2.5 cm (1") root ginger, grated
2 tbsp rogan josh curry paste
225 g (8 oz) beetroot, peeled and diced
450 g (1 lb) tomatoes, chopped
4 tbsp water
125 g (4 oz) frozen peas or fresh courgettes, sliced
Handful of fresh mint, chopped
Salt and freshly ground pepper to taste   (Serves 4-6)

1   Heat the oil in a large pan.
2   Sauté the onions for 5 minutes until golden.
3   Add garlic and ginger and sauté for 2 minutes.
4   Stir in the rogan josh curry paste.
5   Add the beetroot and stir well.
6   Add tomatoes and water, bring to the boil, reduce heat,
    cover and simmer for about 30 minutes or until beetroot
    is cooked.
7   Add the frozen peas or courgettes and mint. Cover and
    simmer for a further 20 minutes until the vegetables
    are tender.
8   Season to taste and serve with rice.

CABBAGE WITH CARAWAY SEED

Jacqui's brother, Harvey, prepared this dish when he came to
stay. Seb enjoyed it and will always eat cabbage if cooked in this
way. Jacqui also tested the recipe with a group of Seb's teenage
friends and, surprisingly, they all liked it too. Jacqui thinks that
cutting the cabbage into thin strips is the key.

450 g (1 lb/2 cups) cabbage, finely sliced into strips
50 g (2 oz/ ½ stick) butter or margarine
2-3 tsp caraway seeds   (Serves 4)

1   Put cabbage into boiling, salted water, bring back to the
    boil, reduce heat and simmer until crisp-tender, about
    5-10 minutes.
2   Drain and set aside.
3   In the same pan, melt the butter or margarine, and add
    the caraway seeds. Fry them for about 1 minute stirring
    continuously. Remove from heat.
4   Add cabbage to pan and stir well.
5   Serve.

CABBAGE WITH POTATOES, CHEDDAR AND FETA CHEESE

450 g (1 lb/2 cups) potatoes, peeled and cut into chunks
25 g (1 oz) butter or margarine
4 tbsp milk
Salt and freshly ground black pepper to taste
1 tbsp olive oil
2 garlic cloves, crushed
450 g (1 lb/2 cups) cabbage, cut into thin strips
Freshly ground black pepper
125 g (4 oz) Cheddar cheese
75 g (3 oz) Feta cheese
½ tsp paprika   (Serves 6)

1   Put potatoes into salted water, bring to the boil, reduce heat and simmer until tender, about 15 minutes. Drain and mash with the butter or margarine, milk and season to taste.
2   In a pan heat the olive oil and sauté the garlic for 1-2 minutes, or until just browned.
3   Add the cabbage and sauté until just wilted, not soft. Add lots of freshly ground black pepper.
4   Grease a baking dish and cover with the mashed potato.
5   Cover with the cabbage. Add the Cheddar and Feta cheese. Sprinkle the top with paprika.
6   Bake for 20-25 minutes in oven, 180°C (350°F/Gas 4), until hot and the cheese has melted.

CABBAGE SPICY SOUP

2 tbsp vegetable oil
2 garlic cloves, chopped
1 onion, chopped
1 red chilli, chopped

225 g (8 oz) cabbage, shredded
40 fl oz (2 pints) vegetable stock
400 g (14 oz) can cannellini beans
Salt and freshly ground black pepper to taste   (Serves 4)

1   Heat oil in a pan and sauté garlic, onion and chilli for 2 minutes.
2   Add cabbage and vegetable stock.
3   Bring to the boil, reduce heat, and simmer for 10-15 minutes or until cabbage is cooked.
4   Add drained cannellini beans and heat for 3 minutes.
5   Season to taste and serve with fresh crusty bread.

CALABRESE IN BATTER

To use up the spare egg whites, why not make Onion Rings, Deep Fried (later in this month's recipes).

2 egg yolks
200 ml (7 fl oz) cold water
125 g (4 oz) plain flour
Extra flour for dusting
Pinch of salt
450 g (1lb) calabrese, in florets or heads
Vegetable oil for frying   (Serves 4)

1   Place egg yolks in a mixing bowl. Add the cold water and mix lightly. Do not beat.
2   Add flour and salt and mix lightly. The batter will be very lumpy.
3   Dust calabrese with the extra flour.
4   Heat oil in a pan until very hot.
5   Dip individual florets or heads of the calabrese in the batter and place in the hot oil, frying only a few at a time.

6 Deep fry for about 3 minutes until golden.
7 Drain on kitchen towels.
8 Continue until all calabrese is used.
9 Serve with mayonnaise, dips and condiments.

CALABRESE WITH COCONUT, GINGER AND SOY SAUCE

450 g (1 lb) calabrese, roughly chopped
2 tbsp vegetable oil
1 tsp sesame oil
1 red chilli, seeded and sliced (optional)
1.25 cm (½") piece fresh root ginger, peeled and finely chopped
2 spring onions, or 1 medium onion, finely chopped
25 g (1 oz) desiccated coconut
1 tbsp soy sauce
1 tsp white wine vinegar
Freshly ground black pepper to taste   (Serves 4)

1 Put the calabrese into boiling, salted water, return to boil, reduce heat and simmer until crisp-tender, about 5-10 minutes. Drain.
2 Heat one tablespoon of vegetable oil and the sesame oil in a pan and fry the chilli (if you like a hot taste), ginger, and onion for about 5 minutes or until softened.
3 Add the coconut and fry over a medium heat for about 3-4 minutes, stirring frequently, until coconut is golden.
4 Add the calabrese, remaining oil, soy sauce, vinegar and pepper. Stir well and serve.

CARROT, CASHEW NUT AND RED LENTIL PATTIES

350 g (12 oz) red lentils
900 ml (1½ pints/30 fl oz) vegetable stock
2 tbsp vegetable oil
2 garlic cloves, crushed
225 g (8 oz/1 cup) carrots, grated
1 medium onion, chopped
4 tbsp mango chutney
125 g (4 oz) cashew nuts, roughly chopped
Salt and freshly ground black pepper to taste   (Serves 4)

1 Put lentils and stock in a pan, bring to the boil, reduce heat and simmer for 15-20 minutes, until lentils are soft and stock is absorbed.
2 Heat half the oil in a pan, sauté garlic, carrots and onion for about 3-5 minutes until the carrots are tender.
3 Add the mango chutney, cashew nuts and lentils and season.
4 Set aside to cool slightly.
5 Using floured hands, shape the mixture into 8 patties.
6 Heat the remaining oil in a pan and sauté the patties for 4 minutes on each side until golden.

CAULIFLOWER, GREEN PEPPER AND SMALL LEAF GREEN SALAD WITH TAHINI

1 medium cauliflower, broken into florets
1 green pepper, de-seeded and sliced thinly or finely chopped
A generous handful of any type of small leaf greens, roughly chopped
1-2 garlic cloves, crushed
3 tbsp tahini
3 tbsp water
Juice of one lemon

Salt and freshly ground black pepper to taste
To garnish: fresh parsley, chopped   (Serves 4)

1   Put the cauliflower into boiling, salted water, bring back
    to the boil and simmer until *al dente*, about 3-5 minutes.
    Drain and cool.
2   Mix the cauliflower with the pepper and small leaf greens.
3   Blend together the garlic, tahini, water, lemon juice,
    salt and pepper so that it has a creamy consistency.
    More water may be needed.
4   Pour the dressing over the vegetables and stir well.
5   Garnish with chopped parsley.
6   Refrigerate before serving.

CAULIFLOWER AND SPINACH WITH TOFU AND DIJON MUSTARD

1 large cauliflower, broken into florets
350 g (12 oz) spinach, stemmed and rinsed well
2 slices wholemeal or whole wheat bread, made into breadcrumbs
1 tbsp olive oil
350 g (12 oz) tofu
2 tbsp Dijon mustard
Salt and freshly ground black pepper to taste
¼ tsp cayenne pepper
75 g (3 oz) Parmesan   (Serves 4-6)

1   Preheat oven to 190°C (375°F/Gas 5).
2   Grease a baking dish.
3   Put cauliflower into boiling salted water, bring back to
    the boil, reduce heat and simmer until tender, about 5-10
    minutes. Drain and rinse under cold water. Set aside.
4   Cook spinach in pan with just rinsing water clinging to
    the leaves, stirring often, until just wilted, about 3-5

    minutes. Drain and rinse under cold water.
    Add to cauliflower.
5   In a bowl, mix the breadcrumbs with the olive oil.
    Stir well. Set aside.
6   In a food processor or blender, combine tofu, mustard,
    salt, pepper, and cayenne pepper and process until
    smooth and creamy.
7   Add Parmesan and blend until just mixed in.
8   Add tofu mixture to cauliflower and spinach and stir well
    to coat vegetables with the sauce.
9   Transfer to greased baking dish, sprinkle breadcrumbs
    coated with oil over the top.
10 Bake until heated through and top is golden brown,
    about 25-35 minutes.

CAULIFLOWER WITH TOMATOES AND FETA

1 large cauliflower, broken into florets
2 tbsp olive oil
1 onion, thinly sliced
2 garlic cloves, crushed
1 tsp dried oregano
2 pinches of ground cinnamon
4-6 tomatoes, chopped
1 tsp honey
Salt and freshly ground black pepper to taste
Juice of one lemon
75 g (3 oz) Feta cheese, crumbled
To garnish: fresh parsley, chopped   (Serves 4)

1   Preheat the oven to 180°C (350°F/Gas 4).
2   Put the cauliflower into boiling salted water, bring
    back to the boil, reduce heat and simmer until just
    tender, about 5-10 minutes. Drain and place in a

greased baking dish.

3   Heat the oil in a pan and add the onion, garlic, oregano and cinnamon, and sauté until the onion is soft, about 5 minutes.
4   Add the tomatoes and cook for about 5 more minutes. Add the honey, salt and pepper.
5   Pour over the cauliflower.
6   Squeeze the lemon juice over the top and add the Feta. Place in oven and bake until the sauce is bubbly and the cheese is browned, about 20 minutes.
7   Garnish with chopped parsley.

COURGETTES WITH GARLIC, LEMON JUICE AND PEANUTS

700 g (1½ lb/3 cups) courgettes, sliced
2 garlic cloves, crushed
1 tbsp lemon juice
25 g (1 oz/¼ stick) butter or margarine
Salt and freshly ground black pepper to taste
350 g (12 oz/1½ cups) peanuts, toasted and
coarsely chopped   (Serves 4)

1   Put courgettes into boiling salted water, bring back to the boil, reduce heat and simmer until tender, about 5-10 minutes. Drain well and transfer to bowl.
2   Add garlic, lemon juice, butter or margarine. Season.
3   Mash ingredients with fork or potato masher. Add more lemon juice if required.
4   Transfer the mashed courgettes to a serving dish and sprinkle with toasted peanuts.
5   Serve with rice or millet.

COURGETTE CURRY PANCAKES

450 g (1 lb/2 cups) courgettes, trimmed and grated
2 spring onions or one medium onion, finely chopped
1-2 cloves garlic, crushed
½ tsp curry powder
½ tsp dried thyme
Salt and freshly ground black pepper to taste
1 egg, beaten
75 ml (3 fl oz) milk
140 g (5 oz/1¼ cups) plain flour
1½ tsp baking powder
Vegetable oil for frying   (Serves 4)

1   Place the courgettes in a colander and sprinkle with salt and mix well. Leave for 20 minutes.
2   Squeeze the courgettes between your hands to extract the water. Place them in a bowl.
3   Add the onions, garlic, curry powder, thyme and seasoning.
4   Mix in the egg and milk.
5   Add the flour and baking powder and mix well.
6   Heat the oil in a frying pan and fry a tablespoon of the mixture for 3 minutes on one side and 1 minute on the other.
7   Repeat until all of the mixture is used up.

COURGETTE PÂTÉ

50 g (2 oz) butter or margarine
450 g (1 lb/2 cups) courgettes, sliced
2 spring onions or 1 medium onion, finely chopped
2 eggs
¼ tsp marjoram
¼ tsp thyme
Salt and freshly ground black pepper to taste   (Serves 4)

1 Melt 25 g (1 oz) butter or margarine in a pan and add the courgettes. Cook gently for about 10 minutes or until they are just cooked.
2 Transfer courgettes to a food processor, but do not blend yet.
3 Melt remaining butter in the pan, and fry the onion. Cook until just soft, about 5 minutes.
4 Add the eggs and scramble them until they are just cooked.
5 Add the marjoram and thyme. Season well.
6 Add the egg mixture to the courgettes in the food processor and blend until roughly mixed.
7 Refrigerate before serving.

DAIKON, CARROT AND FRENCH BEAN STIR-FRY

2 tbsp olive oil
1 medium onion, thinly sliced
2 cloves garlic, crushed
2.5 cm (1") piece of ginger, grated
225 g (8 oz) daikon, peeled and cut into thin strips
225 g (8 oz) carrots, peeled and cut into thin strips
225 g (8 oz) French beans, cut into 2.5 cm (1") lengths
Juice and zest of 1 lime
2 tsp miso
6 tbsp hot water
4 tbsp soy sauce
1 tbsp cornflour
4 tbsp dry sherry   (Serves 4)

1 Heat oil in pan and stir-fry onions, garlic, and ginger for 1 minute over a high heat.
2 Add daikon, carrots and French beans. Fry for a further minute. Add the lime juice and zest.

3 Mix together miso, hot water and soy sauce.
4 Mix cornflour into a paste with sherry and stir into the miso mix.
5 Pour over vegetables and continue to stir-fry until the liquid has evaporated or the vegetables are crisp-tender.
6 Serve with rice.

SPROUT SNIPPET: A daikon is a large winter radish also known as Japanese white radish or mooli. It has a crisp texture and a mild flavour. It is used in salads, soups and stir-fries. All winter radishes have slightly more nutritional value than spring ones.

DAIKON, CARROT AND MISO SOUP

1 tbsp olive oil
½ tsp ginger root, sliced
2 tsp sesame oil
225 g (8 oz) carrots, peeled and cut into thin strips
225 g (8 oz) daikon, peeled and cut into thin strips
600 ml (1 pint/20 fl oz) vegetable stock
2 tbsp soy sauce
1 tbsp miso, preferably mugi

                                    (Serves 4)

1 Heat olive oil in a pan and sauté ginger for 2-3 minutes.
2 Add sesame oil, carrots and daikon. Cover and simmer gently for 15 minutes.
3 Add stock, soy sauce and miso.
4 Bring to the boil, reduce heat and simmer for about 10 minutes.
5 Serve with crusty bread.

SPROUT SNIPPET: Miso is a living food, in the same way that yoghurt is, and contains bacteria and enzymes which are destroyed by boiling. It is therefore usually added as a flavouring at the end of cooking, often mixed with a little warm water so it dissolves easily. The three most commonly available misos are: mugi miso, which is a combination of soya and barley which gives a warm, mellow flavour; hatcho miso, made from soya beans alone and gives a strong flavour; and genmai miso made with rice which is lighter and sweeter.

ELDERBERRY PIE

8 oz shortcrust pastry
700 g (1½ lb) elderberries
125 g (4 oz) sugar
1 pinch salt
3 tbsp lemon juice
2 tbsp plain flour
25 g (1 oz) butter or margarine

1   Preheat the oven to 180°C (350°F/Gas 4).
2   Line a pie dish with half of the pastry.
3   Mix elderberries, sugar, salt and lemon juice together.
4   Put into the lined pie dish.
5   Sprinkle with the flour and dot with butter or margarine
6   Cover the top with remaining pastry.
7   Bake in the oven for about 30 minutes or until brown.
8   Serve warm with a scoop of ice cream.

SPROUT SNIPPET: Elderberries are ripe when the clusters begin to turn upside down, around the middle of September. You must make sure you do not use the green unripe berries, because unripe elderberries contain cyanide and can cause severe diarrhoea. Make sure you wash the berries well. We made this pie with ripe berries, had a large helping each and we were fine. You can add them to other fruit to make a rich fruit salad, try steeping them overnight in red wine – yum. The Russians believe that elder trees ward off evil spirits and it is considered good luck to plant some near the house.

LETTUCE SOUP

225 g (8 oz) lettuce, washed and chopped
50 g (2 oz) butter or margarine
1 small onion, finely chopped
425 ml (¾ pint/15 fl oz) vegetable stock
Salt and freshly ground black pepper to taste
1 pinch sugar
Pinch of grated nutmeg
300 ml (½ pint/10 fl oz) milk
To garnish: croutons

(Serves 4)

1   Pour boiling water over lettuce leaves, add salt and cook for 2 minutes. Drain and set aside.
2   Melt butter or margarine in a pan and sauté the onion for 5 minutes until soft.
3   Add lettuce and stock. Heat to boiling, and add salt, pepper, sugar and nutmeg. Allow the soup to cool slightly and liquidise.
4   Return to pan, add milk and reheat gently. Simmer for 5 minutes.
5   Ladle the soup into bowls and serve with croutons.

ONION RINGS, DEEP FRIED

To use up the spare egg yolks, consider making Calabrese in Batter (earlier in this month's recipes)

Vegetable oil for frying
2 egg whites
6 medium onions, peeled and sliced

25 g (1 oz) plain flour, seasoned with salt and pepper

(Serves 4)

1   Heat the oil in a large pan until very hot.
2   Whisk the egg whites to soft peaks.
3   Toss onion rings in the seasoned flour.
4   Dip in the egg white and fry in the hot oil for 1-2 minutes until crisp and golden.
5   Drain on kitchen towels and keep hot.
6   Repeat until all onion has been cooked.
7   Serve with mayonnaise, dips or condiments.

POTATOES, MUSHROOMS AND SMALL LEAF GREENS WITH BALSAMIC VINEGAR

450 g (1 lb) small potatoes, scrubbed
2 tbsp olive oil
2 garlic cloves, crushed
225 g (8 oz) mushrooms, sliced
2-3 tbsp balsamic vinegar (to taste)
1 spring onion or small onion, sliced
Small leaf greens   (Serves 4)

1   Boil potatoes whole until cooked, about 20 minutes.
2   Drain and cut in half and allow to cool slightly.
3   Meanwhile heat the oil in a pan and sauté the garlic and mushrooms over a high heat for about 5-6 minutes, stirring occasionally until golden.
4   Remove from the heat. Toss with the potatoes, balsamic vinegar, spring onion, or onion and small leaf greens.
5   Serve warm with crusty bread.

SMALL LEAF GREENS, PAK CHOI, OR SWISS CHARD STIR-FRY

2 tbsp olive oil
2 garlic cloves, crushed
450 g (1 lb) of any mixed greens
Salt and freshly ground black pepper to taste
Juice and zest of ½ lime   (Serves 4)

1   Heat the oil in a pan and stir-fry garlic for 1 minute.
2   Add all of the greens, season to taste, and stir to coat in the olive oil for 2-3 minutes.
3   Add the lime juice, stir for 1 more minute and serve.

TOMATO, PESTO, CHEESE AND ROSEMARY SLICES

225g (8 oz) plain flour
125 g (4 oz) butter, diced
125 g (4 oz) Cheddar cheese, grated
3 tbsp pesto
2-3 tbsp cold water
450 g (1 lb) tomatoes, halved
1 tbsp fresh chopped rosemary
Salt an freshly ground pepper to taste (Serves 4-6)

1. Preheat the oven to 200°C (400°F/Gas 6).
2   Put flour in a large bowl and rub in the butter until it resembles fine breadcrumbs.
3   Stir in 75 g (3 oz) of the cheese and half the pesto with the water to form a firm dough.
4   Roll dough out on a lightly floured surface and use it to line a baking tray.
5   Prick all over with a fork and bake for 20 minutes until

crisp and golden.

6   Preheat the grill.

7   Spread the remaining pesto sauce over the pastry and add the tomatoes, rosemary, seasoning and remaining cheese to cover.

8   Grill for 5-6 minutes until the cheese has melted and the tomatoes are heated through.

9   Cut into squares and serve.

RUNNER BEAN PICKLE

This recipe was donated by Joan Pettit, Jacqui's mother.

1.8-2.3 Kg (4 lb-5 lb) runner beans, sliced
1½ pints malt vinegar
450 g (1lb) brown sugar
1 tbsp celery seed
For paste
50 g (2 oz) plain flour
50 g (2 oz) dry mustard
1 tbsp turmeric
4 tbsp malt vinegar

1   Put runner beans into boiling salted water and cook until tender, about 10 minutes. Drain.

2   Put malt vinegar, brown sugar and celery seed in a pan and boil for 5 minutes.

3   Meanwhile mix together flour, mustard, turmeric and vinegar to form a paste.

4   Add paste to boiling vinegar and boil together for 3-5 minutes.

5   Add the cooked runner beans.

6   Put pickle into sterilised jars.

SPROUT SNIPPET: VICTORIA SPONGE. This cake mixture is very useful as a basic recipe. This must have been the first cake recipe that Joan's mother, Alma Noblett, ever taught her. The simplicity of this recipe is that you add the flour, baking powder and eggs into the creamed mixture at the same time. The key is to fold them in lightly and gently as if you were caressing your loved one!

225 g (8 oz) butter or margarine
225 g (8 oz) caster sugar
225 g (8 oz) self-raising flour
1 tsp baking powder
4 eggs, beaten

1   Cream butter or margarine and sugar together in a bowl with a fork until the butter goes pale and the mixture is light and fluffy.

2   Sieve the flour and the baking powder into the creamed mixture, add the eggs, and fold in gently, turning the bowl quarter of a turn with each fold.

3   Grease and flour two 17 cm (7") sponge tins.

4   Spoon the mixture equally between the two tins.

5   Bake in oven 190°C (375°F/Gas 5) for about 20 minutes until the top is firm and the sponge is golden brown.

6   Cool on wire rack.

7   Layer the two cakes with jam and/or cream. Dust the top with icing sugar.

The formula of this sponge allows you to make a mixture for 8 or 80. The number of eggs is the secret. The formula is a 1:2 ratio. That is one egg to 2 oz of butter, sugar and flour. 8 eggs, 16 oz of butter sugar and flour and so on. For the baking powder you need one teaspoon per 8 oz of flour. This formula only works when using imperial measurements.

FARMING REPORT FOR OCTOBER

Potatoes have always featured strongly in the Scottish agricultural – and cultural – calendar. In years gone by the 'tattie harvest' in Scotland required everyone to muck in, and schools would close for the two weeks it took to gather the crop in.

Although today the harvest is done by machine and a few workers, schools still close for the two-week period in October, which is just as well for the EarthShare subscribers. Another of the big harvesting events of the year for EarthShare, the tattie harvest is the time when the subscribers complete their work shifts if they are some hours short. Potatoes are lifted and if – like onions – they are stored properly they form the backbone of the year's boxes. So it's important to get it right. The Clydesdale horses have been used to harvest some of the potatoes. Subscribers love the horses which keep tradition alive and makes the workshifts fun. At one tattie harvest, the horses pulled the children around the fields in a cart, to their delight.

When the tattie harvest is complete, it is time to celebrate another growing year coming to a close with a bonfire party. A huge circle of subscribers gather around a fire. They make music, sing, dance, eat and drink, chat with friends old and new – many made through being a member of EarthShare.

One of EarthShare's big expenses is buying in seed potatoes. Buying in new seed potatoes avoids the viruses that are transmitted via the aphids, which diminish the vigour of the plants. The Irish potato famine resulted from just such conditions. EarthShare buy them in from a certified source to prove that they are disease free. The seed potatoes they buy in come from Northern Scotland and the company they buy from provides seed potatoes all over Britain. The climate in this part of Scotland is windy and the seed potatoes are less prone to aphids.

HARVESTING

EarthShare harvests about 30 tons of potatoes during this month. The pigs complete the potato harvesting by finding all the little tubers and eating them so they do not grow in the middle of the different crops that are planted in their place next year. The first winter cabbage is also harvested, along with cauliflower, red cabbage, carrots, parsnips and leeks and from Cullerne: courgettes, cucumbers, tomatoes and spinach. The first pumpkins from Rafford are lifted out too.

PLANTING

Garlic is planted at Rafford and winter lettuce and Oriental greens in the polytunnels at Cullerne.

WEATHER

Anything from freezing cold to very mild and sunny for this time of year.

Clydesdale horses

Crops growing in Cullerne polytunnel

BEETROOT, CARROT AND CUCUMBER SALAD WITH LIME VINAIGRETTE

2 medium beetroot, scrubbed but not topped and tailed
3-4 medium carrots, peeled and cut into diagonal slices
1 cucumber, sliced

Dressing
6 tbsp olive oil
Juice of 2 freshly squeezed limes
1 tsp dried mixed herbs
2 garlic cloves, crushed
½ tsp ground cumin
Salt and freshly ground black pepper to taste   (Serves 4)

1   Put beetroot into salted water and bring to the boil. Reduce heat and simmer for about 1 hour, or until tender. Drain, cool, peel and cut into bite-size pieces.
2   Put carrots into salted water and bring to the boil. Reduce heat and simmer until tender, about 10-15 minutes. Drain and cool.
3   In a bowl, mix beetroot, carrots and cucumber together.
4   Put dressing ingredients in a jar with a lid. Shake vigorously to blend.
5   Pour dressing over vegetables and stir well. Refrigerate before serving.

CABBAGE AND LEEKS IN A CREAMY SAUCE

50 g (2 oz/½ stick) butter or margarine
½ cabbage, finely sliced into strips
3 medium leeks, washed and sliced
2 garlic cloves, crushed
2 tbsp dry white wine or sherry

For the creamy sauce
25 g (1 oz/¼ stick) butter or margarine
25 g (1 oz) plain flour
300 ml (10 fl oz/½ pint/1¼ cups) milk
¼ tsp grated nutmeg
1 tsp Dijon mustard
Salt and freshly ground black pepper to taste   (Serves 4)

1   Melt butter or margarine in a large pan and add the cabbage, leeks and garlic. Sauté for about 10-15 minutes or until vegetables are just soft.
2   Add white wine or sherry and cook for about another 2 minutes.
3   To make the sauce, melt the butter or margarine in a pan, blend in the flour and cook over a low heat for 2-3 minutes, stirring continuously, with a wooden spoon.
4   Gradually add the milk to the mixture, beating vigorously between each addition of milk. It will be very thick initially.
5   When all the milk has been added, bring to the boil and let it simmer gently for about 2 minutes, stirring frequently.
6   Add the nutmeg, mustard and season to taste.
7   Pour the sauce over the vegetables, and stir well so that vegetables are coated. Serve.

CARROTS, FRIED

2 tbsp vegetable oil
2 garlic cloves, chopped
4 carrots, medium grated
2 tbsp tamari
¼ tsp fresh ginger, grated
Freshly ground black pepper   (Serves 4)

1 Heat oil in a pan and sauté garlic for one minute.
2 Stir in the carrots, tamari, ginger and pepper.
3 Stir-fry for a few minutes until carrots are tender.

CARROT FRITTERS WITH BEER BATTER

For the batter
125 g (4 oz) plain flour
¼ tsp salt
1 egg yolk, slightly beaten
1 tbsp vegetable oil
150 ml (¼ pint/5 fl oz) flat beer (sometimes to be found
in a teenager's bedroom)
1 tsp curry powder
1 egg white, whisked until stiff
225 g (8 oz/1 cup) carrots, peeled and coarsely grated
Vegetable oil for frying   (Serves 4)

1 Combine the flour, salt, egg yolk, vegetable oil and beer
   together and beat to make a smooth batter.
2 Fold in the curry powder and whisked egg white into the
   batter.
3 Gently fold in the carrots.
4 Drop large spoonfuls of mixture in hot vegetable oil, and
   cook for about one minute on each side. The oil does not
   need to be more than 2.5 cm (1") deep.
5 Remove fritters with slotted spoon and let them drain on
   paper towels.

CAULIFLOWER AND CRUNCHY CABBAGE SALAD

450 g (1 lb/2 cups) cauliflower florets, sliced
450 g (1 lb/2 cups) cabbage, finely shredded
1 onion, thinly sliced

225 g (8 oz) mayonnaise
225 g (8 oz) sour cream
1 tsp granulated sugar
1 tbsp white vinegar
1 dash Worcestershire sauce
Salt and freshly ground black pepper to taste   (Serves 4-6)

1 In a large bowl combine cauliflower, cabbage and onion.
2 Mix together mayonnaise, sour cream, sugar, vinegar,
   Worcestershire sauce, and season to taste.
3 Pour over vegetables and mix well.

CAULIFLOWER WITH GINGER AND CORIANDER

4 tbsp olive oil
1.25 cm (½") piece of fresh root ginger, finely chopped
1 large cauliflower, cut into florets
Salt and freshly ground black pepper to taste
4 tbsp fresh coriander, finely chopped
Juice of one lemon   (Serves 4)

1 Heat oil in a pan and add ginger. Stir for about 10 seconds.
2 Add the cauliflower and season well.
3 Cover and cook over medium heat for about 2-3 minutes,
   or until the cauliflower is tender, but still crisp.
4 Uncover and add the coriander and lemon juice. Mix well.

CAULIFLOWER WITH SPICY TOMATOES AND POTATOES

2 tbsp vegetable oil
1 onion, finely chopped
2-3 cloves garlic, crushed
2.5 cm (1") piece fresh root ginger, finely chopped
2-3 tomatoes, chopped

¼ tsp turmeric
½ tsp garam masala
150 ml (¼ pint/5 fl oz) water
1 medium-large cauliflower, broken into florets
2 medium potatoes, peeled and cubed
Salt and freshly ground black pepper to taste   (Serves 4-6)

1 Heat oil and sauté onion, garlic, ginger and tomatoes for
   about 5 minutes or until onion is soft.
2 Add the turmeric and garam masala and cook for about
   2-3 minutes.
3 Add water and stir well.
4 Add the cauliflower and potatoes. Season well.
   Stir to cover the vegetables with the spice mixture.
5 Cover and simmer for about 10 minutes, stirring
   occasionally, until vegetables are tender.
   Add more water if necessary.

COURGETTE AND CABBAGE CRUMBLE
225 g (8 oz/1 cup) rice
1 tbsp olive oil or vegetable oil
3 medium courgettes, sliced thinly
225 g (8 oz/1 cup) cabbage, finely grated
1 egg
150 ml (¼ pint/5 fl oz) milk
Salt and freshly ground black pepper to taste
125 g (4 oz) Cheddar cheese
2-3 slices wholemeal or wholewheat bread,
made into breadcrumbs   (Serves 4)

1 Cook rice according to instructions on the packet. Drain.
2 Heat oil in a pan and sauté the courgettes and cabbage
   for about 10 minutes, until cabbage is soft.

3 Stir the courgettes and cabbage into the rice.
4 Add the egg, milk, seasoning and half the cheese.
5 Put into an ovenproof dish.
6 Mix breadcrumbs with remaining cheese. Spread on top
   of rice mixture and bake in an oven, 180°C (350°F/Gas 4)
   for about 30 minutes or until crust is crisp.

COURGETTE CHUTNEY
700 g (1½ lb/3 cups) courgettes, medium sliced
2 tbsp salt
225 g (8 oz/1 cup) onion, chopped
3 garlic cloves, chopped
350 g (12 oz) Muscovado sugar
900 ml (30 fl oz/1½ pints/3¾ cups) red wine vinegar
225 g (8 oz) raisins
1 tbsp coriander seeds, crushed
2 tbsp brown mustard seeds
1 tbsp fresh root ginger, peeled and finely chopped
2 dried chillies   (Makes approximately 3 x 450 g (1 lb) jars)

1 Mix the courgettes with one tablespoon of the salt and
   leave to drain in a colander overnight. Next day, rinse,
   drain and pat dry.
2 Put the courgettes in a pan and add the onion, garlic,
   remaining salt, sugar, and red wine vinegar. Bring to the
   boil and simmer gently for about 15 minutes, until the
   sugar has dissolved and the vegetables are soft.
3 Add the raisins, coriander seeds, mustard seeds, ginger
   and chillies. Mix well and simmer for another 35 minutes
   or until chutney is thick, stirring frequently.
4 Cool and put into warm, dry jars.

OCTOBER RECIPES

COURGETTE WITH TAGLIATELLE, WHITE WINE AND RICOTTA CHEESE

4 tbsp olive oil
1 onion, thinly sliced
2 cloves garlic, crushed
450 g (1 lb) courgettes, thinly sliced
4 tbsp white wine
450 g (1 lb) tagliatelle
3 tbsp Ricotta cheese
3 tbsp Parmesan, grated
2 tsp balsamic vinegar
Salt and freshly ground black pepper to taste   (Serves 4)

1   Heat the oil in a pan and sauté the onion and garlic for
    about 3-4 minutes.
2   Add the courgettes, and sauté for about 5 minutes,
    or until the courgettes are crisp-tender.
3   Add the wine, boil off the alcohol fumes, then cover and
    simmer for about 5-10 minutes, or until courgettes are soft.
4   Put the tagliatelle into boiling salted water, bring back
    to the boil, reduce heat and simmer for about 5 minutes
    or until cooked. Drain and return to the pan.
5   Add the courgettes, Ricotta and Parmesan.
    Stir briefly over heat for a few minutes and then
    add the balsamic vinegar.
6   Season well and serve.

LEEK, POTATO AND CHEESE PIE WITH FILO PASTRY

105 g (3½ oz) butter or margarine
700 g (1½ lb/3 cups) leeks, washed and sliced
1 onion, chopped
2 medium potatoes, peeled and thinly sliced
Salt and freshly ground black pepper to taste
6 sheets frozen filo pastry, defrosted
50 g (2 oz/½ cup) walnuts, toasted and chopped
175 g (6 oz) grated cheese such as Cheddar or Gorgonzola
(Serves 6)

1   Melt 25 g (1 oz) butter or margarine in a pan. Add the
    leeks and onion, and sauté, stirring occasionally, for
    about 5 minutes or until softened. Remove from the pan
    and set aside.
2   Melt another 25 g (1 oz) butter or margarine in the pan
    and add the sliced potatoes. Sauté for about 5 minutes
    on each side until the potatoes are crisp. Season with
    salt and pepper and add to leeks and onions.
3   Preheat oven to 200°C (400°F/Gas 6).
4   Melt the remaining butter or margarine in a small pan.
5   Place 2 sheets of filo pastry on a 24 cm (9½") greased
    baking tray, allowing the pastry sheets to extend over
    the edge. Brush with a little melted butter or margarine.
6   Add two more layers with the 4 remaining sheets of filo
    pastry brushing with a little melted butter or margarine.
7   Layer the leek, potatoes, walnuts and cheese in the
    centre of the pastry.
8   Gather the filo pastry up over the centre of the pie to
    cover top and pinch together to seal.
9   Brush with melted butter or margarine and bake in the
    oven for about 20 minutes or until the pastry is crisp
    and golden.

LEEKS AND POTATOES WITH WHITE WINE AND ROSEMARY

2 tbsp olive oil
50 g (2 oz/½ stick) butter or margarine

900 g (2 lbs/4 cups) potatoes, peeled and thinly sliced
350 g (12 oz/1½ cups) leeks, washed and chopped
225 ml (8 fl oz/1 cup) vegetable stock
225 ml (8 fl oz/1 cup) dry white wine
1 tbsp fresh rosemary or 1 tsp dried rosemary
Salt and freshly ground black pepper to taste   (Serves 6)

1   Heat oil and butter or margarine in a large pan. Add pota-
    toes and leeks and cook for about 8 minutes, stirring occa-
    sionally, turning potato slices until they become translucent.
2   Add the vegetable stock, wine and rosemary.
3   Season to taste.
4   Bring to the boil, reduce heat, and cook until potatoes are
    tender, about another 10 minutes.
5   Uncover and cook for about a further 5 minutes, stirring
    occasionally, or until most of the liquid is absorbed.

ONION AND LIME SOUP WITH HERB DUMPLINGS

2 tbsp vegetable oil
900 g (2 lb/4 cups) onions, peeled and thinly sliced
2-5 garlic cloves, crushed
1 green chilli, seeded, and finely chopped (optional)
1 large tomato, chopped
1 L (1¾ pints) vegetable stock
Juice and zest of a fresh lime
Salt and freshly ground black pepper to taste

Dumplings

4 oz self-raising flour
¼ level tsp salt
½ tsp dried mixed herbs
50 g (2 oz) shredded vegetable suet
4 tbsp water (approximately)   (Serves 4-6)

1   Heat the oil in a pan. Add the onions and stir to coat them
    in oil. Cover and cook them slowly for about 20 minutes.
2   Uncover the pan, increase the heat slightly and add the
    garlic and chilli (if used). Sauté for about 2 minutes.
3   Add the tomato and stir for about 1 minute.
4   Add the stock, lime juice and zest, and season to taste.
5   Bring the soup to the boil, reduce heat and simmer
    gently, uncovered for about 30 minutes.
6   **For the dumplings**, sieve the flour and salt in a bowl and
    add the mixed herbs and suet. Using a knife, stir in the
    water to form light, elastic dough. Gently knead the dough.
7   Divide the dough into 8, and shape these into balls.
8   When the soup has simmered uncovered for 30 minutes,
    drop the dumplings gently into the soup.
9   Cover the pan with a tight-fitting lid and simmer the
    dumplings gently for about 15 minutes or until cooked.
10 Serve into bowls.

ONION AND ORANGE RICE

3 tbsp water
2 garlic cloves, crushed
1 onion, finely chopped
450 ml (16 fl oz/2 cups) orange juice
450 ml (16 fl oz/2 cups) water
450 g (1 lb/2 cups) long-grain white rice
1 tsp dried oregano
½ tsp ground cinnamon
Salt and freshly ground black pepper to taste   (Serves 6)

1   Heat 3 tablespoons of water in a pan and cook garlic and
    onion until just tender, about 3-4 minutes.
2   Add orange juice, water, rice, oregano, and cinnamon and
    season to taste. Stir well.

3   Bring to the boil, reduce heat and simmer over a low heat until the liquid is absorbed, about 20 minutes.

4   Serve.

The following recipes were given to us by one of EarthShare's subscribers, Marco Solari, who is a professional chef. His parents are Italian, and he grew up in London. He was always in the kitchen with his mum and grandparents who are all wonderful cooks. Marco says, "I believe that cooking and celebrating good food is truly an act of love".

The recipes all make good use of the humble potato. They come from his family roots, which are set in farming, in the mountains of Emiglia Romagna, in particular the villages of Bertonazzi and Cereto.

POTATO BREAD FROM CERETO

Starter dough
2-3 medium potatoes (floury variety), boiled in their skins, peeled and mashed
About 3 tbsp strong white flour
25 g (1 oz) fresh yeast, diluted in a little warm water

Bread dough
1250 g (2¾ lb) strong white flour
1.5 tbsp salt
750-850 ml (1½ pints/30 fl oz) warm water

1   For the **starter dough,** combine the slightly warm mashed potato with about 2 tablespoons of flour to form a dumpling-like dough.

2   Add the diluted yeast and about 1 tablespoon of flour and mix thoroughly to form a soft, slightly wet dough.

3   Put the starter dough in a warm place, covered with a tea towel for 2 hours.

4   For the **bread dough**, combine the flour, salt and warm water with the starter dough.

5   Knead until you have a smooth elastic dough.

6   Return the dough to a lightly floured bowl and cover with a tea towel. Leave to rise until it has doubled in size.

7   Knock the air out of the dough and divide into 4 equal pieces.

8   Form into loaves, and place on trays lined with greaseproof paper.
    NOTE: set them well apart for loaves to grow.

9   Bake in a hot oven 200-220°C (425°F/Gas 7) for 30-40 minutes.

10 Transfer bread onto a cooling rack.

POTATO GNOCCHI WITH TOMATO AND BASIL
(Gnocchi di patate con pomodora e basilico)

Tomato Sauce
1 medium onion, finely sliced
2 garlic cloves, finely sliced
8 tbsp olive oil
80 g (3 oz) butter
500 g carton or jar of good quality Passata
Salt to taste

Gnocchi
1 Kg (2.2 lbs) potatoes (floury potatoes are best), scrubbed
500 g (1 lb 2 oz) plain white flour (sometimes additional flour is needed depending on the potato variety)
A good pinch of salt

To finish
Fresh basil leaves, chopped
Parmigiano Reggiano (Parmesan) cheese, grated   (Serves 4)

1   For the **tomato sauce**, cook the onion and garlic in the olive oil and butter until tender.

2   Add the Passata, a good pinch of salt and continue to simmer for 30 minutes.
3   Adjust seasoning and remove from heat.
4   For the **gnocchi**, cook the potatoes with their skins in boiling water until tender. Allow to cool slightly, remove skins and mash.
5   With the potatoes slightly warm (not hot), incorporate the flour using your hands and work the dough on a well-floured work surface until you have a nice firm and smooth dough. It should not be too sticky.
6   On the floured work surface, roll the dough into long sausage like shapes and cut uniform little pieces of about 3 cm (1¼") x 2 cm (¾") in size.
7   Roll the gnocchi gently but firmly over the inside of a fork to obtain a pattern (optional).
8   Cook the gnocchi in plenty of boiling salted water. When they float to the surface of the water continue cooking for one minute.
9   Lift gnocchi out of the water with a slotted spoon and combine with the tomato sauce, fresh basil and cheese.
10 Serve and enjoy!

SPROUT SNIPPET: Passata is sieved tomatoes.

POTATO TART
(Torta di Patate)
Pasta
225 g (8 oz) strong white flour
150 g (5 oz) semolina
A pinch of salt
2 medium eggs
110 ml-150 ml (¼ pint/4-5 fl oz) cold water (quantity may vary depending on flours, weather, etc.)

Filling
8-9 medium potatoes, scrubbed
(dry variety are good for this recipe)
2 small-medium onions, finely sliced
2 garlic cloves, finely sliced
3-4 fresh rosemary sprigs
6-7 tbsp olive oil
70 g (2½ oz) butter
1.5 tbsp tomato purée
120 g (4 oz) Parmigiano Reggiano (Parmesan) cheese, grated
200 ml (7 fl oz) milk (optional)

(Makes 2 x 26 cm (10½") tarts)

1   **For the pasta**, place flour, semolina and a pinch of salt into a large bowl.
2   Add the eggs and the water, and whisk the ingredients together with a fork.
3   Turn out onto a work surface and knead until you have a pliable dough. You may have to adjust the consistency by adding some extra flour or water.
4   Return this dough to the lightly floured bowl, cover and place in the fridge to rest for at least 30 minutes before using.
5   **For the filling**, place potatoes in a large pot. Cover with water and quickly bring to the boil. Reduce heat and simmer until they are cooked. Drain and set aside.
6   While the potatoes are cooking, sauté the onion, garlic and rosemary in the olive oil and butter thoroughly for at least 15 minutes.
7   Add the tomato purée and continue cooking for a further 2-3 minutes, then set aside.
8   Peel the skins off the potatoes and mash them to a smooth consistency.
9   Remove and disregard the rosemary sprigs from the

onion and garlic mixture.

10 Add mixture to the potatoes along with the cheese. Adjust seasoning with salt. You can add a little hot milk to enrich and slightly soften but the mixture should not be too soft.

11 **To assemble,** grease a tart case with olive oil.

12 Roll out the pasta evenly until very thin, using a rolling pin or pasta machine.

13 Line the tart case with pasta, leaving an overhang of 2.5 cm-5 cm (1"–2").

14 Fill with potato filling making sure not to overfill, 2 cm (¾") height maximum.

15 Fold in overhang, and cover top with another sheet of pasta. Use water to stick pasta sheets together.

16 With a fork, pierce surface of tart all over, then brush with olive oil or beaten egg and bake in a hot oven. 180°C –200°C (375°F/Gas 5) for 30-45 minutes.
NOTE: Turn over half way through cooking to brown both sides evenly.

17 The torta is delicious eaten warm or cold the next day. Ideally store on a wooden board covered with a teacloth.

PUMPKIN STUFFED WITH PARSNIP AND POTATO

Looks spectacular served on Hallowe'en night.

1 small-medium pumpkin
Salt and freshly ground black pepper to taste
1.4 Kg (3 lb/6 cups) parsnips, peeled and diced
450 g (1 lb/2 cups) potatoes, peeled and diced
50 g (2 oz) butter or margarine
½ tsp ground nutmeg
1 tsp mixed dried herbs   (Serves 8)

1 Preheat oven to 190°C (375°F/Gas 5).

2 Cut off top of pumpkin and save.

3 Scoop out the seeds and coarse inner fibres.

4 Season cavity with salt and pepper.

5 Place the pumpkin upright in an ovenproof baking dish with the top next to it.

6 Bake until tender, but firm enough to support filling, about 45 minutes.

7 Remove from oven and keep warm.

8 While pumpkin is cooking, boil parsnips and potatoes together in salted water until tender, about 10-15 minutes. Drain and mash with a potato masher. Add butter or margarine, nutmeg, and season to taste.

9 Fold in 1 tsp mixed dried herbs.

10 Place pumpkin shell on a serving dish. Fill with the mashed vegetables and replace the top.

11 To serve, spoon out the vegetables and scoop out a little of the baked pumpkin.

RED CABBAGE WITH APPLES AND DILL

2 tbsp vegetable oil
1 onion, thinly sliced
1 garlic clove, crushed
1 medium head red cabbage, grated or cut into fine strips
2 medium green apples, quartered, cored and thinly sliced
2 tbsp white wine vinegar
1 tbsp sugar
2 tbsp fresh chopped dill or ¾ tsp dried dill
Salt and freshly ground black pepper to taste   (Serves 4)

1 Heat oil in a pan, add onion and cook for about 4 minutes, or until the onion is soft.

2 Add the garlic, and cook for another minute.

3   Stir in the cabbage, cover and cook for about 5 minutes
    or until the cabbage has wilted.
4   Add the apples, wine vinegar, sugar and dill.
    Season to taste.
5   Stir well and continue to cook until apples are tender,
    about 10 minutes.
6   Serve.

RED CABBAGE, GREEN PEPPER AND CUCUMBER SALAD

450 g (1 lb/2 cups) red cabbage, grated
1 medium onion, finely chopped
1 green pepper, de-seeded and chopped
1 cucumber, diced
4 tbsp olive oil
4 tbsp fresh lemon juice
½ tsp Dijon mustard
1 tsp caraway seeds
½ tsp oregano
Salt and freshly ground black pepper to taste

1   In a large bowl, combine red cabbage, onion, green
    pepper and cucumber. Mix well.
2   In a jar with a lid, add olive oil, lemon juice, mustard,
    caraway seeds, oregano, and seasoning.
    Shake vigorously until blended.
3   Pour dressing over vegetables, and mix well.

VEGGIES IN THE HOLE

1 courgette, sliced
1 medium parsnip, peeled cut into sticks
2-3 medium carrots, cut into sticks
1 green pepper, de-seeded and chopped

1-2 tbsp vegetable oil
Batter
125 g (4 oz) plain flour
Pinch of salt
1 egg, lightly beaten
300 ml (10 fl oz/½ pint/1¼ cups) milk   (Serves 4)

1   Preheat oven to 220°C (425°F/Gas 7).
2   In a roasting tin, coat the vegetables with the oil.
3   Put in the oven and bake for about 10-12 minutes.
    Turn the vegetables once during the cooking time.
    The vegetables should be slightly browned.
4   To make the **batter**, put flour and salt into a large bowl.
    Make the hollow in the centre with a wooden spoon and
    drop in the egg.
5   Slowly pour half the milk into the centre with the egg
    and beat the mixture until it is smooth.
6   Add the rest of the milk beating continuously until the
    batter is bubbly and has the consistency of single cream.
7   Pour the batter over the roasted vegetables and bake
    for about 15 minutes or until it is golden.
8   Cut into slices and serve.

FARMING NEWS FOR NOVEMBER

Potato grading or dressing weekly.

HARVESTING

Beetroot is harvested, netted in sacks and buried in furrows – an old-fashioned form of clamping. This is usually done by hand. The chicory is pulled, its green tops are taken off the root which are then shortened to 6 inches, and planted at Cullerne in a polytunnel under 8 inches of soil. By January or February, chicory will have grown for winter salads. From the fields come green cabbage, curly kale, red cabbage, beetroot, carrots, kohlra-bi, parsnips swede, onions and leeks. Cullerne's last month provides green tomatoes, lettuce, oriental greens and spinach.

MAINTENANCE AND MACHINERY

At Cullerne, the wind-break hedges are weeded and mulched.

WEATHER

The weather – as wet as ever this month – hampers harvesting.

Chinese cabbage

Tomatoes

BEETROOT WITH MOODY BLUE CHEESE AND WALNUT

Pete, who adores blue cheese, but is not keen on beetroot, raved about the recipe and couldn't stop eating it.

900 g (2 lb/4 cups) beetroot, scrubbed but not topped
and tailed
50 g (2 oz/4 tbsp) chopped walnuts
1 tbsp vegetable oil
2 medium onions, chopped
50 g (2 oz/1 tbsp) brown sugar
1-2 tbsp balsamic vinegar
125 g (4 oz/½ cup) crumbled blue cheese   (Serves 6–8)

1 Place beetroot in a saucepan with cold, salted water.
   Bring to the boil, cover the pan and quickly return to the
   boil. Reduce heat and simmer until cooked, about one
   hour depending on size. Drain, rinse under cold water,
   rub off skins and cut into wedges. Set aside.
2 Place chopped walnuts in a dry frying pan over medium
   heat until toasted, about 4 minutes, stirring frequently.
   Remove from pan and set aside.
3 Heat oil in frying pan, add onion and cook for 3-4 minutes
   until soft but not browned. Add beetroot and stir.
4 Combine sugar and vinegar.
5 Add to frying pan and cook for 2 minutes until the
   beetroots are glazed.
6 Either stir in toasted walnuts and blue cheese, or if you
   prefer, put beetroot mixture into serving bowl and
   sprinkle on the walnuts and blue cheese. Serve with rice.

BEETROOT AND CARROT SOUP

2 tbsp vegetable oil
1 onion, chopped
1 medium potato, peeled and sliced
450 g (1 lb) beetroot, peeled and diced
450 g (1 lb) carrots, sliced
1 litre (1¾ pints) vegetable stock
1 pinch of nutmeg
Salt and freshly ground black pepper to taste
To garnish: sour cream   (Serves 6-8)

1 Heat oil in a pan and sauté onion and potato for about 10
   minutes, stirring occasionally.
2 Add the beetroot, carrots, and cook gently for a further
   20 minutes, covered.
3 Add the vegetable stock and nutmeg, bring to the boil,
   reduce heat and simmer for a further 10 minutes.
4 Liquidise and season to taste.
5 Ladle into bowls and swirl sour cream over the top.

BEETROOT ROASTED WITH GARLIC

2 tbsp olive oil
700 g (1½ lb/3cups) beetroot, scrubbed, topped, tailed
and quartered
Salt and freshly ground black pepper
1½ large heads of garlic, peeled
1 tbsp balsamic vinegar
2 tbsp raspberry or red wine vinegar
2 tbsp dry red wine
1 clove
1 tbsp sugar
1 tbsp softened butter or margarine   (Serves 4)

1 Preheat oven to 190°C (375°F/Gas 5).
2 Mix olive oil and beetroot together. Sprinkle with salt and pepper to taste. Place in a glass baking dish.
3 Place in oven for about 40 minutes.
4 Add garlic cloves to pan, mix well and bake for about another 20 minutes or until beetroot is tender.
5 Place in a blender and add remaining ingredients. Purée until smooth. Adjust seasoning.

Serve with mashed potatoes.

BEETROOT WITH HONEY

450 g (1 lb/2 cups) beetroot, scrubbed but not topped and tailed
1 tbsp vinegar
1 tsp salt
1 onion, chopped
50 g (2 oz) margarine or butter
2 tbsp honey
1 tbsp lemon juice
½ tsp salt
¼ tsp ground cinnamon
1 tbsp chopped parsley   (Serves 4)

1 Place beetroot in a saucepan with water, vinegar and salt. Bring to the boil, cover the pan and quickly return to the boil. Reduce heat and simmer until cooked, about one hour depending on size.
2 Remove beetroot skins and root ends and cut into strips.
3 Sauté onion in pan with margarine or butter until onion is tender, about 5 minutes. Stir in beetroot strips, honey, lemon juice, salt and cinnamon and cook until hot, about another 5 minutes.
4 Place in serving dish and sprinkle with chopped parsley.

CABBAGE STRUDEL

1 tbsp vegetable oil
700 g (1½ lb/3 cups) cabbage, finely chopped
1 medium onion, chopped
350 g (12 oz) apples, peeled, cored and diced
125 g (4 oz) pitted dates, chopped
6 tbsp low fat sour cream or yoghurt
1 tsp prepared mustard
8 sheets frozen filo pastry, thawed
4 tbsp vegetable oil or melted margarine for brushing pastry
                                                          (Serves 6)

1 Heat vegetable oil in pan, add cabbage and onion. Cover and cook for 5 minutes.
2 Place apples and dates in a large bowl, add cabbage mixture.
3 Combine sour cream or yoghurt and mustard and mix well. Add to cabbage mixture and set aside.
4 Working with one filo pastry sheet at a time, brush each sheet with vegetable oil or melted margarine, placing one on top of the other, forming a stack.
5 Spoon cabbage mixture lengthwise down one-third of filo stack, leaving a 2.5 cm (1") border on longest sides and 1.85 cm (¾") on shortest sides.
6 Starting with the longest side, roll up stack like a Swiss roll and place seam side down on a greased baking tray. Tuck shortest ends under and brush with melted margarine or vegetable oil.
7 Diagonally cut 0.6 cm (¼") slits about 5 cm (2") apart across top.
8 Bake at 200°C (400°F/Gas 6) for 25–40 minutes or until browned. Let strudel stand for 10 minutes before serving.

CABBAGE WEDGES IN CHEESE SAUCE

450 g (1 lb/2 cups) cabbage, cut into wedges
1 medium onion, peeled and chopped
1 green or red pepper, with seeds removed, chopped
50 g (2 oz) butter or margarine
50 g (2 oz/ ½ cup) plain flour
425 ml (¾ pint) milk
125 g (4 oz/ ½ cup) Cheddar or white cheese, grated
½ tsp powdered English mustard, or 1 tsp ready-made mustard
Pinch of grated nutmeg
Salt and freshly ground black pepper to taste   (Serves 4)

1   Place cabbage wedges and onion in boiling salted water
    and cook until just tender, about 10 minutes.
    Drain and place in baking dish with green or red pepper.
2   Make a white sauce: melt butter or margarine in pan,
    add flour and stir for one minute. Gradually add milk,
    stirring continuously, until sauce thickens. Add grated
    cheese, and stir until melted. Add mustard and pinch of
    grated nutmeg. Season to taste.
3   Pour white sauce over vegetables and bake in the oven
    180°C (350°F/Gas 4) for about 20 minutes, or until
    browned and bubbly. You can add extra cheese or
    breadcrumbs as a topping if you wish.

CARROT COOKIES WITH HONEY

125 g (4 oz) butter or margarine
225 g (8 oz/1 cup) sugar
2 eggs, beaten
3 tbsp honey
1 tsp vanilla essence
275 g (10 oz/2¼ cups) plain flour
2 tsp bicarbonate of soda
½ tsp freshly grated nutmeg
¼ tsp salt
125 g (4 oz) carrots, grated   (Makes about 30 cookies)

1   Preheat oven to 160°C (325°F/Gas 3).
2   Beat together the butter or margarine and sugar until
    light and creamy.
3   Add eggs, honey and vanilla essence
4   Combine flour, bicarbonate of soda, nutmeg and salt.
    Fold dry ingredients into butter or margarine mixture.
5   Fold in carrot.
6   Using well-floured hands, shape rounded teaspoons of
    mixture into 2.5 cm (1") balls.
7   Grease a baking tray and place cookies 5 cm (2") apart and
    bake for 12-15 minutes, or until edges are lightly browned.
8   Place on a wire rack to cool.

CARROTS WITH LEEKS AND DILL

450 g (1 lb/2 cups) carrots, peeled and cut into
0.6 cm (¼") thick pieces
½ tsp dill weed
2 medium leeks, cut in half lengthwise, and then each half
into very thin, long slivers. Wash well
1 tbsp olive oil
1 tsp cider vinegar
Salt and freshly ground black pepper to taste   (Serves 4)

1   Place carrots and dill in a saucepan with cold, salted
    water. Bring to the boil, cover the pan and quickly return
    to the boil. Reduce heat and simmer until tender, about
    10 minutes. Drain.
2   Add leeks to boiling salted water and cook until just
    tender, about 5-8 minutes. Drain.

3 In a pan, combine leeks, carrots, oil, vinegar, salt and pepper. Gently heat through. Serve.

This dish can also be served chilled.

CARROTS WITH LENTILS AND MARJORAM

2 tbsp olive oil or vegetable oil
1 onion, chopped
2 garlic cloves, crushed
450 g (1 lb/2 cups) carrots, sliced into rounds
0.6 cm (¼") thick
225 g (8 oz/1 cup) red lentils
450 ml (16 fl oz/2 cups) vegetable stock
1 tsp dried marjoram
Salt and freshly ground black pepper to taste   (Serves 4)

1 Heat oil in a pan. Add the onion and garlic and sauté until soft, about 5 minutes.
2 Add carrots, lentils and stock. Cover and simmer until lentils are just tender and liquid is absorbed, about 20-30 minutes. More liquid may need to be added so just check from time to time during cooking.
3 Mix in marjoram and season to taste.

CURLY KALE AND CHEESE BAKE

2 tbsp vegetable oil
1 onion, chopped
1 red or green pepper, de-seeded and chopped
450 g (1 lb/2 cups) curly kale, cut into thin strips
Salt and freshly ground black pepper to taste
175 g (6 oz) Cheddar cheese, grated
2 tbsp Parmesan cheese, grated   (Serves 4)

1 Pre-heat oven to 180°C (350°F/Gas 4).
2 Heat oil in pan. Add onion and pepper and cook for about 5 minutes.
3 Add the curly kale and cook until wilted, about 5 minutes. Season to taste.
4 Add the Cheddar cheese, stir well, and transfer to a baking dish.
5 Sprinkle the Parmesan over the top, cover and bake in the oven for about 20 minutes.
6 Uncover and bake for a further 10 minutes, until cheese is brown and bubbly.

CURLY KALE STIR FRY WITH LENTILS

450 g (1 lb/2 cups) curly kale, finely chopped
2 tbsp vegetable oil
2 tbsp sesame oil
1 green pepper, de-seeded and chopped
1 onion, chopped
1.25 cm (½") piece of fresh root ginger, peeled and finely chopped
2 garlic cloves, crushed
2 tbsp sesame seeds
425 g (15 oz) red lentils, cooked
1 tsp soy sauce
3 tbsp water
1 tsp fresh lime juice
Salt and freshly ground black pepper to taste   (Serves 4)

1 Put kale into boiling, salted water. Quickly bring back to the boil, reduce heat, simmer and cook until just tender, about 5 minutes. Drain.
2 Heat the vegetable oil and sesame oil in a pan. Stir-fry the pepper, onion, ginger, garlic and sesame seeds over a high heat for about 3 minutes.

3   Add the kale, lentils, soy sauce, water and lime juice. Season with salt and pepper. Stir well, cover and simmer for about 5 minutes or until the vegetables are tender.

GREEN TOMATO CAKE

450 g (1 lb/2 cups) green tomatoes, skinned and chopped
225 ml (8 fl oz/1 cup) vegetable oil
400 g (14 oz/1¾ cups) sugar
3 eggs
1 tsp vanilla essence
350 g (12 oz/3 cups) plain flour
1 tsp baking powder
1 tsp bicarbonate of soda
Pinch of salt
½ tsp cinnamon
½ tsp ginger
225 g (8 oz/1 cup) raisins
175 g (6 oz/1 cup) walnuts, chopped

1   Preheat oven to 180°C (350°F/Gas 4).
2   To skin tomatoes, place them in a bowl of boiling water, leave for about 2-3 minutes, then remove skin.
3   Using a wooden spoon beat together oil, sugar, eggs and vanilla essence until light and creamy.
4   Add sieved flour, baking powder, bicarbonate of soda, salt, cinnamon and ginger. Mix well.
5   Add skinned, chopped tomatoes, raisins and walnuts to cake mixture.
6   Pour mixture into a greased loaf or cake tin and bake for about 1 hour or until cooked. A knife inserted into the middle of the cake should come out clean when the cake is cooked.

GREEN TOMATO PIE

Pastry
150 g (5 oz) soft margarine
225 g (8 oz) plain flour
2 tbsp water
Sugar mixture
125 g (4 oz/½ cup) sugar
2 tsp plain flour
Grated rind of one lemon
¼ tsp ground allspice
¼ tsp salt
Green tomato layer
900 g (2 lb/4 cups) green tomatoes, sliced
1 tsp lemon juice
25 g (1 oz) butter or margarine   (Serves 6)

1   To make the pastry, put margarine with 2 tablespoons of flour and the water into a bowl. Cream with a fork until well mixed.
2   Still using the fork, work in the rest of the flour to form a manageable dough.
3   Turn onto a floured board and knead lightly until smooth.
4   Roll out and line a pie dish with two-thirds of the pastry.
5   To make a sugar mixture, blend the sugar, flour, lemon rind, allspice and salt together. Sprinkle a little of this on top of the pastry in the pie dish.
6   Arrange the tomato slices, a layer at a time, and put some sugar mixture, lemon juice and a dot of butter or margarine between each layer of tomatoes. Keep layering until all tomatoes and sugar mixture are used.
7   Roll out the remaining pastry, cut into strips and make a lattice top.
8   Bake in oven 180°C (350°F/Gas 4) for about 30 minutes, or until tomatoes are cooked and pastry is golden brown.

KOHLRABI WITH APPLES

50 g (2 oz/ ½ stick) butter or margarine
450 g (1 lb/2 cups) kohlrabi, peeled and cut into thin slices
225 g (8 oz/1 cup) cooking apples, peeled, cored and cut into thin wedges
Salt and freshly ground black pepper to taste   (Serves 4)

1   Melt butter or margarine in a pan and add kohlrabi slices. Sauté until just soft and starting to brown, stirring frequently, about 15 minutes.
2   Add the apple wedges, salt and pepper to taste and continue to sauté until the apple is cooked, stirring frequently.
3   Serve.

KOHLRABI AND CARROT SALAD WITH PAPRIKA AND HORSERADISH

3 tbsp white wine vinegar
1 tbsp paprika
150 ml (¼ pint/5 fl oz) olive oil
2 tsp creamed horseradish
1½ tsp sugar
Salt and freshly ground black pepper to taste
450 g (1 lb/2 cups) kohlrabi, peeled and grated
225 g (8 oz/1 cup) carrots, peeled and grated   (Serves 4-6)

1   Mix vinegar and paprika in a bowl. Whisk in the oil until blended.
2   Mix in the creamed horseradish and sugar. Season with salt and pepper.
3   Place kohlrabi and carrot in a bowl. Add the dressing and stir well.
4   Serve.

KOHLRABI WITH CINNAMON AND HERBS

700 g (1½ lb/3 cups) kohlrabi, peeled and diced
1 onion, chopped
1 tsp cinnamon
1 tbsp vegetable oil
1 tsp dried mixed herbs
Salt and freshly ground black pepper to taste
125 g (4 oz) fresh breadcrumbs
25 g (1 oz) butter or margarine   (Serves 4-6)

1   Place kohlrabi in a saucepan with salted water. Bring to the boil, cover the pan and quickly return to the boil. Reduce heat and simmer until just tender, about 15 minutes. Drain and cool.
2   Place kohlrabi in a bowl and mix in onion, cinnamon, oil, mixed herbs and seasoning to taste.
3   Put into a greased baking dish.
4   Mix breadcrumbs with butter or margarine and sprinkle over kohlrabi.
5   Bake in oven 180°C (350°F/Gas 4) until golden, about 15-20 minutes.

LEEK AND POTATO SOUFFLÉ

50 g (2 oz) fresh breadcrumbs
175 ml (6 fl oz/ ¾ cup) milk
450 g (1 lb/2 cups) potatoes, peeled and quartered
350 g (12 oz/1½ cups) leeks, sliced and washed well
1 tbsp olive oil
2 garlic cloves, crushed
½ tsp dried oregano
½ tsp dried parsley
120 g (4 oz) Parmesan cheese
4 eggs, separated

Salt and freshly ground black pepper to taste   (Serves 6)

1   Preheat oven to 180°C (350°F/Gas 4).
2   In a small bowl, soak breadcrumbs in milk.
    Reserve for topping.
3   Place potatoes in a saucepan with salted water. Bring to
    the boil, cover the pan and quickly return to the boil.
    Reduce heat and simmer until cooked, about 15 minutes.
4   Drain, mash and keep warm.
5   Put leeks into boiling salted water and cook until tender,
    about 10 minutes. Drain and finely chop.
6   Heat olive oil and add garlic. Cook for about 2 minutes,
    but do not brown. Add leeks, oregano and parsley and
    cook for 2 more minutes. Take off heat.
7   Mix together leek mixture, mashed potatoes, Parmesan,
    egg yolks and seasoning.
8   Beat egg whites until stiff and fold into leek mixture.
9   Spoon mixture into 30.5 cm (12") round baking dish and
    smooth out. Top with breadcrumbs and bake until golden,
    about 30 minutes. Serve immediately.

LETTUCE, LEEK AND TARRAGON SOUP

50 g (2 oz/½ stick) butter or margarine
700 g (1½ lb/3 cups) leeks, sliced and washed well
1 garlic clove, crushed
950 ml (32 fl oz/1¾ pints/4 cups) vegetable stock
1 head of lettuce, washed and sliced into 2.5 cm (1") strips
1½ tsp dried tarragon
Salt and freshly ground black pepper to taste
To garnish: Crème fraîche, sour cream or double cream
                                                   (Serves 6)

1   Melt butter or margarine in a pan. Add leeks and garlic.

Sauté until leeks have softened and are beginning
    to turn golden, about 10 minutes.
2   Add stock, bring to the boil, reduce heat and simmer
    for about 15 minutes.
3   Stir in lettuce. Cook uncovered until lettuce has wilted,
    about 5 minutes.
4   Stir in tarragon and season to taste.
5   The soup can be served like this or liquidised if you
    prefer a smooth texture.
6   Put soup into individual bowls and swirl a little crème
    fraîche, sour cream or double cream over the top.

ONIONS CURRIED AND BAKED

700 g (1½ lb/3 cups) onions, sliced
25 g (1 oz) butter or margarine
2 tbsp plain flour
¼ tsp cayenne pepper
½ tsp curry powder
¼ tsp paprika
2 tsp bouillon
225 ml (8 fl oz/1 cup) milk
75 g (3 oz) mature Cheddar cheese, grated
6 slices wholemeal bread, cut in triangles and toasted
                                                   (Serves 6)

1   Place onions in a pan with enough water to cover them.
    Bring to the boil, reduce heat and simmer for about
    10 minutes or until onions are soft. Drain.
2   Melt the butter or margarine in a pan. Over a gentle
    heat, stir in the flour with a wooden spoon until it makes
    a thick paste.
3   Add the cayenne pepper, curry powder and paprika.
    Add the bouillon and stir in the milk gradually until you

have a thick sauce.

4   Add the cheese, reserving 2 tablespoons for the top. Stir until the cheese has melted.
5   Place the toast in a buttered casserole dish. Cover with the drained onions.
6   Pour the sauce over them and sprinkle with remaining cheese.
7   Bake in the oven (180°C (350°F/Gas 4) for about 20 minutes or until the cheese is bubbly and browned.

PARSNIP CHIPS (FRENCH FRIES)

900 g (2 lb/4 cups) parsnips, peeled and cut into chips
Vegetable oil for frying
1 tbsp celery salt
1½ tsp dried dill
½ tsp freshly ground black pepper   (Serves 4-6)

1   Fry the parsnips in hot vegetable oil until golden brown. Transfer with a slotted spoon onto paper towels to drain.
2   In a small bowl mix the celery salt, dill and pepper and sprinkle over parsnip chips.

PARSNIP CURRY WITH PEANUTS

1 onion, chopped
1 tbsp vegetable oil
½ tsp ground cumin
½–1 tsp chilli powder
1½ tsp turmeric
½ tsp cayenne pepper
150 ml (¼ pint/5 fl oz) water
Salt and freshly ground black pepper to taste
450 g (1 lb/2 cups) parsnip, peeled and cubed
125 g (4 oz/ ½ cup) peanuts

To garnish: 1 medium green pepper, cut into thin strips
(Serves 4)

1   Sauté onion in oil for about 5 minutes, or until golden.
2   Add cumin, chilli powder, turmeric, and cayenne pepper. Cook, stirring, for one minute.
3   Add water, salt, pepper and parsnips, bring to the boil, cover, and simmer over a low heat for about 15–20 minutes until parsnips are tender but not mushy. The sauce will become quite thick. Add more water if necessary.
4   Add peanuts and heat through.
5   Transfer to a serving dish and garnish with strips of green pepper.
6   Serve with rice, chutneys and desiccated coconut.

PARSNIP AND POTATO GRATIN

450 g (1 lb/2 cups) parsnip, peeled and sliced
450 g (1 lb/2 cups) potato, peeled and thinly sliced
300 ml (½ pint/1¼ cups) double cream
2 tsp creamed horseradish
Salt and freshly ground black pepper to taste
90 g (3 oz) grated cheddar cheese   (Serves 4-6)

1   Combine all ingredients except cheese in a heavy-bottomed saucepan. Bring liquid to boil, reduce heat and simmer gently for about 5 minutes.
2   Transfer mixture into baking dish.
3   Top with grated cheese and bake in 180°C (350°F/Gas 4) for about 30–40 minutes or until potatoes are tender.

PUMPKIN WITH LEMONY LENTILS

600 ml (1 pint/2½ cups) vegetable stock
1 medium onion, chopped

225 g (8 oz/1 cup) lentils
350 g (12 oz/1½ cups) pumpkin, peeled and diced
3 tbsp lemon juice
½ tsp dried parsley
¾ tsp ground ginger
¼ tsp ground cumin
Salt and freshly ground black pepper to taste   (Serves 4–6)

1   Put vegetable stock into a large pan, add onion and
    lentils. Bring to the boil, reduce heat, cover and simmer
    for about 15 minutes, stirring occasionally.
2   Add the pumpkin, lemon juice, parsley, ginger, cumin, salt
    and pepper. Stir well and cook the mixture until the
    pumpkin is tender, about 20 minutes.

Serve with herb roasted potatoes on page 165.

PUMPKIN SWEET AND SOUR
1 x 1.4 Kg (3 lb) pumpkin, peeled, seeded and cut into
2.5 cm (1") cubes
1 tsp dried mint
4 tbsp water
1 medium onion, chopped
3 tbsp cider vinegar
2 tbsp brown sugar
Salt and freshly ground black pepper to taste   (Serves 6–8)

1   Preheat oven to 180°C (350°F/Gas 4).
2   In a large bowl, mix all of the above ingredients
    together.
3   Transfer to a 5 cm (2") deep baking dish. Cover, put in
    the oven and bake for 30 minutes.
4   Remove from the oven and uncover. If mixture seems

dry, add a little more water, re-cover and return to oven.
If it seems watery, return to oven uncovered. Continue
to cook until pumpkin is tender, about another 15
minutes. Taste for seasoning and serve.

Serve with crunchy roast potatoes and green vegetables.

RED CABBAGE WITH RED WINE
1 onion, peeled and sliced
900 g (2 lb/4 cups) red cabbage, sliced finely
900 g (2 lb/4 cups) apples, unpeeled, cored and sliced
225 ml (8 fl oz/1 cup) vegetable stock
4 tbsp red wine
4 tbsp red wine vinegar
4 tbsp brown sugar
Salt and freshly ground black pepper to taste   (Serves 6)

1   In a large pan, place onion, red cabbage, apples and
    vegetable stock, bring to the boil, cover, reduce heat
    and simmer until cabbage is crisp-tender.
2   Add red wine, red wine vinegar, brown sugar, salt and
    pepper. Cover and continue simmering over a low heat,
    stirring occasionally until vegetables are tender.

SPINACH WITH CHEESY MASHED POTATOES
900 g (2 lb/4 cups) fresh spinach, washed
1.4 Kg (3 lb/6 cups) potatoes, peeled and chopped
120 g (4 oz/½ cup) butter or margarine
300 ml (½ pint/1¼ cups) milk, warmed
180 g (6 oz) Swiss cheese (can use Cheddar cheese)
Salt and freshly ground black pepper to taste   (Serves 6)

1   Place washed spinach in a large pan with no extra water.

Sprinkle with a little salt, cover and cook gently until it wilts, about 5 minutes. Drain and set aside.

2 Place potatoes in a saucepan with salted water. Bring to the boil, cover the pan and quickly return to the boil. Reduce heat and simmer until tender, about 15 minutes. Drain and return to pan.

3 Mash the potato and add the butter or margarine and milk gradually. Mix until smooth.

4 Add cheese and spinach, stirring until cheese melts. Season with salt and pepper.

SPINACH WITH COCONUT AND GINGER

1 tbsp vegetable oil
1 tsp mustard seeds
½ tsp whole cumin seeds
1 tbsp brown sugar
2 tsp grated fresh ginger or 1 tsp ground ginger
900 g (2 lb/4 cups) fresh spinach, washed and trimmed
125 g (4 oz/½ cup) desiccated coconut
Salt and freshly ground black pepper to taste
2 tbsp water
Pinch of nutmeg
To garnish: lemon wedges   (Serves 4)

1 Heat oil in large pan. When hot, add mustard seeds, cumin seeds and brown sugar. Fry until the seeds darken and the sugar caramelises.

2 Add the ginger, spinach, coconut, salt and pepper. Cover, reduce heat to low and cook for about 10 minutes.

3 Uncover, stir and add a little water if necessary, and cook for a further 5- 10 minutes. Stir in the nutmeg.

4 Garnish with lemon wedges.

SPINACH AND RICE BAKE

700 g (1 ½lb/3 cups) fresh spinach
125 g (4 oz/½cup) rice
125 g (4 oz/½ cup) Cheddar cheese, grated
2 eggs, beaten
300 ml (½ pint/1¼ cups) milk
50 g (2 oz) butter or margarine
1 medium onion, chopped finely
1 tbsp Worcestershire sauce
1 tsp dried thyme or 1 tbsp fresh thyme   (Serves 4)

1 Place washed spinach in a pan with no extra water. Sprinkle with a little salt, cover and cook gently, shaking the pan occasionally for about 5 minutes. Drain and set aside.

2 Put the rice into boiling salted water. Boil rapidly until cooked. Drain the rice in a sieve and rinse it under hot water. Return to the pan.

3 Combine the spinach with the rice and the rest of the ingredients in a large bowl.

4 Pour into a greased baking dish. Cover and bake at 180°C (350°F/Gas 4) for about 20 minutes.

5 Uncover and bake for 5 minutes more, or until browned.

SWEDE CURRY

3 tsp desiccated coconut
3 tsp ground almonds
3 tsp poppy seeds
3 tsp coriander seeds
150 ml (¼ pint/5 fl oz) plain yoghurt
1 tsp ground ginger
½-1 tsp chilli powder
2 tbsp vegetable oil
225 g (8 oz) onions, peeled and sliced

3 garlic cloves, crushed
450 g (1 lb/2 cups) swede, peeled and diced
4 tbsp water
Salt and freshly ground black pepper to taste   (Serves 4)

1   Dry roast the coconut, almonds, poppy seeds, and
    coriander seeds in a frying pan and grind to a fine paste.
2   Add the yoghurt, ground ginger and chilli powder. Set aside.
3   Heat oil, add onions and garlic and fry until light brown.
4   Add the swede to the pan and fry until light brown.
5   Add yoghurt mixture and cook for about 5 minutes,
    stirring occasionally.
6   Add water, salt and pepper, cover and simmer gently for
    a further 15-20 minutes, or until the swede is tender and
    the sauce is thick.

SWEDE WITH POPPY SEEDS AND PAPRIKA

50 g (2 oz) butter or margarine
900 g (2 lb/4 cups) swede, peeled and diced
2 tbsp poppy seeds
1-2 tsp paprika – more if you like a hot taste
4 tbsp red wine vinegar
Salt and freshly ground black pepper to taste   (Serves 4-6)

1   In a large pan, heat the butter or margarine.
    Add swede and stir to coat well.
2   Add poppy seeds and sauté until light golden brown,
    about 10 minutes.
3   Add paprika and stir well.
4   Add vinegar and cook until evaporated, about 5 minutes,
    or until swede is cooked. You may need to add a little
    water. Season to taste.
5   Remove from heat and serve.

"Many CSA subscribers say their participation has led them to try new things that are infrequently found in supermarkets, foods such as kale, and kohlrabi. While this variety has caused some families to drop their CSA membership, it is welcomed and praised by others. The rhythm and the variety typical of CSAs is thus both a blessing and a burden."

From 'Farms of Tomorrow Revisited'
by Trauger Groh & Steven McFadden

SPROUT SNIPPET: WHAT IS THE DIFFERENCE BETWEEN A PUMPKIN, A SQUASH AND A GOURD?
They are all members of the cucurbit family. With a few exceptions, the groups differ largely in culinary characteristics and the age of the rind when picked. **Summer squash** is usually eaten as a vegetable and is picked when the rind is immature and soft, and the plant is still living. Zucchini, or courgette and **crookneck** squash are in the summer squash group. In comparison, **winter squash** is also eaten as a vegetable but is harvested after the plant has died and the rind has matured and become hard. Examples of this group include **butternut** and **acorn** squash. **Pumpkins** can be described like winter squash and have a hollow seed cavity and a thick rind. In the UK it is eaten as a vegetable and is also suitable for carving into Halloween lanterns. The pumpkin recipes in this book can also be used for winter squash. Courgette recipes can be used for summer squash. **Gourds** have a much harder rind than winter squash or pumpkin and are used for their ornamental value and are often used to make bowls and oil lamps.

FARMING NEWS FOR DECEMBER

EarthShare is now settling into the winter routine. Part of this routine is potato grading or dressing.

HARVESTING
From the fields, Brussels sprouts, red and white cabbage curly kale, carrots, parsnips, swede and kohlrabi are harvested.

MAINTENANCE AND MACHINERY
At EarthShare, general maintenance of machinery. At Cullerne, preservative stain is put on the wooden cold frames and doors of the tunnels. Christopher also plans next year's crops and orders seeds.

WEATHER
It is definitely going to be cold, with varying degrees of rain, snow and wind.

Latest farming news: Mathis and Marianne Rosenbusch are starting a FruitShare Scheme in partnership with EarthShare. This is an unusual and creative response to the request from subscribers for more fruit. The FruitShare box will contain oranges, tangerines, lemons, almonds, walnuts in shells and olives in brine, plus a surprise. This will be available to subscribers in early March.

They are restoring a traditional Spanish farmhouse in the Alpujarra Valley, Andalucia, Spain, and are living and farming here between November and February. They have 10 acres of land with 130 black olive trees from which they are producing single farm virgin olive oil. Single farm virgin olive oil is the olive oil equivalent to single malt whisky.

Olives from their groves are picked, sometimes with the help of neighbours, and taken to the local mill straight away. This ensures that they are pressed when freshly picked. Mathis stays at the mill while the oil is being pressed so that his olives are not mixed with those from other farms. Once pressed, it is poured into 25 litre cans. Because the oil is unfiltered from the press, it is left to settle for about 4-6 weeks before bottling. The main benefit is that the olives are not rotting before they are pressed and this makes high quality oil. Mathis and Marianne believe that small-scale production results in a quality product. The fruit and nuts are grown on their own farm with some coming from their neighbours as they do not have enough trees yet.

Brussels Sprouts

BEETROOT WITH HORSERADISH

450 g (1 lb/2 cups) medium to small beetroot,
scrubbed but not topped and tailed
150 ml (¼ pint/5 fl oz) sour cream
½ tbsp creamed horseradish
1 tbsp chopped chives or parsley
Coarsely ground black pepper   (Serves 4)

1 Place beetroot in a saucepan with salted water. Bring to
   the boil, cover the pan and quickly return to the boil.
   Reduce heat and simmer until cooked, about one hour
   depending on size. Drain and peel.
2 Mix sour cream and horseradish sauce together.
3 Place beetroot onto serving dish and make a deep
   cross-shaped cut into each beetroot and pour the
   horseradish mixture over.
4 Garnish with chives or parsley and coarsely ground
   black pepper.

BEETROOT, ORANGE GLAZED

450 g (1 lb/2 cups) beetroot, scrubbed but not
topped and tailed
50 g (2 oz) butter or margarine
1 tbsp flour
2 tbsp brown sugar
150 ml (¼ pint/5 fl oz) fresh orange juice   (Serves 4)

1 Place beetroot in a saucepan with salted water. Bring to
   the boil, cover the pan and quickly return to the boil.
   Reduce heat and simmer until cooked, about one hour
   depending on size. Drain, peel and slice.

2 In a small saucepan melt the butter or margarine,
   add flour and stir well. Add the brown sugar and
   gradually the orange juice. Stir until thickened.
3 Add the beetroot to the sauce and serve immediately.

BEETROOT AND ORANGE SOUP

450 g (1 lb/2 cups) beetroot, with leaves
1 litre (1¾ pints) vegetable stock
2 tsp red wine vinegar
½ tsp ground coriander
Salt and freshly ground black pepper to taste
225 ml (8 fl oz/1 cup) fresh orange juice
To garnish: orange slices and fresh coriander   (Serves 4)

1 Cut the leaves off the beetroot, wash and chop them and
   put them in a large pan.
2 Scrub beetroot well. Finely grate beetroot in a food
   processor or on a grater.
3 Add beetroot to the pan with the leaves and vegetable stock.
4 Bring to the boil, cover and simmer for about 25 minutes.
5 Add vinegar, coriander, seasonings and orange juice.
6 Soup can be served like this, or blended in a food
   processor if smooth consistency is preferred.
7 Garnish with a slice of orange and fresh coriander.

BRUSSELS SPROUTS WITH CHESTNUTS

700 g (1½ lb/3 cups) Brussels sprouts, washed and trimmed
225 g (8 oz) chestnuts
1 tbsp vegetable oil
½ tsp dried rosemary
½ tsp dried tarragon
½ tsp ground cumin
1 tbsp cornflour

275 ml (½ pint/1¼ cups) vegetable stock
Salt and freshly ground black pepper to taste   (Serves 6)

1   Bring salted water to the boil, add Brussels sprouts, cover the pan and quickly return to the boil. Reduce heat and simmer for about 5 minutes, just to take the rawness away. Drain.
2   Take chestnuts, and with a sharp knife, make an X on the top of each one. Brush each chestnut with oil and bake in the oven 200°C (400°F/Gas 6) for about 15 minutes or just cooked. Cool and shell.
3   Mix sprouts with chestnuts, rosemary, tarragon, and cumin, and transfer to a baking dish.
4   Mix the cornflour with the vegetable stock and cook until it thickens. Season to taste. Pour thickened stock over vegetables.
5   Bake in oven 180°C (350°F/Gas 4) for about 20 minutes.

BRUSSELS SPROUTS WITH ORANGE LIQUEUR

450 g (1 lb/2 cups) Brussels sprouts, washed and trimmed
25 g (1 oz) butter or margarine
2 tbsp orange-flavoured liqueur (can use fresh orange juice instead)
Salt and freshly ground black pepper to taste   (Serves 4)

1   Bring salted water to the boil, add Brussels sprouts, cover the pan and quickly return to the boil. Reduce heat and simmer until just tender, about 10 minutes. Drain into a serving dish and keep warm.
2   Heat butter or margarine in a small pan, add orange-flavoured liqueur or orange juice. Heat one minute longer. Season to taste.
3   Pour over Brussels sprouts, mix well and serve.

BRUSSELS SPROUTS ORIENTAL STYLE

900 g (2 lb/4 cups) Brussels sprouts, washed and trimmed
1 tsp soy sauce
Salt and freshly ground black pepper to taste
25 g (1 oz) butter or margarine
150 g (5 oz) tinned water chestnuts, drained and sliced
                                           (Serves 6-8)

1   Bring salted water to the boil, add Brussels sprouts, cover the pan and quickly return to the boil. Reduce heat and simmer until just tender, about 10 minutes. Drain and return to pan.
2   Add other ingredients and heat through gently.
3   Transfer to serving dish.

CABBAGE AND CARROT BHAJI

1 tbsp coriander seeds, crushed
½ tsp cumin seeds
1-2 dried chillies or ½ tsp chilli powder
450 g (2 cups) cabbage, chopped finely or grated
225 g (8 oz/1 cup) carrots, diced
90 g (3½ oz) tomatoes, chopped
¼ tsp turmeric
Salt and freshly ground black pepper to taste   (Serves 4)

1   Dry-fry coriander, cumin seeds, chillies or chilli powder for about 1-2 minutes.
2   Add cabbage, carrots, tomatoes and turmeric.
3   Mix thoroughly.
4   Season to taste.
5   Reduce heat, cover and simmer for about 15-20 minutes. Vegetables should be a little crunchy. You may need to add a little water.

CABBAGE, CARROT AND ONION CURRY

1 tbsp vegetable oil
2 large onions, peeled and cut into small pieces
2-4 garlic cloves (to taste), chopped or crushed
¼ tsp mustard seeds
½ tsp ground cumin
¼ tsp ground coriander
¼ tsp turmeric
450 g (1 lb/2 cups) carrots, cut into thin rounds
450 g (1 lb/2 cups) cabbage, cut into small pieces
¼ tsp chilli powder
¼ tsp cinnamon
1 tin (400 ml) coconut milk
Salt and freshly ground black pepper to taste   (Serves 4)

1   In a medium sized pan, heat oil and sauté onion and garlic
    until soft.
2   Add mustard seeds, cumin, coriander and turmeric.
3   Add carrots to the pan and cook with the lid on for
    about 5 minutes.
4   Now add cabbage and mix well.
5   Add chilli powder, cinnamon, and coconut milk. Season to taste.
6   Put lid back on and cook for about 15 minutes or
    until cooked.
7   Serve hot with rice.

CABBAGE WITH GIN AND JUNIPER

450 g (1 lb/2 cups) cabbage, cut lengthwise into 6 wedges,
leaving core intact
2 shallots or one medium onion, chopped finely
50 g (2 oz) butter or margarine
1 tsp dried mixed herbs
6 juniper berries

75 ml (3 fl oz) gin
Salt and freshly ground black pepper to taste   (Serves 4)

1   Bring 1 litre (1¾ pints) of salted water to the boil.
    Add cabbage, bring back to the boil, reduce heat and
    simmer for about 10 minutes until just cooked.
    Drain and put aside.
2   Sauté shallots or onion in butter or margarine with the
    mixed herbs and juniper berries over a moderate heat,
    stirring occasionally, until soft.
3   Add the gin, salt and pepper to taste and cook for
    about one minute.
4   Add cabbage wedges, cut sides down, and cook them,
    turning once carefully for about 6 minutes.
5   Transfer the cabbage with a slotted spoon to a heated
    serving dish and pour the pan juices over it.

CARROT CHRISTMAS PUDDING

225 g (8 oz/1 cup) brown sugar
120 g (4 oz/1 stick) butter or margarine
1 egg
225 g (8 oz/1 cup) carrots, peeled and grated
225 g (8 oz/1 cup) potatoes, peeled and grated
225 g (8 oz/1 cup) apples, cored and grated
225 g (8 oz/1 cup) raisins
225 g (8 oz/1 cup) currants
150 g (5 oz/1¼ cups) plain flour
1 tsp bicarbonate of soda
1 tsp allspice
1 tsp cinnamon
½ tsp nutmeg, grated
1 pinch clove, grated
½ tsp salt   (Makes 2 puddings)

1 Cream together sugar, butter or margarine and egg.
2 Add carrots, potatoes, apples, raisins, and currants.
   Mix well.
3 Combine flour with bicarbonate of soda, allspice,
   cinnamon, nutmeg, clove and salt.
4 Fold into the creamed mixture.
5 Divide mixture into two buttered pudding bowls;
   leave at least 5 cm (2") at the top.
6 Cover with a double thickness of greaseproof paper and
   place string tightly around the outside of the bowl.
7 Place each pudding bowl in a pot of boiling water –
   fill up to the neck of the bowl.
8 Boil for 3 hours.
9 Can be frozen. Steam to re-heat.

CARROTS WITH COCONUT

4 tbsp desiccated coconut
450 g (1 lb/2 cups) carrots, cut crosswise into slices
50 g (2 oz) butter or margarine
1 tsp salt
½ tsp ground nutmeg   (Serves 4)

1 Sprinkle coconut evenly on an ungreased baking tray and
   toast in the oven 180°C (350°F/Gas4) until golden brown
   – about 10 minutes. **Watch carefully** so that the coconut
   does not burn. Remove from oven and set aside.
2 Put carrots in salted water in a medium-sized pan, bring
   to the boil, reduce heat and simmer until cooked, about
   15 minutes. Drain and put back into pan, add the
   butter or margarine and stir until melted.
   Add salt and ground nutmeg.
3 Put carrots into serving dish, and sprinkle toasted
   coconut over the top.

VARIATION: After boiling carrots and adding butter or margarine, instead of coconut, add 2 tsp grated orange rind and
crushed seeds from 8 cardamom pods. Add salt to taste.

CARROT COINS

450 g (1 lb/2 cups) carrots, peeled and sliced into
thin rounds or coins
150 ml (¼ pint/5 fl oz) water
2 tbsp brown sugar
25 g (1 oz) butter or margarine
1 tsp cider vinegar
Salt and freshly ground black pepper to taste   (Serves 4)

1 Place prepared carrots in a medium-sized pan with the
   water. Cover and cook on medium heat for about 7
   minutes, or until water has nearly evaporated and the
   carrots are soft.
2 Uncover carrots and add sugar, butter or margarine,
   and cider vinegar.
3 Turn up the heat and sauté, stirring for 2–3 minutes.
   A copper-coloured glaze will form over the carrots.
   Season and serve immediately.

CARROT AND HONEY CUSTARD

4 eggs
125 g (4 oz/½ cup) honey
¼ tsp salt
600 ml (1 pint/2½ cups) milk
175 g (6 oz/¾ cup) carrots, finely grated
2 tbsp sherry (optional)
Grated peel of 1 orange
¼ tsp ground cinnamon   (Serves 4)

1 Beat the eggs with the honey and salt until frothy and light, then stir in milk.
2 Add carrots, sherry (if used), orange peel and blend well.
3 Pour mixture into greased baking dish and sprinkle top with cinnamon.
4 Put baking dish in a baking pan and add water to the pan so it is halfway up the baking dish.
5 Bake at 180°C (350°F/Gas 4) for about 40 minutes or until custard is firm.

CARROT AND ONION SOUFFLÉ

1 medium onion, chopped
225 g (8 oz/1 cup) carrots, grated
1 clove garlic, crushed
2 tbsp water
300 ml (½ pint/1¼ cups) skimmed milk
50 g (2 oz) oat bran
2 tbsp fresh parsley, chopped
2 pinches ground nutmeg
Salt and freshly ground black pepper to taste
4 eggs, separated
225 g (8 oz/1 cup) Cheddar cheese, grated   (Serves 4)

1 In a large saucepan, combine onion, carrots, garlic and water. Bring to boil, reduce heat. Cover and simmer for about 10 minutes or until vegetables are tender, stirring occasionally. Do not drain.
2 Stir in milk, oat bran, parsley, nutmeg and seasoning. Bring to boil over medium heat, stirring constantly. Cook and stir for 2 minutes. Stir in egg yolks and remove from heat.
3 Stir in cheese until melted. Cool slightly.
4 In a large bowl, beat egg whites until stiff peaks form.

Fold in vegetable m
5 Pour into a greased so
(325° F/Gas 3) for 40-5
and a knife inserted near t
6 Serve immediately.

CARROT, PARSNIP, POTATO A
ROASTED WITH HERBS

125 g (4 oz) each of swede, carrots, parsnips,
peeled and cut into wedges
2 medium onions, peeled and cut into quarters
1–3 cloves garlic, chopped or crushed
3 tbsp olive oil
1 tbsp chopped, fresh mixed herbs or 1 tsp dried herb
Salt and freshly ground black pepper to taste.   (Serves 4-6)

1 Place prepared vegetables in large bowl, add crushed garlic, olive oil, mixed herbs and seasoning. Mix well to make sure the vegetables have a good coating of oil.
2 Place in oven 180°C (350°F/Gas 4) and bake for 25-35 minutes or until cooked. Stir at least once during cooking.

CARROT PÂTÉ

450 g (1 lb/2 cups) carrots, sliced
1 medium onion, chopped
1–3 garlic cloves, chopped
¼ tsp dill
2 tbsp olive oil
1 tbsp cornflour made into paste with 1 tbsp water
1 tbsp bouillon
1 tbsp tahini
Salt and freshly ground black pepper to taste   (Serves 4)

onion, garlic and

, cover, and

t 10-15 minutes.

mooth.

l seasoning

ed carrots.

, and cook until

f the pan.

onto a lightly

, raw vegetables.

(rotated text, partially obscured) ...xture. ...uffé dish. Bake in oven 160°C ...0 minutes or until top is brown ...e centre comes out clean. ...potatoes, ...ND SWEDE

1 tbsp vegetable oil
225 g (8 oz/1 cup) carrots, diced
1 medium onion, sliced
2 cloves garlic, crushed (optional, for light flavour omit garlic)
450 g (1 lb/2 cups) rice
½ tsp ground turmeric
3 tbsp dark raisins
12 pitted dates, chopped
Freshly ground black pepper   (Serves 4–6)

1   Heat 1 tablespoon of oil in pan and fry carrots and
    onion and garlic (if used) over a medium heat for about
    3 minutes. Remove and set aside.
2   Place rice into boiling salted water. Boil rapidly until just
    cooked. Drain and rinse under cold water, and add to
    carrots and onion.
3   Put 2 tablespoons of oil in a pan, add 2 tablespoons water

and turmeric. Mix well.

4   Mix rice, carrots, onion, raisins and dates together
    and add to the oil and turmeric mixture. Stir well.
5   Cover pan and cook over low heat for 5 minutes.
    Sprinkle remaining oil over top. Cover again and cook
    for a further 5–10 minutes. Serve warm.

CARROTS, ROASTED WITH BALSAMIC VINEGAR

450 g (1 lb/2 cups) carrots, cut diagonally into
2.5 cm (1") pieces
4 tbsp balsamic vinegar
2 tsp olive oil
Salt and freshly ground black pepper to taste   (Serves 4)

1   Preheat oven to 180°C (350°F/Gas 4)
2   Combine carrots, balsamic vinegar, oil and seasoning in a
    bowl. Stir well.
3   Place onto a greased baking tray and bake for about 25
    minutes until carrots are soft and browned. Stir once
    during cooking.

CLOOTIE DUMPLING

A clootie dumpling is made according to a very old traditional
Scottish pudding recipe, dating back to pre-oven days when most
food was cooked in a pot over an open fire. It is considered to
exemplify a mother's love for her children. It is tradition to wrap
small silver coins and trinkets in greaseproof paper and place
them in the mixture before cooking. Ingredients were placed in a
floured cloth or 'cloot' – which is the old Scottish word for cloth
– and boiled in water for several hours, hence the name, clootie
dumpling. You may want to try this instead of traditional
Christmas pudding.

2 eggs, beaten
2 tbsp black treacle
110g (4oz) wholemeal flour
170g (6oz) fine brown breadcrumbs
110g (4oz) vegetable suet, finely chopped or butter
110g (4oz) sultanas
110g (4oz) currants
1 large cooking apple
1 lemon, juice and zest
1 tsp baking powder
1 tsp ground cinnamon
1 tsp ground ginger
1 tsp ground nutmeg
1 tsp ground cumin
Fresh orange juice to mix   (Serves 8-10)

1   Boil a square of cotton or linen cloth, about 60 cm (24")
    square for a few minutes.
2   Spread it out on a table, sprinkle with a tablespoonful of
    wholemeal flour, tossing the flour to coat the main centre
    of the cloth quite thickly.
3   Place the eggs and treacle into a bowl, beat lightly together.
4   Add the remaining ingredients and mix well to a stiff
    consistency, adding a little water, if needed.
5   Place the mixture in the middle of the cloth.
6   Bring up the edges and tie with a string, leaving a little
    space for expansion.
7   Hold the tied ends of the cloth and gently pat the
    dumpling to produce a rounded shape.
8   Place the pudding into a saucepan of boiling water,
    which should reach halfway up the side.
9   Cover and simmer gently for 4 hours, checking occasionally
    and top up the water as needed.

10 Once cooked plunge into cold water for about one
    minute to release it from the cloth.
11 Put onto a plate and place the pudding into a hot oven
    for a few minutes to dry off the skin.
12 Serve hot with custard.

CURLY KALE AND BACON GRATIN

Although our main focus is on the vegetables in the box, not
everyone in our families is vegetarian. So we have decided to
include a handful of favourite recipes with meat. This recipe is
very quick and easy to make and is very popular with children.

12 curly kale leaves, roughly torn into pieces
1 tbsp olive oil
1 onion, chopped
8 smoked bacon rashers cut into 1cm (¼") cubes or
225 g (8 oz) or smoked tofu
300ml (½ pint/10 fl oz/1¼ cup) double cream
½ tsp Tabasco
Freshly ground black pepper
125 g (4 oz) Gruyère cheese, grated   (Serves 4)

1   Plunge kale into boiling water just long enough for it to wilt.
2   Drain and refresh in cold water. Drain again and gently
    squeeze, then lay on kitchen paper.
3   Heat oil in a pan and gently sauté the onion until soft,
    about 5 minutes. Transfer to a bowl.
4   In the same pan, fry the bacon or tofu until just
    beginning to brown.
5   Transfer to the bowl containing the onion.
6   In the same pan, boil the cream until it thickens.
7   Return the onion and bacon to the pan and add the
    kale and Tabasco.
8   Season with black pepper. Stir over a low heat until

mixed well.

9　Transfer to an ovenproof glass dish, sprinkle with the cheese, and brown under the grill.

CURLY KALE WITH GARLIC, PARSLEY AND PARMESAN

2 tbsp olive oil or vegetable oil
2 garlic cloves, crushed
1 onion, finely chopped
350 g (12 oz/1½ cups) curly kale, cut into fine strips
1 tbsp parsley, chopped
4 tbsp water
Salt and freshly ground black pepper to taste
50 g (2 oz) Parmesan cheese, grated　　　　　(Serves 4)

1　Heat the oil in a pan and fry the garlic and onion for about 2 minutes.
2　Add the curly kale and parsley. Stir for a few minutes so that the kale is coated in oil.
3　Add about 4 tablespoons of water. Bring to the boil, cover and simmer until kale is tender. Stir occasionally during cooking and do not allow the pan to boil dry. Add a little more water if necessary.
4　Once the kale is cooked, bring the liquid to boil and allow the excess water to evaporate and then stir in the Parmesan cheese. Season.

CURLY KALE AND POTATO SOUP

1 tbsp olive oil or vegetable oil
1 onion, chopped
2 garlic cloves, crushed
450 g (1 lb/2 cups) potatoes, peeled and sliced
0.6 cm (¼") thick

1.5 L (2¾ pints/6 cups) vegetable stock
225 g (8 oz/1 cup) curly kale, roughly chopped
Salt and fresh ground black pepper to taste　　　(Serves 4)

1　Heat oil in a pan. Add the onion and garlic and cook for about 2 minutes.
2　Add the potatoes and cook for a few minutes, stirring occasionally.
3　Add the stock and bring to the boil. Reduce heat and simmer, covered for about 20 minutes, or until the potatoes are just cooked.
4　Add the curly kale, salt and pepper. Bring back to the boil and simmer until kale is cooked, about 5-10 minutes.
5　Serve. This soup can also be liquidised if you prefer a smooth texture.

CURLY KALE AND SOFT BLUE CHEESE PASTY

225 g (8 oz) flaky or shortcrust pastry
175 g (6 oz) curly kale, cut into fine strips
1 onion, finely chopped
225 g (8 oz) Gorgonzola or other soft, mild, blue vein cheese
Salt and freshly ground black pepper to taste
1 egg, beaten　　　　　(Serves 4)

1　Preheat oven to 400°F (200°C/Gas 6).
2　Roll pastry into a long rectangle.
3　Combine curly kale, onion, cheese and season to taste.
4　Spoon mixture into centre of pastry.
5　Brush edges of pastry with half the egg.
6　Bring edges of pastry together and crimp shut. Brush with rest of the egg, place on a baking tray and bake in the oven for about 40 minutes, or until golden.

KOHLRABI AND CARROTS ROASTED WITH CARDAMOM AND ORANGE GLAZE

700 g (1½ lb/3 cups) kohlrabi, peeled and cut into wedges
700 g (1½ lb/3 cups) carrots, peeled and cut into chunks
4 tbsp vegetable oil
Finely grated rind of one orange
Salt and freshly ground pepper to taste
For the glaze
4 tbsp sugar
Juice of 4 oranges
Seeds from 6–8 cardamom pods, crushed   (Serves 6-8)

1 Preheat oven to 190°C (375°F/Gas 5)
2 Put oil into roasting tin and put in oven until very hot.
3 Place vegetables into roasting tin. Sprinkle with orange rind, season and stir to coat vegetables in the oil. Roast for about 25 minutes, turning once.
4 To make the glaze, heat the sugar and orange juice in a pan, stirring until sugar has dissolved. Bring to boil and simmer for a few minutes until glaze is slightly syrupy and darker in colour.
5 Remove from the heat and stir in cardamom seeds.
6 Pour glaze over the vegetables and roast for about 10 minutes more, stirring once making sure that the glaze doesn't burn.

KOHLRABI GRATIN WITH BUTTERY CRUST
Very popular with children because of the 'crunch factor'.

900 g (2 lb/4 cups) kohlrabi, peeled, halved vertically and cut into thinly sliced semi-circles
3 tbsp fresh parsley
Finely grated rind of one lemon

Salt and freshly ground black pepper to taste
90 g (3 oz) butter or margarine
300 ml (½ pint/10 fl oz) carton single cream or fromage frais
90 g (3 oz) white breadcrumbs
1-3 garlic cloves, finely chopped
120g (4 oz) Gruyère or Edam cheese, grated
                    (Serves 4 as main dish, 6 as side dish)

1 Preheat oven to 190°C (375°F/Gas 5).
2 Lightly grease 1.5 litre (2¾ pints) gratin dish.
3 Arrange **half** the kohlrabi in the bottom of dish. Sprinkle with **half** the parsley and lemon rind. Season.
4 Dot kohlrabi with ½ oz butter or margarine.
5 Make second layer with remaining kohlrabi, parsley and lemon rind, and season again.
6 Pour cream or fromage frais over the mixture and dot another ½ oz butter or margarine over the top.
7 Loosely cover the gratin with foil and bake for about 40 minutes until kohlrabi is just tender.
8 Meanwhile, melt 50 g (2 oz) butter or margarine in frying pan, add the breadcrumbs and garlic and fry over a medium heat for 2–3 minutes until crumbs have absorbed butter or margarine and are beginning to go crisp. Season.
9 Remove foil from gratin, first sprinkle over cheese, and then breadcrumbs, and bake uncovered for about another 15 minutes.

PARSNIP AND CARROT WITH PEANUT DRESSING
1 litre (1¾ pints/4½ cups) water
4 tsp red wine vinegar
225 g (8 oz/1 cup) parsnips, peeled and cut into thin strips
225 g (8 oz/1 cup) carrots, peeled and cut into thin strips

1-2 tbsp peanut butter
1 tbsp soy sauce
¼ tsp sugar
Salt and freshly ground black pepper to taste   (Serves 4)

1   In a medium saucepan, combine water and one teaspoon
    red wine vinegar.
2   Bring to boil and add parsnips and carrot. Return to boil,
    reduce heat and simmer for about 5-10 minutes until
    vegetables are just tender. Drain.
3   In a bowl, combine peanut butter, soy sauce, sugar, and
    remaining 3 teaspoons red wine vinegar. Season if neces-
    sary. Add drained vegetables and toss until just combined.

PARSNIPS IN MUSTARD AND WHISKY SAUCE

450 g (1 lb/2 cups) medium parsnips, peeled and
sliced diagonally
45 g (1½ oz) butter or margarine
2 tbsp Dijon mustard
1 tsp honey
3 tbsp whisky
Salt and freshly ground black pepper to taste   (Serves 4)

1   Preheat oven to 190°C (375°F/Gas 5).
2   Place parsnips in a saucepan with salted water. Bring to
    the boil, cover the pan and quickly return to the boil.
    Reduce heat and simmer until just tender, about 10
    minutes. Drain.
3   Place parsnips in greased shallow baking dish.
4   Melt the butter or margarine in a pan and slowly add the
    mustard, honey and whisky.
    Cook gently for about 4 minutes.
5   Pour sauce over the parsnip and sprinkle with salt and

pepper to taste and bake for about 10 minutes until
sauce is bubbly.

PARSNIP PIE

225 g (8 oz/1 cup) parsnips, peeled and sliced
25 g (1 oz) butter
Salt and freshly ground black pepper to taste
2 eggs
2 tbsp sugar
½ tsp nutmeg
225 ml (8 fl oz/1 cup) milk
24 cm (9½") pie dish lined with shortcrust pastry   (Serves 4)

1   Place parsnips in a saucepan with salted water. Bring to
    the boil, cover the pan and quickly return to the boil.
    Reduce heat and simmer until cooked, about 10 minutes.
    Drain and mash.
2   Add the butter, salt and pepper.
3   Beat the eggs, add the sugar and nutmeg. Add the milk.
4   Stir into the parsnip mixture and mix well.
5   Line the pie dish with pastry and pour in the parsnip
    mixture.
6   Sprinkle with nutmeg and bake in oven, 190°C (375°F/Gas 5),
    for about 30 minutes or until the parsnip is browned.

POTATOES BAKED WITH HERBS AND CHEESE

25 g (1 oz) butter or margarine
1 onion, finely chopped
1 garlic clove, crushed
2 eggs
300 ml (½ pint/10 fl oz) crème fraîche or double cream
125 g (4 oz) Gruyère cheese, grated

700 g (1½ lb) potatoes, peeled and cut into matchsticks
2 tsp dried mixed herbs
Pinch of grated nutmeg
Salt and freshly ground black pepper to taste   (Serves 4-6)

1   Preheat oven to 190°C (375°F/Gas 5).
2   Grease an ovenproof dish.
3   Heat butter or margarine in a pan and fry the onion and garlic until softened. Remove from heat.
4   In a large bowl, whisk together the eggs, crème fraîche or cream and half the cheese.
5   Stir in the onion mixture, potatoes, herbs, nutmeg and season to taste.
6   Put mixture into the ovenproof dish and sprinkle over remaining cheese.
7   Bake for 50-60 minutes or until browned.

POTATOES ROASTED WITH LEMON AND HERBS
4 tbsp olive oil
2 tbsp fresh lemon juice
Salt and freshly ground black pepper to taste
1 tsp fresh oregano or ½ tsp dried oregano
1 tsp fresh thyme or ½ tsp dried thyme
¼ tsp paprika
900 g (2 lb/4 cups) potatoes, peeled and quartered
(Serves 6-8)

1   Combine olive oil, lemon juice, salt, pepper, oregano, thyme and paprika together in a large bowl and mix well.
2   Add potatoes and toss.
3   Transfer to greased shallow roasting pan and bake for about 35 minutes until tender and well browned. Stir twice during cooking.

Serving suggestions: Excellent with scrambled eggs, omelettes, or pumpkin and lemony lentils on page 150.

RED CABBAGE WITH CHESTNUTS AND RED WINE
900 g (2 lb/4 cups) chestnuts
3 tbsp olive oil
1 medium onion, finely chopped
900 g (2 lb/4 cups) red cabbage, cored and cut into medium strips
350 ml (12 fl oz/1½ cups) dry red wine
350 ml (12 fl oz/1½ cups) vegetable stock
2 tbsp red wine vinegar
¼ tsp nutmeg
Salt and freshly ground black pepper to taste   (Serves 6)

1   Make a cross on the flat side of each chestnut with a sharp knife. Parboil them in boiling water for ten minutes, drain and remove outer and inner skins.
2   Preheat the oven to 180°C (350°F/Gas 4).
3   In a large pan, heat oil and sauté the onion for 5 minutes.
4   Stir in the cabbage and cook for 10 minutes.
5   Add the wine, vegetable stock, vinegar, nutmeg, salt and pepper.
6   Transfer to an oven dish. Cover and place in the oven for about one hour. Check part way through the cooking that the liquids are not cooking too fast, if so, add more vegetable stock.
7   Gently stir in the chestnuts and cook, covered for another hour or until the cabbage is tender and most of the liquid is absorbed. Adjust seasoning and serve.

SWEDE WITH BLUE CHEESE

This dish even improved with reheating and the family liked it.

450 g (1 lb/2 cups) swede, peeled and sliced paper thin
1 medium onion, peeled and finely sliced (optional)
4 tbsp vegetable oil
150 ml (¼ pint/5 fl oz) whipping cream
¼ tsp ground nutmeg
Salt and freshly ground black pepper to taste
125 g (4 oz/½ cup) Roquefort or Stilton or other
blue cheese, crumbled   (Serves 4)

1   Preheat oven to 190°C (375°F/Gas 5).
2   Mix together swede, onion and vegetable oil and place in
    a baking dish. Cover and place in oven for about 30-45
    minutes or until cooked.
3   In a small pan, combine cream, nutmeg, salt and pepper.
    Bring to the boil and let cook for one minute.
4   Remove swede and onion from the oven, remove cover
    and pour over cream mixture. Sprinkle with the blue
    cheese and return to the oven, uncovered.
5   Continue to cook in the oven for about another 15-20
    minutes or until cheese is melted and golden brown and
    crisp. In fact, the crisper the better.

SWEDE WITH BUTTER BEANS

225 g (8 oz/1 cup) swede, peeled and sliced into
0.6 cm (¼") thick pieces
225 g (8 oz/1 cup) butter beans, cooked
1 tbsp vegetable oil
1 medium onion, finely chopped
1 tsp soy sauce
50 g (2 oz) walnuts, chopped

1 tsp dried mixed herbs
4 tbsp water
Salt and freshly ground black pepper to taste   (Serves 4)

1   Preheat oven to 190°C (375°F/Gas 5).
2   Lightly grease a baking tray with vegetable oil.
3   Cook swede in boiling salted water until just tender. Drain.
4   Place swede onto baking tray.
5   Combine cooked butter beans, vegetable oil, onion, soy
    sauce, walnuts, herbs, water and seasoning.
6   Spoon over swede.
7   Bake in the oven for about 15 minutes.

SWEDE AND BRUSSELS SPROUTS, WITH HAZELNUTS

Robin meets Jacqui – Robin's pet hate is swede and Jacqui's pet
hate is Brussels sprouts. Does this recipe work for them?

700 g (1½ lb/3 cups) Brussels sprouts, halved lengthwise
550 g (1¼ lb/2½ cups) swede, peeled and cut into slices
25 g (1 oz) butter or vegetable oil
1 medium onion, chopped
75 g (3 oz) hazelnuts, chopped
1 tsp dried thyme
3 garlic cloves, crushed
Salt and freshly ground black pepper to taste   (Serves 6-8)

1   Put Brussels sprouts into boiling salted water and cook until
    crisp-tender, about 5-10 minutes. Drain and keep warm.
2   Place swede in a saucepan with salted water. Bring to the
    boil, cover the pan and quickly return to the boil.
    Reduce heat and simmer until crisp-tender, about 10
    minutes. Drain and keep warm.

3 Melt butter or vegetable oil in a pan. Add onions and hazelnuts. Cook until nuts begin to brown, about 3 minutes.
4 Add thyme and garlic. Cook until nuts are golden, about 2 minutes.
5 Add Brussels sprouts and swede, cover and cook until heated through, stirring occasionally, about 5 minutes. Season with salt and pepper, transfer to a bowl and serve.

Louise Frazier, an author and experienced chef, has observed the development of CSA for nearly a decade. She believes that the reason CSA growth is strong but not explosive, is that members have to do inner work – to make an inner shift as well as an outer shift. "*It is really about a lot more than vegetables*", she says.

From 'Farms of Tomorrow Revisited'
by Trauger Groh & Steven McFadden

NOTES:

FOOD PRESENTS

Jacqui first made her own gifts 30 years ago when money was tight and imagination was rich. Fresh from studying art, she managed to create original Christmas gifts for her family and friends. Since then she has made many gifts, so the idea of making some from the EarthShare box was obvious to her.

This chapter shows how, with a bit of planning during the year, a sackful of original presents can be made to ease the strain on purse strings at Christmas, make bountiful birthdays, or just to say a special 'thank you'. Collect attractive jars and bottles, create your own labels and enjoy giving them to people. If you have any ideas for presents, contact us on our website www.theboxingclevercookbook.co.uk.

BEETROOT, CARROT AND APPLE JUICE WITH GINGER

Make this delicious drink on the day you want to give it to someone. It will not keep for more than three days tightly sealed in the fridge.

1 medium raw beetroot, washed, topped and tailed and
cut into pieces
2 carrots, washes and split lengthhwise
1.25 cm (½") fresh root ginger, peeled
2 apples, unpeeled and cut into small pieces

1   Put the beetroot, carrots, ginger and apples in a juicer. Enjoy the colour effects and the sweet, spicy taste.
2   Pour into an attractive jar, label and refrigerate.

CARROT, LEMON AND CORIANDER MARMALADE

This is one of Pam Rodway's specialities. When we tested the marmalade on friends and family, most people thought that it contained oranges. A useful recipe when you have a glut of carrots.

700 g (1½ lb/3 cups) organic carrots
700 g (1½ lb/3 cups) organic lemons
900 ml (1½ pints/3¾ cups/30 fl oz) water
1.4 kg (3 lb/6 cups) organic sugar
1 small tsp freshly ground coriander
(Makes approx 5 x 450 g/1 lb jars)

1   Peel carrots and medium-grate.
2   Peel skin off lemons with potato peeler and chop skin into thin strips, or medium-grate.
3   Cut lemons in half and squeeze juice.
4   Save pips and pith and tie in a muslin cloth.
5   Put carrots, lemon peel and juice, water and muslin bag into a preserving pan and cook until softened (about ½ hour).
6   Add sugar, and stir until dissolved.
7   Add freshly ground coriander and boil quickly until set. To check if set, put a teaspoonful of the marmalade onto a cold plate. After 2 minutes, push finger through sample and if it wrinkles, it is set.
8   Remove muslin bag and squeeze excess liquid gently into pan (mind, it's hot!).
9   Skim the marmalade, then leave to cool for about 30 minutes, stirring occasionally to distribute the peel evenly.
10 Pour into sterilised dry warm jars, cover with paper discs, waxed side down, before putting the lid on.

CARROT AND RHUBARB PRESERVE

Jacqui made this and Robin was discovered on several occasions in the fridge, spooning it out of the jar. Sam and Zac never got chance to test this recipe but Robin gave it 10 out of 10.

1 Kg (2.2 lb) carrots, peeled and sliced
1 Kg (2.2 lb) rhubarb, sliced
1 Kg (2.2 lb) granulated sugar

1   Place carrots in a pan with enough water to just cover them.
2   Bring to the boil, reduce heat and simmer with lid on until tender. Drain reserving 125 ml (4 fl oz/½ cup) of liquid.
3   Purée carrots and liquid.
4   Transfer to a large pot and add rhubarb and sugar. Stir until sugar has dissolved.
5   Bring to a slow boil, reduce heat and simmer for about 20 minutes or until preserve starts to thicken.
6   Remove from heat and pour into warm sterile jars.
7   Seal and store in a cool place.

CASSIS

This cassis tastes fabulous and is so simple to make. Drink it on its own or make Kir. Traditional Kir combines cassis and white wine. For that special occasion try a Kir Royale, which is a mixture of cassis and champagne. We tried it with a dry Spanish Cava and it tastes just as good as champagne. Simply put one tablespoon of cassis into the bottom of a tall tulip glass, add chilled white wine or champagne/Cava and stir gently to mix. Garnish with a twist of lemon zest.

550 g (1 lb 4 oz) fresh blackcurrants
700 ml (70 cl) bottle gin
450 g (1 lb) granulated sugar
1 cm (½") piece cinnamon stick
1 clove

1   Place all of the ingredients into a jar with a lid.
2   Shake the jar gently once a day for the first few days or until the sugar has dissolved.
3   Store for one month.
4   Strain through double muslin, squeezing the juice from the pulp, then bottle.
5   Label and date the bottle.
6   You can drink it straight away, but it improves with age.

ELDERBERRY KETCHUP

900 g (2 lb) elderberries
Vinegar to cover
225 g (8 oz) granulated sugar
1 tbsp allspice
1 tbsp cloves
¼ tsp cayenne pepper
1 tsp salt
1 tsp cinnamon

1   Cook the elderberries in vinegar until the berries burst.
2   Sieve the berries and put the strained liquid in a pan. Discard contents of sieve.
3   Add the sugar, allspice, cloves, cayenne pepper, salt and cinnamon.
4   Bring to the boil, reduce heat and simmer until ketchup thickens.
5   Pour in sterilised jars and seal.

SPROUT SNIPPET: Make sure you use ripe elderberries because unripe ones contain cyanide and can cause severe diarrhoea. The berries are ripe when the clusters begin to turn upside down, about the middle of September. Do not use any green berries.

HERB VINEGARS

Herb vinegar makes an attractive gift and it is also a way of using up fresh herbs from your vegetable box. Many types of vinegar can be used such as white vinegar, cider vinegar, white wine vinegar, red wine vinegar or rice vinegar. They all work very well, although our preference is for white wine vinegar. You can also be creative and make up your own recipes.

The basic recipe below tells you to heat the vinegar and put into sterilised bottles. Some cooks do not bother with this and use room temperature vinegar, sealing the bottles straight away without sterilising them, and say that this works just as well.

Once the herb vinegar is made, it can be stored for up to one year, but often lasts even longer.

1   Choose your herbs, and if you wash them, pat them between kitchen towels and let them dry thoroughly as any water left on the herbs will make your vinegar cloudy.
2   Heat vinegar in a glass or enamel pan, but **do not boil** it.
3   Add the fresh herb sprigs to your sterilised bottles, then pour the heated vinegar over the top. Three to four sprigs per bottle are usually enough.
4   Let the vinegar cool and then put the lid on.
5   Label, date, and decorate the bottle and store in a cool, dark place.

You can also add multicoloured peppercorns, whole cloves of garlic and flower petals to the bottle. The following are some suggestions. Experiment a little and see.

➤   Basil, bay leaf and marjoram in white wine vinegar
➤   Fennel leaves, parsley and garlic cloves in white wine vinegar
➤   Tarragon, marjoram and nasturtium flowers in white wine vinegar
➤   Sage, parsley, peppercorns and chives in red wine vinegar
➤   Rosemary, orange peel, raisins and garlic in red wine vinegar
➤   Garlic cloves, dill and nasturtium flowers in cider vinegar
➤   Garlic cloves, oregano and red chillis in cider vinegar
➤   Cardamom seeds, violet petals and lemon peel in white vinegar
➤   Rose petals, violet petals and orange peel in rice vinegar
➤   Lavender flowers (not stalks), rose petals and orange peel in rice vinegar

LEMON ZEST LIQUEUR (LIMONCELLO)

We haven't tested this recipe yet, because our FruitShare does not arrive until March 2003, so any feedback, drunken or otherwise, would be welcome! This recipe was given by an Italian, Guido, from Alicante.

Zest from 13 large lemons, well scrubbed and dried
2 x 750 ml bottles vodka (ideally 100% proof)
1 Kg (2.2 lb) granulated sugar
2 Litre (3½ pints) water

1   Remove zest from the lemons carefully, with a sharp vegetable peeler to avoid any pith.
2   Put the vodka and the zest into a glass container with a lid, and leave for about a week or until the zest becomes crackly and brittle.
3   Strain through muslin. Add sugar and water, stir until sugar has dissolved, bottle and leave for 12 weeks.

ONION MARMALADE

1 Kg (2.2 lb) onions, peeled and sliced
4 tbsp olive oil
125 g (4 oz/½ cup) caster sugar
350 ml (12 fl oz/1½ cups) white vinegar
3 cloves
2 tbsp tomato paste
2 pinches of cayenne pepper
Salt and freshly ground black pepper to taste

1 Sauté the onions in the the olive oil until soft, about 5 minutes.
2 Add the remaining ingredients, bring to the boil, reduce heat and simmer gently for about one hour or until mixture reaches a jam like consistency.
3 Remove from heat, and pour off any surplus oil.
4 Put into hot sterilised jars and seal.
   Keeps for 3-4 months.

PUMPKIN JAM

2 Kg (4.4 lb) pumpkin, peeled, seeded and cut into thin slices
2 lemons, washed and cut into thin slices
1.5 Kg (3¼ lb) granulated sugar

1 In a large bowl, alternate pumpkin, lemons and sugar.
2 Cover and put in the fridge overnight.
3 Next day, transfer pumpkin, lemon and sugar mixture to a pan, bring to the boil and simmer for about 40 minutes or until it starts to darken and slips off the spoon slowly.
4 Remove from heat, cool a little and pour into sterilised jam jars.
5 Put lids on when jam is still hot, as this helps to form a vacuum in the jar.
6 Label and store in a cool place.

RASPBERRY VODKA

1 L (1¾ pints) vodka
1200 g (2 lb 11 oz) fresh raspberries
900 g (2 lb) granulated sugar
2 tbsp lemon juice

1 Put all ingredients into a glass container and stir gently until the sugar dissolves.
2 Cover tightly and put in a cupboard for 3 weeks.
3 After 3 weeks, sieve liqueur into a clean sterilised container, pressing the fruit through with a wooden spoon.
4 Strain the sieved liqueur through double muslin. Leave for a couple of hours to allow sediment to settle, then strain again and bottle.

SLOE OR DAMSON GIN

450 g (1 lb) sloes or damsons
1 x 70 cl bottle gin
250 g (9 oz) granulated sugar

1 Wash the sloes or damsons and prick each one about 12 times.
2 Place them in a lidded jar with the gin and sugar.
3 Shake the jar regularly over a period of 6-8 weeks.
4 When the liqueur is a deep red colour, strain through muslin and bottle.
5 Leave for a further month before drinking.

PLAYBACK MENUS

Playback Theatre is an original form of improvisational theatre in which audience or group members tell stories from their lives, and watch them enacted on the spot. Playback Theatre affirms the importance and dignity of personal experience, enables people to view their lives in new ways, and draws people closer as they see their common humanity. First created in 1975, the form was developed by JONATHAN FOX and JO SALAS and the original Playback Theatre Company in the Hudson Valley of New York.

The story of our friendship and the cookbook began when we met in the Universal Hall at the Findhorn Foundation in January 1999 when we attended the first of many Playback Theatre courses with trainers Veronica Needa and Anna Chesner. We went on to become founder members of the Findhorn Playback Theatre Company and are now an active company along with four other members, Gwyneth Bowman, Mary Gillespie, Saille Mawson, and Francine Rietberg.

This cookbook and Playback have gone hand in hand so much so that we ended up catering for a yearly 10-day Playback Theatre Practice in April 2001 in Findhorn. This cemented our commitment to the book and we dedicate this chapter to Jo Salas and our fellow Playbackers.

We took on the catering because we had a glut of vegetables from the box and garden, and saw it as a golden opportunity to clear the back log, and start researching recipes and trying them out. The connection between CSAs and Playback became apparent; they both serve and enrich community.

We have included some of the menus and recipes. The rest are available on our website www.theboxingclevercookbook.co.uk.

MENU 1
Starter
CURRIED PARSNIP SOUP
Main course
BROCCOLI/MUSHROOM STROGANOFF WITH RICE
Dessert
CARROT CAKE

MENU 2
Starter
SAMBUSAK WITH GREEN SALAD
Main course
SWEET ONION AND POTATO PIE
CARROT AND ORANGE SALAD
Dessert
LEMON MERINGUE PIE AND DUKE OF CAMBRIDGE TART

MENU 3
Starter
SPINACH AND POTATO TORTILLA
Main course
AFRICAN CHICK PEA, DATE AND LIME STEW WITH ROASTED HERB POTATOES
Dessert
BOILED FRUIT CAKE
SELECTION OF WESTER LAWRENCETON CHEESES AND OATCAKES

PLAYBACK MENU I

CURRIED PARSNIP SOUP

Donated by Helen Powell from a Dairy Diary bought from the milkman in the 1970's.

50 g (2 oz) margarine
1 medium onion, chopped
1 large garlic clove, crushed
450 g (1 lb) parsnips, peeled and sliced
1 small potato, peeled and diced
1 large dessert apple, peeled, cored and diced
1-2 tsp mild curry powder
¾ tsp turmeric
850 ml (1½ pints) vegetable stock
Salt and freshly ground black pepper to taste
To garnish: toasted croutons   (Serves 4)

1   Melt margarine in large pan.
2   Sauté onion, garlic, parsnip and potato for about
    5 minutes, stirring frequently
3   Add apple and cook for a further 5 minutes until the
    vegetables and apple are just tender
4   Stir in the curry powder and turmeric and sauté for
    another minute.
5   Add stock, bring to the boil, reduce heat and simmer for
    about 15 minutes.
6   Leave to cool slightly. Purée in a food processor or sieve,
    return to the pan and reheat gently.
7   Add seasoning to taste and serve immediately with croutons.
8   To make croutons remove crusts on 1.25 cm (½") thick
    slice of bread. Cut into cubes and toast or fry in a little
    butter until crisp and golden. Serve in a separate dish or
    sprinkle over the soup.

MUSHROOM OR BROCCOLI STROGANOFF

This recipe is from Joan's good friend Jan Ferguson who, with her husband Matthew, has run an award-winning bed and breakfast near Aviemore for 14 years.

50 g (2 oz) butter or margarine
2 tbsp olive oil
450 g (1 lb) mushrooms, or broccoli, chopped
1 tbsp brandy
1 red onion, finely chopped
1 tsp paprika
225 ml (8 fl oz) vegetable stock
50 g (2 oz) creamed coconut
150 ml (5 fl oz) crème fraîche
1 tbsp parsley, chopped   (Serves 4)

1   Heat half the butter and olive oil in a pan.
2   Sauté mushrooms or broccoli until soft.
3   Add brandy and ignite. Remove from pan and set aside.
4   Melt the rest of the butter and olive oil in pan, fry onion
    and paprika for 30 seconds.
5   Add stock and coconut.
6   Boil and reduce by one-third.
7   Add crème fraîche and thicken.
8   Add mushrooms or broccoli and simmer for 5 minutes
    until thick and creamy.
9   Sprinkle with parsley and serve with rice.

CARROT CAKE

This is an American recipe measured in cups. As long as the same cup or mug is used throughout, it works. Everything goes in together and it is a great way of using up gluts of carrots and it can be frozen very successfully.

1½ cups sugar
1½ cups sunflower oil
4 large eggs
2 cups self-raising flour
2 tsp bicarbonate of soda
2 tsp cinnamon
1 tsp salt
3 cups carrots, grated
½ cup chopped mixed nuts
1 tsp vanilla essence
Topping: 200 g crème fraîche and 1 tbsp fresh orange juice

1   Preheat oven to 180°C (350°F/Gas 4).
2   Mix together sugar and oil.
3   Add eggs and beat well.
4   Add sifted dry ingredients and mix in.
5   Add carrots, nuts and vanilla essence.
6   Line a large roasting tin 30 cm (11") square with foil and pour in mixture.
7   Bake for about 50 minutes until firm and golden brown.
8   For the topping, flavour the crème fraîche with orange juice and pour over cooled cake.

PLAYBACK MENU 2

SAMBUSAK

This is a Middle Eastern dish. Robin's mum, Angeline Shohet, cooks these and they are absolutely delicious. They are like samosas. She makes them in delicate bite-sized moon shapes (she has more patience!) whereas Joan makes them 4 times as big, like small croissants.

Filling
450 g (1 lb) chickpeas, soaked overnight
3 small onions
1 tbsp mild curry powder
2 tbsp vegetable oil
Dough
450 g (1 lb) self-raising flour
1 tbsp sunflower oil
Warm water (from the cooked chickpeas) to mix
(Makes about 30 small sambusak)

1   For the filling, cook soaked chickpeas in a pan of water until soft, drain, and skin (optional).
2   Grind coarsely in a food processor.
3   Fry onions and curry in oil until tender.
4   Add the chick peas to onion mixture and fry, adding more oil if required.
5   Set aside.
6   For the dough, mix flour, oil and enough warm water to form a soft dough.
7   Cut the dough into balls and roll them with your hands, then roll out into small circles with a rolling pin.
8   Fill with 1tbsp of the filling, bring the edges together and close tightly.
9   Heat oil in a frying pan and fry sambusak on both sides until golden brown.

Meat option: Can add 225 g (8 oz) cooked chicken, added at number 4 above.

SWEET ONION AND POTATO PIE

4 large potatoes, peeled
Large knob of butter
1 tbsp olive oil
3 large onions, sliced
2 tsp Demerara sugar
225 g (8 oz) puff pastry, thawed if frozen
1 egg yolk
Salt and freshly ground black pepper to taste   (Serves 6)

1   Preheat oven to 200°C (400°F/Gas 6).
2   Put potatoes in salted water. Bring to the boil reduce
    heat and simmer until just cooked, about 10 minutes.
3   Heat butter and olive oil and fry onion until dark golden
    brown. Add sugar and continue to cook until completely
    caramelised. Season.
4   Roll out pastry into two circles, one 20 cm (8") and the
    other 25 cm (9¾") in diameter.
5   Place smaller circle onto a baking tray lined with
    non-stick paper.
6   Arrange a layer of potatoes on the pastry circle leaving a
    2 cm (¾") border.
7   Top with a thin layer of caramelised onions.
8   Continue until all potatoes and onions are used and it is
    dome shaped.
9   Brush around the edge of the pastry with egg yolk and
    cover with the other pastry disc.
10 Seal edges and brush pie with egg yolk.
11 Bake for 20-25 minutes until golden brown.

CARROT AND ORANGE SALAD

Grate 4 medium carrots. Add a handful of raisins and 2-3
tbsp orange juice and mix.

DUKE OF CAMBRIDGE TART

125 g (4 oz) shortcrust pastry
125 g (4 oz) raisins
50 g (2 oz) glace cherries, chopped
75 g (3 oz) butter or margarine
75 g (3 oz) caster sugar
2 egg yolks (you can add the spare whites to the
lemon meringue pie recipe below)
2 tbsp of rum or brandy
Fresh cream

1   Preheat oven to 190°C (375°F/Gas 5).
2   Line an 18 cm (7") pie dish with pastry.
3   Prick with a fork and blind bake for about 10 minutes.
4   Cover raisins with cold water and bring to the boil.
5   Allow to stand for 5 minutes and then strain.
6   Put raisins and cherries into the lined pie dish.
7   Melt butter or margarine and sugar in a pan and bring to
    the boil.
8   Remove from heat and add egg yolks and rum or brandy.
9   Pour over the raisins and cherries and bake for about
    40 minutes.
10 Serve with fresh cream.

LEMON MERINGUE PIE

This recipe was donated by Alma Noblett, Joan's mother. It beats
the packet variety and is just as easy.

225 g (8 oz) shortcrust pastry
2 lemons
(35 g (1¼ oz) cornflour
25 g (1 oz) butter or margarine
4 oz caster sugar
2 eggs (separated)

1 Preheat oven to 190°C (375°F/Gas 5).
2 Roll out pastry and line an 18 cm (7") round pie dish.
3 Prick the base of the pastry with a fork and bake blind for about 5-10 minutes until pale brown.
4 Grate the zest of the lemons into a pan.
5 Squeeze the juice of the lemons, add water to make up 12 fl oz (1½ cups), and add to the pan.
6 Mix cornflour with a little of the lemon liquid to form a slightly runny paste.
7 Put the rest of the lemon liquid on to boil and then pour over paste, stirring continuously. Put mixture back into the pan on a low heat and stir until it thickens.
8 Add the butter or margarine, stirring until melted.
9 Add half the sugar.
10 Add egg yolks to the pan, stir and remove from the heat.
11 Allow to cool for about 2-3 minutes and pour into the pastry case.
12 Whisk the egg whites until stiff and fold in rest of sugar and spread the mixture over the lemon base.
13 Bake in slow oven for about 20 minutes or until it is golden brown.

PLAYBACK MENU 3

SPINACH AND POTATO TORTILLA

This recipe was given to us by Sandra Fraser, fabulous Playgroup leader, cook and lover of all things Italian. (Yes we *do* know that this recipe is Spanish!)

450 g (1 lb) potatoes, scrubbed and sliced
2 tbsp olive oil
2 onions, chopped
1 garlic clove, crushed
225 g (8 oz/1 cup) fresh spinach, cooked and chopped
6 eggs

Salt and freshly ground black pepper to taste

1 Put potatoes in a pan of salted water, bring to the boil, reduce heat and simmer until tender, about 10-15 minutes.
2 Heat oil in a pan and sauté onions for about 5 minutes until transparent.
3 Add garlic and potatoes and sauté until just browned.
4 Add spinach and cook for one minute.
5 Whisk eggs with seasoning and pour into the pan with the vegetables and stir gently to mix together.
6 Cook gently for about 10 minutes until nearly set.
7 Place under a hot grill for about 3 minutes until brown.
8 Let the tortilla stand for about 1-2 minutes, turn out onto a plate and serve.

AFRICAN CHICKPEA, DATE AND LIME STEW

1 tbsp olive oil
1 medium onion, finely chopped
1 large garlic clove, chopped
1 tbsp fresh ginger root, chopped
350 g (12 oz) fresh tomatoes, chopped
2 tsp ground cumin
1 tsp ground coriander
Salt and freshly ground black pepper to taste
¼ tsp cayenne pepper
400 ml (14 oz) tin of chickpeas, drained
150 ml (¼ pint) water
1 tbsp clear honey
175 g (6 oz) pitted dates, chopped
1 tbsp lime juice

1 Heat oil in a pan and sauté onion, garlic and ginger for about 5 minutes.

2   Add tomatoes and cook for 5 minutes.
3   Add cumin, coriander, salt, pepper, and cayenne pepper and cook for one minute.
4   Add the chickpeas, water, honey and dates. Cover, bring to boil, reduce heat and simmer for about 15 minutes.
5   Just before serving, stir in lime juice.

BOILED FRUIT CAKE

Joan's sister, Joy, gave us this recipe. She makes many exotic cakes. However, this one is made in a saucepan and is very practical.

300 ml (½ pint/1¼ cups) milk
50 g (2 oz) margarine
175 g (6 oz) Demerara sugar
275 g (10 oz) mixed fruit
2 tsp mixed spice
1 tsp bicarbonate of soda
280 g (10 oz) self-raising flour
1 egg

1   Place milk, margarine, sugar, mixed fruit, and mixed spice in a pan and boil for 5 minutes.
2   Remove from the heat and add bicarbonate of soda whilst mixture is still hot.
3   Leave to cool.
4   Add the flour and the egg and mix well.
5   Bake for 1½ hours in the oven, 180°C (350°F/Gas 4).

Wester Lawrenceton cheese

177

You have now reached the end of The Boxing Clever Cookbook. We hope it *has* taught you to box clever with your veggies and you, like us, have had many more happy moments in the kitchen and around the table with family and friends because of it.

If, however, you are still struggling with your box, try this way of making it work, courtesy of the Viennese Vegetable Orchestra.

Forget the Stradivarius and Yahamas, the Viennese Vegetable Orchestra consists exclusively of vegetable-based instruments. The musicians blow carved-out carrots, tap turnips, clap with eggplant cymbals, twang on rhubarb fibres, and rustle parsley and greens. Where necessary, additional kitchen utensils such as knives or mixers are employed.

As if that was not bizarre enough, after the concert the stage is left to the cooks who turn the instruments into a tasty vegetable soup, enjoyed at a post-performance party by both the audience and musicians.

POSTSCRIPT

In our next edition we hope to bring a Mediterranean flavour to the boxes as we follow Mathis to his new FruitShare scheme in Spain. Recipes will include almonds, olive oil, citrus fruits and romantic weeding shifts in cossies, rather than wellies!

Instruments in the making

CONVERSION TABLES

The tables below give three measurements, metric, imperial and American cups. The equivalents given are approximate only, but are close enough to ensure successful results in the kitchen.

WEIGHT

METRIC	IMPERIAL	AMERICAN
15 g	$1/2$ oz	
25 - 30 g	1 oz	
45 g	$1 1/2$ oz	
50 - 60 g	2 oz	$1/4$ cup
75 g	3 oz	
90 g	$3 1/2$ oz	
100 - 125 g	4 oz	$1/2$ cup
150 g	5 oz	
175 g	6 oz	
225 g	8 oz	1 cup
275 g	10 oz	
325 - 350 g	12 oz	$1 1/2$ cups
400 g	14 oz	
450 g	1 lb	2 cups
700 g	$1 1/2$ lb	3 cups
900 g	2 lb	4 cups
1.1 kg	$2 1/2$ lb	5 cups
1.4 kg	3 lb	6 cups
2 kg	$4 1/2$ lb	9 cups
2.3 kg	5 lb	10 cups

LIQUID CAPACITY

METRIC	IMPERIAL	AMERICAN
25 ml	1 fl oz	
50 ml	2 fl oz	$1/4$ cup
75 ml	3 fl oz	
100-125 ml	4 fl oz	$1/2$ cup
150 ml	5 fl oz/$1/4$ pint	
175 ml	6 fl oz	$3/4$ cup
200 ml	7 fl oz	
225 ml	8 fl oz	1 cup
250 ml	9 fl oz	
275-300 ml	10 fl oz/$1/2$ pint	$1 1/4$ cups
350 ml	12 fl oz	$1 1/2$ cups
425 ml	15 fl oz/$3/4$ pint	
450 ml	16 fl oz	2 cups
500 ml	18 fl oz	$2 1/4$ cups
575-600 ml	20 fl oz/1 pint	$2 1/2$ cups
650 ml	24 fl oz	3 cups
725 ml	27 fl oz	
850-900 ml	30 fl oz/$1 1/2$ pints	$3 3/4$ cups
980 ml	35 fl oz/$1 3/4$ pints	
1 litre	36 fl oz	$4 1/2$ cups

1 metric cup = 250 ml   1 American cup = 236.59 ml
1 metric tbsp = 15.625 ml   1 American tbsp = 14.79 ml

LENGTH

METRIC (Centimetres)	IMPERIAL (Inches)
0.6 cm	$1/4$ in
1.2 cm	$1/2$ in
1.9 cm	$3/4$ in
2.5 cm	1 in
3.2 cm	$1 1/4$ in
3.8 cm	$1 1/2$ in
4.5 cm	$1 3/4$ in
5 cm	2 in
12.7 cm	5 in
22.8 cm	9 in
25.4 cm	10 in
30.5 cm	12 in

OVEN TEMPERATURES

°C	°F	GAS MARK
130	250	$1/2$
140	275	1
150	300	2
160-170	325	3
180	350	4
190	375	5
200	400	6
210-220	425	7
230	450	8
240	475	9

USEFUL RESOURCES AND REFERENCES

Jacqui Jones and Joan Wilmot
Email: jj@theboxingclevercookbook.co.uk
Tel: 01309 672001
Website: www.theboxingclevercookbook.co.uk

J & J Publishing
Mains of Struthers Farm, Kinloss, Forres, Moray, Scotland IV36 2UD
Tel: 01309 672001

EarthShare
65 Society Street, Nairn, Moray, Scotland IV12 4NL
Email: earthshare@macunlimited.net
Tel: 01667 452879
Website: www.earthshare.co.uk

Wester Lawrenceton Farm
Forres, Scotland IV36 2RH
Tel: 01309 676 566

Soil Association Scotland
18 Liberton Brae, Tower Mains, Edinburgh EH16 6AE
Email: contact@sascotland.org
Tel: 0131 666 2474
Website: www.soilassociationscotland.org

Soil Association
Bristol House, 40-56 Victoria Street, Bristol BS1 6BY
Email: info@soilassociation.org
Tel: 0117 929 0661
Website: www.soilassociation.org

Cultivating Communities
Soil Association, Bristol House, 40-56 Victoria Street, Bristol BS1 6BY
Email: csa@cuco.org.uk
Tel: 0117 914 2425
Website: www.cuco.org.uk

Our local wholefood shop who also stock a good selection of books and goods available through mail order:

The Phoenix Centre
The Park, Findhorn, Moray, Scotland IV36 3TZ
Tel: 01309 690 110
Email: phoenix@findhorn.org

International Playback Theatre Network (ITPN)
Website: www.playbacknet.org

Where is your nearest organic vegetable box scheme?
Find out in **The Organic Directory.** Published by Green Books with the Soil Association. Green Books Ltd, Foxhole, Dartington, Totnes, Devon TQ9 6EB
Website: www.theorganicdirectory.co.uk
ISBN 1 903998 10 7

'Farms of Tomorrow Revisited'
Community Supported Farms - Farm Supported Communities
By Trauger Groh and Steven McFadden.
Published by:
Biodynamic Farming and Gardening Association Kimberton PA
ISBN: 0-938250-13-2

INDEX OF RECIPES

WHY JOIN THE SOIL ASSOCIATION?

The Soil Association needs **your** help to build an organic future.

The Soil Association is an independent not-for-profit body that sets organic standards, supports and advises organic farmers and works to change the way the UK farms. If you want to end disasters like BSE and are against the commercial planting of GM crops ñ if you want organic food and a living countryside ñ please join us today.

As a charity we rely on public support to do much of our work. The giant biotech companies lobby hard to protect their profits. We must lobby harder. We urgently need support from people that believe in farming that works with nature, not against it ñ people like you.

Benefits of joining

Free. The Truth about Food, a 44 page booklet revealing the facts about what you eat, yours with a monthly payment.

Free. Regular editions of the award winning Living Earth magazine

All supporters receive regular updates about our activities and events.

YES, I'll join the Soil Association

CLEVER1

TITLE   FORENAME   SURNAME

ADDRESS

POSTCODE

We promise that your details will be used for Soil Association purposes only. If you would rather not receive additional special offers please tick here ☐

I would like to give a monthly gift of:

| £3 | £5 | £10 | £20 | £ other |

Instruction to your bank or building society to pay by Direct Debit

DIRECT Debit

Please fill in the whole form and return to Soil Association, Bristol House, 40–56 Victoria Sreet, Bristol BS1 6ZY

TO THE MANAGER OF   BANK/BUILDING SOCIETY

BRANCH ADDRESS

POSTCODE

NAME(S) OF ACCOUNT HOLDER(S)

ACCOUNT NO.   SORT CODE

Originator's identification no.   9 4 0 3 7 4   Ref. no. (office use only)

Please pay the Soil Association Direct Debits from the account detailed on this instruction subject to the safeguards assured by the Direct Debit guarantee. I understand this instruction may remain with the Soil Association and, if so, details will be passed electronically to my bank/building society.

SIGNATURE(S)   DATE

Banks and building societies may decline to accept instructions to pay Direct Debits from some types of accounts.

Registered charity no. 206862

NOTES